There's **hope** For Today

Daily Devotional

Presented by Book of Hope

Daily devotionals by David B. Crabtree

Pastor, Calvary Church, Greensboro, North Carolina

There's Hope for Today
Published by Book of Hope International
© 2002 Book of Hope

Some photos used in this publication are representative of the people whose stories are told.

Book of Hope
3111 SW 10th Street
Pompano, FL 33069
1-800-GIV-BIBL (448-2425)

info@bookofhope.net
www.bookofhope.net

Book of Hope UK
PO Box 6558
Olbury
West Midlands
B69 4JP
0121 601 6678
david.lherroux@virgin.net
www.hopenet.net

A Personal Word From
Founder Bob Hoskins &
Executive Director Rob Hoskins

The theme of this year's edition of *There's Hope for Today* is "Plant a seed."

Our choice is whether to plant seeds of death or seeds of life.

In Angola, the seeds of death have already been planted: it is the most land-mined nation in the world, and families are few that do not have at least one member lost to the accidental explosions. Millions more have lost limbs.

When the *Book of Hope* arrived in Angola, one of the local Christian leaders told us that after so much death, these books are seeds of hope.

Of course, Angola has not cornered the market on seeds of death. The devil is reaping his fatal harvest around the world.

Across many nations of Africa, Asia and even South America, war and its bloody aftermath continues to claim lives, devastate families and kill children.

Think of Sudan, where a brutal conflict between the north and the south has wiped out over two million people in that nation, with the remnant surviving either as slaves in Northern Sudan or starving slowly in the bare and arid mountains.

Across Africa, AIDS is also devastating the population. In South Africa alone, predictions are that if no cure is found, by the year 2010, six million people will die from AIDS-related illness every year. To put that in tragic perspective: it is the equivalent of five 9/11 disasters every day, every week, every year.

Satan has planted the seeds of death in the hearts and lives of child abusers – those that abandon, abuse, neglect or molest their own children, and the pedophiles who fuel the child prostitution industry of nations such as Cambodia, Thailand and India.

Little girls and boys as young as five or six-years-old have been kidnapped or sold into sexual slavery to live out their short, unhappy lives in perpetual pain and humiliation.

The list goes on. Poverty in poor nations such as India, drug addiction in almost every nation on earth, epidemic alcoholism among young men in Russia, totalitarian regimes such as Castro's Cuba, religious terrorism in the Middle East and nations such as Indonesia and the Philippines ...

Our adversary the devil has sown his seeds of death far and wide, and the daily harvest he reaps is a horror that we can hardly fathom.

But we have known ever since the Garden of Eden that Satan would stop at nothing in his twisted mission to steal, kill and destroy. And we have known since the cross of Christ that his power can be and will ultimately be utterly destroyed!

The Bible predicted of these days, "This is the spirit of the antichrist, which you have heard is coming and even now is already in the world. You, dear children, are from God and have overcome them, because the one who is in you is greater than the one who is in the world" (1 John 4:3-4).

Our God is greater than the spirit of this age, and by the power of His Word, the seeds of death can be swallowed up in seeds of life!

Our desire is for this devotional to plant seeds of hope in your life, each and every day of the year ... and to remind you that when we together plant the *Book of Hope* as a seed for hope in the hands of a needy child, it can grow into a harvest of new life in Christ.

We hope that day by day throughout the year, this devotional helps you recognize that God is at work through His Word to raise up a harvest of life, from the seeds we are planting together.

Thank you for your partnership in this mission to affect the destiny of the next generation by providing God's Word to every child and youth in the world.

You have chosen to plant seeds of life, and we are grateful for your help! Keep in mind that any time you want to plant a seed of faith in this ministry, your gift will place God's Word into the hands of students around the world.

Every dollar provides the *Book of Hope* for three children or youth, so you can sow seeds of hope today, and through God's Word plant a legacy for the future, and for eternity! •

David B. Crabtree
Pastor, Calvary Church
Greensboro, North Carolina

Preface by
David B. Crabtree

When life's passions meet at points of opportunity, the end result is joy. Writing "There's Hope for Today" has been a happy convergence of my love of writing and short-term missions. I serve in the role of Senior Pastor at Calvary Church, an Assemblies of God fellowship. I write, of necessity, every day. My pastoral role has also opened up the world of short-term missions teams with Book of Hope International. I go, wherever they will send me, every year. To combine writing and missions has been particularly enriching for me. I am indebted to visionary leaders who partner with me at Calvary Church. We do chaos better than anyone in town!

At this writing, I have finished my eight hundredth devotional. I am keenly aware that I have only begun to scratch the surface of the incredible depths of truth revealed in the Bible. Every text is a treasure. Every Scripture truth is eternal. Every verse is profitable. Every word is loaded with potential. In my commentaries, stories, and parallels, I strive to open a window through which the reader looks deeper into the Word of God. If one column causes you to open your Bible, that's reward enough for me.

I am grateful for the vision and passion of Bob and Rob Hoskins. They took me to Russia in 1991 and changed my life and ministry with a simple paperback Gospel and a few thousand Russian school children. When it comes to "Book of Hope," I'm a lifer!

I grew up with a love of language. My father is an orator/preacher. My mother is a voracious reader. They raised me in a house filled with books, and wonder, and faith, and love. They continue to provide inspiration and encouragement, along with a thousand unpublished stories that can't possibly be told in two hundred word columns.

My heart belongs to my wife, Cheri. In our early years she insisted that I buy books. No one has encouraged me more. To this day, I cannot fathom why she chose me. Our daughters reflect all of her best qualities. Of all the labels I wear, I'm most proud of the one that says "Dad."

I'm thankful for every friend of Book of Hope. I write first for Him, and then for you. I hope these daily devotionals will cause you to think, to laugh, to search, to pray, to question, to share, to go, to give, and to pause each day to thank God for the most incredible words ever written: the living Word of God.

*"Come unto me, all ye that labour and are heavy
laden, and I will give you rest."*
Matthew 11:28 KJV

LIMA, PERU: Vilma Escudero carried the title of "principal." In her heart, she carried the burdens that weigh down large inner-city schools. Discipline was a constant challenge. Immorality was bearing its bitter fruit among the students. Her teachers were offering constant complaints about their low salaries and lack of materials. Parent trouble, teacher trouble, funding shortfall, and a general lack of support left her carrying a tremendous load for the two thousand students at Augusto Gutierrez School.

One afternoon Pastor Elmer Zavaleta visited the school and asked for permission to distribute the *Book of Hope*. Vilma did not hesitate to open the door. The books were well received and Pastor Zavaleta felt great freedom to extend an invitation for salvation at the end of the presentation. Almost all of the students raised their hands, and several teachers joined them in a sinner's prayer. Vilma Escudero raised her hand, too.

Vilma now attends an Evangelical Church where she is growing in faith. She boldly tells her colleagues that school problems dropped sharply after the *Book of Hope* was distributed.

God's Word can make a difference in your workplace too. Pray for open doors.

In the beginning God created the heaven and the earth.
Genesis 1:1 KJV

God's economy with words is staggering. With the first ten words in the Bible He establishes Himself as Lord over all sciences.

"In the beginning." There was one – a premeditated starting point and preparation for man's immediate appearance in a lifeless universe. "In the beginning God." Four words establish the eternal fact of God and His legitimate paternity. "In the beginning God created." Neither we nor the universe are products of random and accidental occurrences. Creation is a divine conspiracy. "In the beginning God created the heaven." Here we have a complete cosmology. "And the earth." Here we have the ultimate truth of biology. Every emerging science is predicated on Genesis 1:1. Every truth we discover in the Bible is rooted in God's first and foundational claim. Every "natural" process has a supernatural starting point in God's great and sudden creation.

Stand fast on the first ten words of the Bible. Without an unshakable faith in Genesis 1:1, we have no basis for faith at all.

"If you have run with the footmen, and they have wearied you,
Then how can you contend with horses?"
Jeremiah 12:5 NKJV

Take the measure of your problems. Are you facing a giant, or are the little things ganging up on you?

Jeremiah was alarmed when he saw the people struggling with the little things. He wondered how they would make it when the stakes were raised. We should win some small victory every day, whether it be the curbing of our appetites or the choosing of our attitudes. Small victories prepare us for big achievements. A man is a fool who sets out to run a marathon when he has not yet run a mile.

The only way to successfully run the big race is to train hard for lesser distances. Tackle little problems with diligence. Expect a little pain along the way – training is hard work. Don't allow bitterness to fester or small challenges to go unmet. Train hard over the short haul; you are conditioning yourself for greater victories in the long race of life.

Submit yourself to God and appropriate His daily strength. In the end, it's not about manpower or horsepower; it's about God's power.

Please Pray for Colombia   Population under age 18: 16,235,000

Crime and violence is epidemic. Pray for peace and safety for the children and believers who are distributing the *Book of Hope*.

Out of the Ruins of a Violent Past in Colombia, a New Life for Leide

When Leide was 12-years-old, she joined a gang in her rough neighborhood of Medellin, Colombia. Her home life was troubled, and the gang members became her new family.

They did drugs together, drank alcohol together, and even lived together in the streets. But when Leide was 13, the gang demanded that she prove herself truly worthy to be a member. They said she had to kill another girl. And Leide did it.

From that moment, Leide's young heart was frozen into stone. She became a hardened delinquent, involved in more violent crimes, robberies, immorality, drug abuse, and more. Nothing mattered to her anymore.

But then Leide came to the town of Quibdo, and last October, the *Book of Hope* came to Quibdo, too. Leide did not have any interest in the book, but her school adopted it as their textbook for a course on personal development, so Leide had to read it.

She attended a Book of Hope summer camp, and there she accepted Christ as her Savior and began a process of healing and rehabilitation.

Today, Leide is a vibrant 15-year-old Christian girl. She has given up drugs and alcohol, has a renewed relationship with her family, and is coming to terms with her past. Although she deeply regrets the evil that she did, she knows that Jesus has forgiven her – and she has hope for the future!

Brethren, I count not myself to have apprehended: but this one thing I do, forgetting those things which are behind, and reaching forth unto those things which are before, I press toward the mark for the prize of the high calling of God in Christ Jesus.
Philippians 3:13-14 KJV

The old high school stirred up bad memories and a cloud of regret settled on me.

I graduated from high school without distinction and the old building reminded me of what could have been. I thought of scholarships I might have earned, the leader I might have been, the witness I might have shared had I not sold out to mediocrity. I would have passed by, until I noticed the old track.

I could have been a winner there too, but I didn't take running seriously. I was almost past the gap in the chain link fence when an inspiration pierced my darkness. I turned toward the track carrying all my regrets and wasted opportunities. One lap . . . one final lap on the high school track to close the books and shelve my shortcomings forever. I picked up the pace and clicked off a lap. My spirits began to rise. One last look at the old high school and I turned for home, closing a chapter called regret. I left it all behind on that final lap.

No one was watching and my time was not recorded, but if you ask me, my finest run was a one-lap race when hope broke through and regret failed to place.

*David arose from the ground, washed and anointed himself, and
changed his clothes; and he went into
the house of the LORD and worshiped.
2 Samuel 12:20 NKJV*

Most people have the luxury of locking their night-
mares in tight little closets. For this man, there was
no hiding place.

Idle time, lustful thoughts, sexual sin, a botched
cover-up, premeditated murder, a somber wedding, a
dying child – all this in the life of a man after God's heart.
Who can imagine his shame, his humiliation? Lying on
the floor of the palace begging God for grace – for judgment deferred, he held on to the hope that his illegitimate
child would be spared. For seven days he cried and
prayed, and then, it was over! "Is the child dead?" King
David asked. "Yes." It was over. Facing circumstances he
could not change, and having received forgiveness he
could not earn, David got off the floor and went to the
house of the Lord to worship. With a sober heart, he
closed the book on his sin and moved on.

Few people do that. Rather, they settle within sight
of their failures. Awash in tears of confession, they never
see the light on the far side of repentance. God never
intended such a waste of life.

When it's over, and lessons have been written on the
heart, there is nothing to be gained at the tomb of sin
forgiven ... not a moment to be lost on the road that
leads beyond.

And he brought him to Jesus. Jesus looked at him and said,
"You are Simon son of John. You will be called Cephas"
(which, when translated, is Peter).
John 1:42 NIV

Hope is a powerful motivator. I experienced the power of hope a few years ago when we put our home on the market.

For the hope of a better place, we radically changed the way we looked at our old home. As long as we were living without expectation of a change, needed projects languished, the carpets were tolerable, the paint was adequate and the cabinets were just fine. But when expectations changed, all projects became urgent: the carpet had to go, the paint was awful, and the cabinets demanded attention. Hope caused us to fix it, paint it, clean it, carpet it, power-wash it, pitch it, replace it, change it, spray it, and sell it. When hope fades, our spiritual house falls into disrepair, routine wears us threadbare, and procrastination robs us of needed maintenance. When hope is gone, life fades to gray. Victorious living requires that we no longer see the world through the eyes of ownership, but through the eyes of the One who has purchased us!

It's His vision of who we can be that inspires us to change. Don't give up; look up. Don't back up; rise up. You don't have to stay the same. He's going to take you on to a better place.

Come unto me, all ye that labor and are heavy laden,
and I will give you rest.
Matthew 11:28 ASV

We are tired these days, and proud of it. We work hard and pay for it with chronic fatigue. We are living in the fast lane, but are we living well?

There are times when we have to burn the candle at both ends, but I wonder if the perpetually tired are victims of the grind, or of poor priorities? People who are overworked and overtired hurry along a road of diminishing returns. There is nothing I do that is improved by fatigue; on the contrary, much is diminished. If tired was a virtue, we might be the most virtuous generation to ever populate the planet, but it can be argued that our generation is the most irresponsible, selfish, and unfeeling generation to ever work overtime.

The Lord invites those who are weary to rest because we need it! Everything breaks down unless you take care of daily maintenance. Back off, sharpen your saw and reassess your priorities.

Abundant living requires more than stress tabs and eight hours sleep – it requires a quieted heart.

*"When your days are over and you rest with your fathers,
I will raise up your offspring to succeed you."*
2 Samuel 7:12 NKJV

And what remains when the "amen" is spoken at our gravesides? What of our labor yet brings a harvest? What lives outside our selfish human spheres? Don't get me wrong – I'm not thinking about dying so much as I am about living. I know that I will step from this temporal world into His presence when He calls, but what will remain?

My investments for Christ in people will remain. Therefore I must increase my spiritual deposits. My prayers will live forever before God's throne. Therefore I must pray more, and pray for the generations that may follow. My life story may, somehow, live on to inspire another. Therefore I must live out God's script in faithfulness, excellence, and godliness. My giving may enable a mission school to thrive, a ministry to grow, a lost one to be found.

Therefore, I must give of what I earn, and give even to sacrifice when I see a need that I can meet. My children carry my physical and spiritual DNA. I must know that they know Him. I must know that they love Him – I must, that the faith of my fathers lives to touch another generation.

Consider what lives on when you are gone. Live beyond your life span.

So I spoke to you; yet you would not listen.
Deuteronomy 1:43 NKJV

My head was swimming in business as I pulled into rush hour traffic.

Talk radio poured out a steady stream of bad news. My mind was on other things. I worried about things I could not control and people I could not change. I determined, I resolved, I retrenched as I listed all my illegitimate cares and their cures. Almost lost in the background was the voice of my six-year-old passenger. "Hey Dad ... Daddy, hey Dad!" – she was excited. She was giving me a complete rundown of her day and I responded with the occasional, "Oh really," but I wasn't listening.

It didn't hit me until we arrived at home – she was still talking. She had chattered non-stop for fifteen minutes about her little world. She asked questions, hummed melodies, discussed her friends, and I couldn't recall a single word. I couldn't help but think that the day will come when she might not want my attention so much anymore. I repented before God and asked my little girl to tell it all again. She didn't hesitate for a moment, and I listened with rapt attention.

God speaks to us constantly by His creation and by His Word. It is our great loss when distractions rob us of golden moments with the One who loves us most.

Honor one another above yourselves.
Romans 12:10 KJV

Kids offer a refreshing transparency. At a birthday party, it came time to serve the cake. A little boy name Brian blurted out, "I want the biggest piece!" His mother quickly scolded him. "Brian, it's not polite to ask for the biggest piece." The little guy looked at her in utter confusion, and asked, "Well then, how do you get it?" Brian wasn't going to allow his appetite to be suppressed by something so trivial as proper etiquette. He saw his mother's rebuke as a temporary setback.

While I admire Brian's determination, I've often seen the grown-up version of this attitude wreak havoc in friendships and organizations. Watch out for the guy who has to have the biggest piece of the pie. He'll slash away with fork and knife to gain his objective. I've seen grown men throw away their families, and scuttle their reputations in their scrambling to get the biggest piece of the cake. Paul instructed the Romans to honor others above themselves. We catch glimpses of Paul modeling this noble behavior in his praise for Timothy, Luke, and Epaphroditus.

Can you think of a time when you've stepped aside to let another have the big piece of cake? I think there may be a connection between big slices and small people.

Those who look to him are radiant;
their faces are never covered with shame.
Psalm 34:5 NIV

We can look to Jesus with hope. As a little boy, I looked to my Dad with supreme confidence. No matter where I was or what I was going through, if I could see my Dad, I knew that I would be all right.

You see, Dad could fix stuff, kill bugs, bait hooks, drive a boat, lift loads, chase strays, buy burgers and shakes and pay the bills. Dad made sure I knew I was special, his only son. He seemed to glow with pride when he would introduce me and I looked up at him with something close to worship. The combination of love, loyalty, confidence, and grace set my Dad on a very high pedestal. But there is One higher than the world's greatest Dad. He fixed everything for us for all eternity. There isn't anything He cannot do, and He loves to work on His children's behalf. There is no load so heavy that He cannot lift it; no soul so lost that He cannot rescue it; no heart so broken that He cannot mend it.

When we look to Him our faces should be radiant and our hearts joyful, for we are His dearly loved children and He will never stop caring for His own.

Jesus said to him, "I am the way, the truth, and the life.
No one comes to the Father except through Me."
John 14:6 NKJV

Missions trips have given me a new appreciation of the choices we enjoy in America.

During a recent visit to the grocery store, I stopped counting dry cereal varieties when I passed one hundred ... everything from flakes to pops, loops, fruits, nuts and whole grains. I quit counting pickle varieties at fifty. My grocer stocks more than seventy-five meal choices for the discriminating canine. Multiple-choice is all the rage today, even in the church. We are besieged by consumerism that demands an expanded menu of ministries with drive-up service. Tolerance demands that we accept everything in the name of unity, turning a blind eye to truth. In the Old Testament, the children of Israel strayed into idolatry by blending religions rather than worshipping the one true God. Their option-driven religion resulted in moral collapse and God's judgment.

Truth only comes in one flavor. God can only be known through Jesus Christ who said, "You will know the truth and the truth will make you free." Variety is the spice of life, but when it comes to eternal life, there is no multiple-choice.

Direct my steps by Your word,
And let no iniquity have dominion over me.
Psalm 119:133 NKJV

One of England's finest preachers determined that his wife's failing health must keep him from ministering at a prestigious conference in America. Although he had purchased his ticket and concluded all arrangements, the ship would sail without him. Thus, J. Stuart Holden missed a golden opportunity in the prime of a preaching career.

A devoted husband, Holden gave himself to caring for his wife and tried not to think of what he was missing on the other side of the Atlantic. We are too easily disappointed when our plans fall through; too easily discouraged when a grand opportunity is missed. Our plunge to the pits of despair exposes a lack of intimacy with God. When we walk close to Him we live with a sure knowledge that we are immortal until His plan is completed in us. Delay is often the protective hand of a loving Father. Disappointment is often the precursor of great blessing. Hardship always precedes the highest summit.

Until the day he died, J. Stuart Holden resolved to never question God's timing. The unused ticket he held as a reminder for the rest of his life reserved his passage on a new luxury liner – the H.M.S. Titanic.

But God demonstrates His own love toward us,
in that while we were still sinners, Christ died for us.
Romans 5:8 NKJV

The old Bible lay on a bargain table amidst hundreds of tattered books. Many people picked it up and thumbed through its faded pages. It wasn't in very good shape – certainly not worth two pounds, so it was cast aside.

But then a man picked up the Bible and stifled a shout. He rushed to the counter and paid the paltry sum for the old book. It was an original Gutenberg, estimated to be worth more than one million dollars. I wonder who turned it over to the "last chance" booksellers? How many times did the old Bible change hands before its redemption? Someone cast it aside, unaware of its value.

We do the same thing with people. Seeds of greatness are often buried deep within unpromising characters that abruptly change course and change history. In truth, we were all passed over when Jesus saw something of value in us. Rather than paying a bargain price, He paid the highest price.

A different world would appear before our eyes if we would see every man and woman as a precious treasure that God just couldn't live without.

This is my comfort in my affliction,
for Your word has given me life.
Psalm 119:50 NKJV

SANTA CRUZ, BOLIVIA: Daniela is a ten-year-old student at the Cristo Rey School. She wrote to Book of Hope concerning her recent conversion. She paints a bleak picture of life before coming to know Christ. You may ask, "How bad can it be for a ten-year-old girl?"

Daniela confesses a list of what some might call childish infractions, but it is punctuated by the devastation and loneliness she felt when her parents separated. This tragedy broke her heart. As her little world was falling apart, Daniela was given a copy of the *Book of Hope* at school. She read the book, and believed God's Word. "Jesus came to my life just when I needed Him the most," she said. Daniela began to pray that God would bring her family back together again. Never underestimate a child's faith. "God granted me my wish," she writes. Daniela's mother has now become a Christian, too. Together, they are believing God for the salvation of the entire family. Of her father Daniela writes, "I know one day he'll change."

God's Word in the heart of a ten-year-old girl has power to change an entire family. If we will take the Word of God to all the children of the world, we can heal broken families; we can change the world.

"Show me, O LORD, my life's end and the number of my days;
let me know how fleeting is my life."
Psalm 39:4 NIV

When the nurse called me from the waiting room, I knew we were in trouble. The EKG was abnormal and the doctor wasn't treating it lightly.

I had seen my wife fill multiple roles with elegant grace. She had been a wife, mother, teacher, musician, and homemaker. Now she was a heart patient. With one phone call, a cardiologist entered our most intimate circle of friends. With one report, nameless technicians held our rapt attention. With one test, our perspective changed. The decks were cleared for whatever the doctor suggested. In a moment, importance took the lead and "urgent" dropped out of sight.

How is it that the "urgent" always rules? Running hard to keep pace, we lose sight of importance and lose touch with our higher values. Yet, when big storms threaten, we secure everything, and trim down to simple necessities. In so doing, we live on a higher plane with a sharper sense of purpose. In our case it took an abnormal EKG to un-clutter our priorities.

What will it take for you to stop living like a reactor? Empower the important and refuse to be led by the urgent. Get centered on vital relationships and eternal values. Your quality of life will improve, even in the midst of the storm.

And he saith unto them, Follow me,
and I will make you fishers of men.
And they straightway left their nets, and followed him.
Matthew 4:19-20 KJV

When the teacher asked if he might use his boat, the fisherman was happy to oblige. He had fished all night but no repair was needed for his old nets, only cleaning. Anchored in the cove, the teacher's words carried over the water to a crowd on the shore.

The fisherman sat in the back of the boat, listening intently as he ran the nets through his fingers. The crowd was leaving when the teacher said, "Put out into deep water, and let down the nets for a catch." "Why not?" he thought, "Maybe my luck will change." With practiced skill he cast the net, completely unprepared for what happened next. The boat lurched. The net was filled with fish. It was only with the help of his friends that the catch was saved. By the time the bow scraped the sandy shore, his net was in tatters; a total loss. What would he do tomorrow? Staring at the tangled netting, he heard the teacher say, "Follow me." He dropped the net, and followed.

We might learn a lesson from the fisherman. Impulsive, but wise, he lay down the tattered remains of his old life and followed Jesus. In the end Peter traded his job for a cause, and two boat loads of fish for a crown.

"Look, I am about to die," Esau said.
"What good is the birthright to me?"
Genesis 25:32 NIV

Esau was hungry. The hunt consumed all reserves and his brain bowed to his stomach. In that moment he cared more for Jacob's stew than for Isaac's blessing.

Thus Esau is forever remembered in the Scripture as a stupid, brutish man. He lived by his passions and acted without forethought. He valued the wrong things, married the wrong women, and acted for all the wrong reasons. His brother was a con man, but Esau was a fool. His appetites devoured all reason and in the rush of passion, he cared only for the here and now. He sold his birthright for a bowl of pottage, despising his little brother with every bite.

Years would pass; surely Jacob would forget Esau's empty words ... but Jacob didn't forget and Esau lost his father's choice blessing. For Esau, all values were relative to his desires. He found out too late that some values in life are absolute. Jacob's swindlers stew goes down in the annals of time as the consummate bad deal.

When desires are screaming, we would do well to remember that instant gratification makes the rich man a debtor.

*If you, then, though you are evil, know how to
give good gifts to your children, how much more will
your Father in heaven give good gifts to those who ask him!*
Matthew 7:11 NIV

It was the kind of place every kid should have memories of … an old log cabin on a New England lake sheltered by tall oaks and soft pines – hot enough in August to appreciate the shade at noon and cool enough in the evenings for a fire in a pot belly stove.

It was swimming and water skiing and camping with Dad on an island overgrown with blueberries. It was two weeks every summer on Lake Lucerne. Schedules were cast aside and every day was treasured.

When the third week of August arrived and we packed to go home, I grieved. While Dad loaded the car I would walk to the dock for one last look at the lake, wishing somehow I could take it all with me.

I guess some wishes come true, because I still carry that place with me now after twenty-seven years. I can still smell the damp pine needles after a rain. I can still hear the early morning sounds of the lake; the call of the loon, the high pitched singing of an outboard motor.

My folks knew how to make great memories that live on in the hearts of their children forever. What kind of memories are you making?

That the man of God may be complete,
thoroughly equipped for every good work.
2 Timothy 3:17 NKJV

On a cold February morning we started our three-day bicycle tour of the Outer Banks of North Carolina.

Driving rain, unforgiving head winds, and cold damp mornings added a few challenges along the way. I would gladly take the trek from Kitty Hawk to Beaufort again, but I'll be better prepared next time.

In short – I'll buy better gear! I'll have brand new tires; two flats in two hours got my attention. I'll buy the best in rain gear; wet and cold translate to grumpy and blistered. I'll be ready next time for anything short of a blizzard.

When you're not well equipped, life's journey always seems longer. We endure what we should have enjoyed; survive when we should have thrived; finish when we should have won. Poor equipping leads to a poor life experience.

The Apostle Paul offers a complete equipment catalog of the highest quality in Ephesians 3:11-20. Get yourself outfitted with this gear and you'll be ready for battles, rains, winds, drought or flood.

And God said unto Jacob, Arise,
go up to Beth-el, and dwell there.
Genesis 35:1 ASV

What do you do when you've lost your way; when your integrity is blown; your security is breached? Where do you go when your homestead has become hostile and your welcome has been rescinded?

These questions haunted Jacob at Shechem. Almost every bend in Jacob's road had been marked with deceit. He learned the con early in life and played it well. Now the con man was getting old and mending his ways, but his sons had learned deceit from the old master and coupled it with wanton violence. By the hands of Jacob's sons, a city lay in slaughter and Jacob felt the cold hand of fear grip his heart. *Surely the Canaanites would rise up and avenge the massacre at Shechem.* In his despair God whispered in Jacob's ear, "Go to Bethel." So Jacob journeyed back to the place where he had once met with God; where he had once received a heavenly vision; where he had first known the security of the covenant. Jacob returned to Bethel and made an altar there.

What do you do when you've stumbled and fallen? Get back to the place where your faith was strong. On your knees build an altar ... and dwell there.

His fame spread far and wide, for he was greatly
helped until he became powerful. But after Uzziah
became powerful, his pride led to his downfall.
2 Chronicles 26:15-16 NIV

Who has not watched the spectacular flameout of a promising sports star?

The yellow brick road to stardom is littered with the burned out hulks and speedsters who parlayed fame to fortune, only to turn their fortunes to dust. Legendary basketball coach John Wooden said, "It is best not to drink too deeply from a cup full of fame. It can be very intoxicating, and intoxicated people often do foolish things."

Uzziah was just such a man. He was marked for greatness from his youth. He flew higher and ruled longer than most kings, but fame ultimately clipped his wings. He died a leper.

If you have a measure of fame, treat it like bottled nitroglycerin. If you yearn for fame, beware that your yearnings do not make you a fool. If fame is unlikely to touch your life, guard your heart against other forms of pride that work to strip the believer of spiritual discernment and power.

To borrow John Wooden's analogy, pride is a powerful inebriant. If you drink much at all, you'll go blind. When Christians embrace sobriety and humility, our gifts display God's glory. Prideful indulgence leads to a wasted life.

*And not many days after the younger son gathered all together,
and took his journey into a far country.*
Luke 15:13 KJV

On April 15, 1992 Chris McCandless hitched a ride out of South Dakota to begin his great escape to the Alaskan wilderness.

Chris sought a solitary existence … a season of self-discovery. He gave himself a new name and left his last human contact in the area of Mt. McKinley. He tramped down the stampede trail to the place he thought he had been looking for all his life. Four months later, he died from starvation. His tragic tale is told in Jon Krakauer's book, "Into the Wild."

Though Chris is a most severe example, he is not unlike so many who go seeking a new life or enlightenment through an illicit relationship; a drug experience; abandoned responsibility; a pleasure spree or uncontrolled spending. When the far country is finally attained, our plunge to despair begins. When the magic is gone, bitterness finds a home in us. We weep for our disappointments and sing the anthem of my generation: *"I still haven't found what I'm looking for."*

As long as we are searching out new horizons for meaning and peace, we are cursed to disappointment and grief. What we need is not to be found in the far country, but with Father at home.

"... give me my share of the estate."
Luke 15:12 NIV
"... make me like one of your hired men."
Luke 15:19 NIV

Two attitudes speak to a wrong and right relationship with the Father.

The arrogant young man demands an early distribution of his inheritance. His complete absence of humility and submission, as well as his intention to pursue a wasteful course leave little to be desired. Two words mark him for his greed and impertinence – "Give me." And so, the Father gave him what he asked for and the party began.

It's amazing how foggy things become in affluence and how clear in poverty. His vision is finally restored in a pigpen. His position is perilous. Deciding to go to his Father, he demonstrates a true change of heart. Rather than saying, "Give me another chance," or "Give me back my place and title," he says, "Make me."

Our daily prayers often mirror the darker side of the prodigal son. We spend much of our time before our Father pleading – "Give me." Rather we should pray, "Make me, Lord. Make me what You want me to be."

The adolescent and wayward son submits demands. The wise son submits himself.

*"... the younger son got together all he had, set off for a distant
country and there squandered his wealth in wild living ...
So he went and hired himself out to a citizen of that country,
who sent him to his fields to feed pigs."*
Luke 15:13,15 NIV

He sat in my office, his head in his hands, his life in tatters.

"I had it all," he muttered, "I had it all and I threw it away." The tears that fell that afternoon were bitter. The sorrow that escaped in sobs was genuine. She was gone; the house was gone; the kids were gone; his job was gone; all for a selfish and foolish indulgence.

Good times don't always add up to a good life. The pleasures of sin are for a season, but seasons change. The prodigal ran from one party to the next consuming his own future. He denied himself nothing, like the preacher in Ecclesiastes (Ecc. 2:10), and found himself diminished for it. His raging pursuit of good times dropped him from the pinnacle of financial power to the lowest pit of poverty. His life of adventure was soon replaced with one of drudgery and demoralization. He went from being a man sought out to being a man avoided.

It's not a long way from the party life to the pigpen. A cavalier dalliance with drugs, alcohol, or illicit pleasure can so suddenly consume.

Choose wisely and be sober. Good living always outlives good times.

I will arise and go to my father.
Luke 15:18 ASV

Two words are necessary for change – I will.

The prodigal son made that foundational resolution, and it changed his life. No one gets far in life without resolve. Where there is no resolution there is no revolution. The prodigal would have missed the feast had he not resolved to go to the father. Daniel would have never risen to power had he not resolved to follow God's diet plan. The four lepers at the gate of Samaria would have starved had they not resolved to take their chances with the Arameans.

Neglecting needed change is accepting a life sentence without parole. Indecision is a very efficient jailor. Don't run from resolutions; run to them. Set goals, seek the help of the Lord, have others hold you accountable, step out in faith, and celebrate the wins. If not, you can just keep feeding the pigs and dreaming of what could have been.

The Apostle Paul said, "I can do all things through Christ who gives me strength." People who trust the Lord saying, "I can" and "I will" become, by His grace, people who say "I am" and "I did."

But when he was still a great way off,
his father saw him.
Luke 15:20 NKJV

Every day it was the same. The old man would rise early, say his prayers, and then walk out to the gate to gaze down the same dusty track that held his most painful memory.

His youngest son had walked down that track and over the far hills, pursuing a foolish and youthful dream. By now his inheritance was surely gone and his shattered pride would bring him back ... if he survived the big city after all. By now, he must realize that life at its highest and best is lived at home. The father shakes his head in disbelief, "I never imagined that he would stay gone so long." The sun is up and responsibilities move him back to the business that once gave him joy ... now it just marks time. He'll walk out to the gate again just after noon, and again to watch until sunset. Some would say the kid deserves a bitter taste of the big bad world. Others would tell the old man to get on with his own good life. But his heart is for his son, and nothing can pull him away from the gate.

So it is with our Heavenly Father who has so often been rejected for the fleeting delights of some "far country." He has every right to forget and move on, but this Father's heart is for His children too, and as long as there is life, He'll be standing at the gate ... watching and waiting.

The older brother became angry and refused to go in.
Luke 15:28 NIV

It was the biggest party the servants had ever seen.

Neighbors were asked to come at once. Ranch hands and cooks were hard at it to prepare for everyone from the servant's child to the valley barons. The Master's wayward son had come home, broken and humbled, an answer to the Master's prayers. The house pulses with new energy. The servants are singing. The Master is beaming. But something is out of place; something is not quite right.

The elder brother cannot be found. The Master is bursting to tell him the good news, but he has vanished. See that big house dancing with excitement, and now – see big brother sulking behind a sheep shed. He heard it first from a servant and darkness fell upon his soul.

What a study in contrast. The joy of the father is matched by the pettiness and self-pity of the eldest son. He is forfeiting a chance to be even greater in his father's eyes. He is losing the opportunity to be truly noble. This could be his greatest moment, but anger is making it his worst.

The elder son reminds us that of all this world's wretchedness, selfishness is the greatest misery of all.

The entrance of thy words giveth light;
it giveth understanding unto the simple.
Psalm 119:130 KJV

IGRA TOWNSHIP, RUSSIA: Arkadiy was a thirty-six-year-old homeless man living at the town dump. His younger years were spent wandering Siberia, working on roads and power plants. When the jobs ran out, Arkadiy ended up at the Igra garbage dump. He fashioned a small hut from the rubble and soon gave up all hope of a brighter day. It is hard to imagine a more hopeless situation.

In the fall of 1999, Book of Hope distributors from Izhevsk targeted Igra township. They distributed books wherever they could find an open door. While giving the books out on the streets, they heard that there were people living at the dump. When they arrived, the dump was empty. Disappointed, they decided to leave a book anyway in hopes that someone would find it. They prayed together and left the book by faith.

Arkadiy saw the bright colored book on the way to his hut. As he read, light pierced the darkness of his wandering soul. He began to weep, and for the first time, he prayed. God heard his prayer.

Today Arkadiy works in service ministries through the Igra church. He is about to be married. What a turnaround! We must never underestimate the power of God's written Word.

"My master has withheld nothing from me except you,
because you are his wife. How then could
I do such a wicked thing and sin against God?"
Genesis 39:9 NIV

If anyone ever deserved a little pleasure in life, it was a boy named Joseph.

He was sold into slavery by his brothers, robbed of his homeland, and stripped of his heritage. Serving in the household of Potiphar, an Egyptian officer, things started looking up. God blessed Joseph and Potiphar put him on the fast track to success. In short order, he was in charge of a large household.

When Potiphar's wife propositioned this young servant, he should have been an easy mark. He had risen above his peers. He enjoyed a measure of success, and success is the cocaine of the spirit. Entrusted with power, Joseph was certainly tempted with pleasure.

A lesser man would have fallen, but Joseph resisted temptation because he set absolute boundaries. In answer to the seductive advances of Potiphar's wife, Joseph resisted and fled. Joseph knew his boundaries.

Unless we establish clear boundaries and refuse to cross the lines, we will soon fall. The proud man, in hot pursuit of power or pleasure, ignores the boundaries. He is soon far from home and storing up regrets. Absolute boundaries keep us centered and safe, even against the strongest temptations.

But pity the man who falls and has no one to help him up!
Ecclesiastes 4:10 NIV

To whom can you bare your soul? Are there confidants among your acquaintances? Too many dark secrets make the heart a mausoleum.

James instructs us to confess our sins to one another. Confession is the enlistment of a friend to aid us in the fight against temptation. It's the unlocking of a prison door. It is also a hedge against pride, which precedes a fall. We often resist accountability because of a violated trust. Past betrayal convinces us to go it alone. We reason along these lines: "Because I've been burned I'll never risk again."

If we were so short-sighted in other arenas, we would never learn to walk, sing, dance or write. Trial and error, even painful error, accounts for much of our learning. If we lock the doors and close the shutters because somebody let us down, we live in darkness, never seeing the light of forgiveness and restoration that dawn with the encouragement of a friend.

Choosing one with whom to share your struggles should be a prayerful, careful, and thoughtful decision. Choosing to go it alone insures disaster.

Cuba has lost economic ground since the fall of the USSR, and the people are poor. Pray that God will provide for the children and the local church members who are distributing the *Book of Hope.*

Saved from the Brink of Suicide by the Gift of HOPE!

In Cuba, a lonely woman had just made her decision to end it all. In fact, she had taken an overdose of drugs that she knew would kill her. Life was too lonely and painful for her to carry on. Now all she had to do was wait for death to come ...

That's when the Book of Hope team arrived at her door. In Cuba, where not all the schools are open to the Christian teams, local churches have organized to go door to door, community by community, and personally contact each household in the city with God's Word.

When there are children in the home, they leave the *Book of Hope* with the kids, then they return later and collect the knowledge reviews at the end of each section. They correct these, then come back to discuss the answers to the questions and lead the children and their families to Jesus.

But in this house, they found no children – just one lonely woman who seemed very depressed. So they began to talk with her and tell her about Jesus, and His plan for salvation and eternal life. Suddenly the suicidal woman saw a glimmer of hope for her future! She said she wanted to accept Jesus as Savior right then!

The team prayed with her to lead her to the Lord. Then she told them about the drug overdose she had taken minutes before. They were able to get a doctor to come to the house, and the woman's life – and her soul – were saved!

Hope can save lives, and Jesus' love can mend broken hearts.

All we like sheep have gone astray;
we have turned every one to his own way.
Isaiah 53:6 KJV

A thirty-two-year-old investment banker lies on the couch searching his memories for childhood wounds.

A Lexus in the parking lot and a Wall Street portfolio brings no peace to his troubled mind. The analyst probes and questions while soft jazz helps fill the awkward silences. They're getting close now ... the banker remembers another broken promise ... another missing piece of the puzzle and the analyst nods knowingly. A father's broken promises and frequent absences have ruined this poor soul. It's time to let the young man off the hook. "It's not your fault," says the good doctor, "It's just not your fault." Tears roll down the banker's cheeks as he gains release from the guilt he's carried through two divorces and countless bare-knuckled brawls on his way to the top. Absolved of all responsibility for his own choices, he firmly shakes the hand and gladly pays the fee of the man who helped him lay his guilt on the shoulders of a dead father.

We can easily justify remaining the same as long as we can lay it on someone else's doorstep. Sure ... we are influenced by our beginnings, but each and every one of us will stand before God to give our own account; no excuses; no exceptions; no scapegoats.

And Elijah came to all the people, and said,
"How long will you falter between two opinions?
If the Lord is God, follow Him."
1 Kings 18:21 NKJV

The wedding was planned to perfection. The music and photographer were chosen months in advance. The honeymoon was extravagant. The grand event was a grand success.

The wedding lasted an hour – the marriage lasted a year. Hindsight revealed fatal flaws and everyone said, "How sad." It was soon forgotten; just another pothole in the fast lane of American culture. They chose what they wanted only to find that they didn't want what they had chosen. The solution was obtained with the help of a lawyer and the stroke of a gavel: game over – choose again! The blessings of living in a multiple-choice culture are obvious; the curses less so. With the ever-changing winds of choice, there is always the promise of something new, and rarely a thought for something lost. The virtues of commitment, honor, and persistence are long gone ... gone with the winds. Rather than submitting to disciplines and enduring hardship, many just walk away; away from a church, a family, a promise.

We live in a culture that cannot make up its mind. Surrounded by a million broken vows, the Christian stands to remind the world that there are some choices we make only once ... and forever.

A father to the fatherless, a defender of widows,
is God in his holy dwelling.
Psalm 68:5 NIV

Before he was born he was abandoned.

He's an innocent victim – he's the scene of the crime. He's been robbed of a father and he's forever looking for the dad he never had through the windows of a broken heart. Through that window he sees healthy families, loving fathers, and happy sons. Through the window he sees the fishing trips and baseball games they might have shared. He sees the man he dreamed would come home and correct this terrible mistake ... but that man remains on the other side of the glass, oblivious to the longing eyes at the window.

Nothing in life has been able to pull a curtain on that window or gain him access to the other side. He needs a father. Nothing can replace father; someone to heal the wounds of rejection; to silence the roar of loneliness.

At the window, he's unaware of the One who stands at his side. The Father he longs for; the Father he didn't know he had stands by, waiting for an introduction.

Surely this is the work of the church in a "dysfunctional" world: to turn his eyes from the window of longing to find the Father who knows the pain of unrequited love, and sees us through the windows of a broken heart.

"Forget the former things; do not dwell on the past."
Isaiah 43:18 NIV

I think I'm losing my memory!

I leave things home when I leave for the office, especially when I have set them out ahead of time. I reach into my gym bag to find that I have clean socks but no towel. I am seated in a restaurant enjoying my first bite when I catch a vision of my money clip on the night stand at home. Not long ago I reached a new plateau in my ascent to cognitive nirvana. I arrived home late in the evening and was greeted by my wife with an odd question: *"Where's Ashley?"* She was referring to our eldest daughter. I was supposed to pick her up after my meeting. I was suddenly aware that I had crossed a new threshold in forgetfulness. But then, I'm not sure if it's worse to forget, or to be unable to forget.

A world without forgetting would be a horrible place. What if time didn't soften the blow or blur the edges? What if our perspective couldn't be altered, or our attitude elevated? What if there were no new vantage points to steal away our affections and attentions? Life would be a numbing monotony, a constant rehearsing of yesterday's pain and trouble.

Enjoy the warm pleasure of precious memories while rejoicing in the grace of things forgotten.

I am with you always.
Matthew 28:20 NKJV

I'm miles from home on a Sunday morning. Two time zones have me sipping coffee while my church is about to begin the first service.

I suddenly want to be there. I worry about everything from staffing to starting on time. When I take the pulpit here, my congregation will be enjoying a Sunday afternoon. It's a strange feeling, as though life slipped out of sync and I'm out of place.

I'll bet you've felt this way . . . out of sync? Maybe you feel that way this morning. Your job description was rewritten and you've become a stranger at your own desk. Your last child left for college and the house has lost that "homey" feeling. Your husband made you a divorcee and you can't let go of the married life you loved. Your mother left the rest home for heaven and suddenly you don't feel so at home here on earth. What do you do when life slips out of gear? Get closer to the Changeless One.

AT&T used to tell us to "reach out and touch someone." It's good advice when life seems out of sync. Though miles from home and surrounded by strangers, a minute prayer, a psalm of thanks, a whispered petition, and life begins to work again. Surely, one of the great treasures of the Bible is the word "always!"

... but this one thing I do, forgetting those things which are behind,
and reaching forth unto those things which are before,
I press toward the mark for the prize of
the high calling of God in Christ Jesus.
Philippians 3:13-14 KJV

If, indeed, some things are best forgotten, how shall we discriminate between what to keep and what to throw away? Here are a few touchstones along the way.

We should forget anything that God has forgotten. His promise to "remember our sins no more" is one of the crown jewels of grace. Holding ourselves captive to forgiven sin is sheer folly. We should forget anything that centers on self. Paul summed up his former life of personal ambition and achievement with a pungent word: dung.

We should forget the sins of others against us. Jesus said that if we would not forgive our brothers, then the Father would not forgive us. We should forget whatever the past held of sorrow and wrong. Most of our regretting is wasted emotion. We should forget our finest moment to make room for something better. When we settle in around our successes, we rob ourselves of the new frontier.

Paul admonished the church to make the most of every opportunity. When we can't let go, we make a mess of every opportunity.

But when the young man heard that saying,
he went away sorrowful: for he had great possessions.
Matthew 19:22 KJV

He is a shining example to his community: so young, and already a judge in the court system.

He married well and everything he touches turns to gold. His three-car garage holds two eighty thousand dollar marvels built in the Black Forest, and a luxury S.U.V. He lives a clean life and plays by the rules. He's living the American Dream, yet he is constantly awakened to a simmering discontent: *"Shouldn't I be happy? Shouldn't I feel better about myself? Why can't I find peace and why do I need more?"* His search for contentment goes on even as his stocks rise and windfalls are re-invested. He'll try anything to find an answer. If someone can point him to the answer, he'll come running.

Take the modern factors out of the story and you're left with the rich young ruler. Financially sound … his whole life before him … positioned for power; yet empty. He came so close to the discovery of eternal life, but in the end his holdings held him fast and his condition remained unchanged.

You can have it all and have nothing. You can reach the top only to wonder why you climbed.

*"For we have no power against this great multitude that is coming
against us; nor do we know what to do,
but our eyes are upon You."*
2 Chronicles 20:12 NKJV

What do you do when your manageable conflict becomes a raging crisis? What do you do when you are suddenly surrounded and outnumbered? What do you do when you don't know what to do?

Some people panic, others resign, still others resort to desperate schemes – wasting their energies while impending doom hangs like a dark cloud. King Jehosophat found himself in an impossible situation. Human ingenuity couldn't save him; armed warriors couldn't defend him; his allies couldn't reinforce him; and his creativity failed him. Here is a man at the end of the road: *"We have no power ... we don't know what to do."* Rather than succumb to fear, Jehosophat made a great proclamation of faith: *"But our eyes are upon You."* While others might have focused on the strategic positioning of the enemy, or the organization of the local militia, Jehosophat focused on God.

When hope is fading, turn your eyes to heaven. Fix your eyes on Jesus, the redeemer of every hopeless cause, and trust Him absolutely. When He is entrusted ... we are protected.

*And we pray this in order that you may live a life worthy of the
Lord and may please him in every way: bearing fruit in
every good work, growing in the knowledge of God.*
Colossians 1:10 NIV

Most of us wouldn't think of making a cross-country journey without a map and timetable, and yet most people have no map or timetable for the journey of life.

Structured learning takes us through the first quarter century, and from then on it's passive learning or on-the-job-training. Weariness of the classroom and impatience for the future rob us of wisdom and understanding. We become spiritual and emotional pygmies ... stunted in our growth and frustrated in our purpose.

God has given us an incredible capacity to learn. It seems a great waste that for many, the pursuit of knowledge ceases at graduation. Take a few hours with your Bible and concordance and study the passages that deal with understanding, wisdom, learning, teaching, etc. You'll find that every believer should be determined to grow.

Draw up a life plan today. Think through your goals ... sort out your priorities ... stop waiting for life to happen and start doing the things that will fulfill God's plan in your life. You really can't afford to put it off. If you fail to plan, you are unknowingly planning to fail!

"For some time you have wanted to make David your king.
Now do it!"
2 Samuel 3:17-18 NIV

I once asked a friend whose great administrative gift I envied, "How do you get so much done?" His answer was simple: "Do it now! I eliminate procrastination in my decision making process." I've since found that peace and progress are two immediate by-products of the "Do it now" maxim.

The dragons that slay us are the ones we allow to grow in the backwaters of procrastination. They start out as minor, messy, annoying little reptiles, but soon they're snorting fire, scorching our hopes, and eating up our opportunities.

Procrastination is an expensive luxury. If I put off minor dental work, I will soon be facing major expenditures. If I fail to consistently discipline a child, I will raise a monster. What we ignore usually finds a brutal way to get our attention. A valiant warrior named Abner once challenged the divided house of Israel to quit procrastinating – "Now do it!" he said.

That's sound advice. Make a list; stick to it; get organized; close chapters; say "yes" or "no" finish what you started. Each of us must decide whether we will slay our dragons or serve them.

Jesus wept.
John 11:35 NKJV

It was such an emotional display that the locals talked about it. Why did He weep?

Some will tell you it was because of the grief He saw in Mary and Martha. Others say He wept because he knew that Lazarus would have to come back to the struggles of life. To me, it doesn't matter what triggered this flow of emotion. What matters is that Jesus wept.

God broke down and cried. He proved himself the forever-faithful high priest suffering with His people. To Mary it seemed that God was running late. Her words betray her deep disappointment. It would seem that the "Great One" was coming to grips with His first failure. But then the Master wipes His eyes, clears His throat and says, "Roll away the stone." What a moment! Here we have a God who weeps with us in our pain, and then "rolls away the stone" of suffering. Here is both Friend and Deliverer, Brother and Master, Sympathy and Salvation. This moment was the perfect "bridging" of God to man. He cried out of His humanity, then He spoke out of His divinity, and the dead lived again.

Where is God when we hurt? He weeps with us; He walks with us; and He works in us. Don't doubt Him, not even for a minute – He can still roll away the stone.

For though I am absent from you in body,
I am present with you in spirit and delight to see how
orderly you are and how firm your faith in Christ is.
Colossians 2:5 NIV

SMOLENKA, SIBERIA: In this small town on the outskirts of Chita, the site of the distribution of the 100 millionth copy of the *Book of Hope,* a church is rising up.

The impact of the *Book of Hope* in the community has drawn favorable attention to the sponsoring church in Chita. The church, in turn, has launched a church planting for Smolenka. Land has been donated, leaders have been appointed, a core group has been established, and a new church has been welcomed into the community.

The 100 millionth distribution will now live far beyond its date on the calendar. A church rises up to light the darkness. In time, the 100 millionth celebration will be forgotten as the little school we invaded in Smolenka greets class after class of first graders. We will one day celebrate the billionth distribution in another city, in another land . . . but a church in Smolenka will continue to bring in the harvest until Jesus comes.

Affect Destiny Teams go beyond the mere distribution of books. Churches are encouraged, churches are planted, goodwill is established and Christianity often gets a sec-ond look. We hold eternal hope for short-term encounters. This summer morning, hope is rising in Smolenka.

Set your minds on things above,
not on earthly things.
Colossians 3:2 NIV

We choose a radio station by tuning the dial. We select a television channel by clicking a channel. We search for a website that meets a distinctive need for information or retail.

We discriminate every day between restaurants, clothiers, bookstores, gas stations, and dry cleaners. We have determined what is good and bad; what meets our needs; where service is best.

Every day we make choices ... none so important as our mind-set. Paul offers the Philippians selected categories for mental health in Philippians 4:8. He challenges the Colossians to "set" their minds.

Are you setting the range and focal point of your thinking, or are you allowing your mind free reign to wander all over the dial? Are you discriminatory in rejecting lines of thought that are evil, wasteful, or selfish? Are you heavenly minded? Do thoughts of the Lord intrude in every corner of your thought life? We are what we think. What we do is ultimately traced back to the headwaters of the thought life.

We need to take time every morning to establish presets for the mind. Determining where we will tune in will help define what we should tune out.

*And we know that in all things God works for the good
of those who love him, who have been called
according to his purpose.*
Romans 8:28 NIV

The doctor gave you bad news, and the question formed immediately: "Where are You, Lord?" You thought you had job security when your manager called you in. Now you're unemployed and the question troubles you: "Where are You, Lord?"

You can't quite put your finger on it, but you can't escape the feeling that your teenage daughter is slipping away from you. Her new friends don't share your values and her new attitudes are keeping you awake at night: "Where are You, Lord?"

You're in good company. David must have wondered where God was when Saul was hunting him like an animal. Elijah wondered where God was when Jezebel threatened his life.

The truth is that God is there, and He is working – always. He is making something out of nothing. He is in the early stages of transforming your heartache to a heartsong. He is making something glorious out of something hideous.

Quiet your heart and renew your faith. Regain your focus and take a new grip. God never checks out on anybody. You can't see it and you don't feel it, but you *must* believe it: God is working – and He is working all things for your good.

That I may gain Christ and be found in him.
Philippians 3:8-9 NIV

"Who *am I?*" This is a bedrock question that every believer needs to answer daily.

You see ... the culture tells me I'm just another brick in the wall; the biologist tells me that I'm DNA; the evolutionist tells me that I'm an ascending animal; the boss tells me I'm replaceable; the government tells me that I'm a taxpayer and medical liability; the mirror tells me I'm older; the law tells me that I'm a sinner; the bank tells me that I'm a breadwinner; my father calls me son; my wife calls me sweetheart and my kids call me Daddy ... but every day I need to turn my heart toward heaven and be reminded of who I really am.

I am a child of the One and Only, Almighty God – creator of the universe and lover of my soul. I am the purposed creation of the ultimate craftsman. I am fearfully and wonderfully made. I am here for God's good pleasure. I am alive in the flesh – this outer shell, but I am also alive in the Spirit. I am a sojourner in this world – a citizen of heaven.

I am owned by God; loved by God; filled with His Spirit; guided by His hand; used for His purpose and crowned with His glory!

And we know that to them that love God all things work
together for good, even to them that are called
according to his purpose.
Romans 8:28 ASV

My flight was delayed – then cancelled. I missed my meeting. I couldn't get an aisle seat. The guy next to me looked like he had a fever. My tray table was broken. My luggage didn't make it. The hotel was out of non-smoking rooms. The mattress must have been purchased from prison supply. Have you ever had a day like that?

Sometimes things don't work out. Paul wanted to take Barnabas on his second missionary journey but it didn't work out. He wanted to go to Asia, but that did not work out either; flight cancelled. Next, he tried to enter Bythinia but that didn't work out either; God said no (Acts 16:6-7). Finally, the doors opened up for Paul to go to Macedonia, a place it had never occurred to him to visit. Paul's great travel disaster turned into one of his great missionary conquests. Sometimes God's leadership can be most clearly seen in the things that don't work out. Press on when it seems that circumstances are conspiring against you.

God's creative genius is at work amidst disappointments, cancellations, obstructions and delay. Now you call it disaster, but one day you may call it grace.

But none of these things move me;
nor do I count my life dear to myself.
Acts 20:24 NKJV

When James Calvert went out as a missionary to the cannibals of the Fiji Islands, the captain of the transport ship sought to turn him back. As the long boat bobbed in the green waters, ready to row the small party ashore, the captain called out, "You will lose your life and the lives of those with you if you go among such savages." Calvert looked up from the long boat and ended all discussion with a simple reply, "We died before we came here."

Paul was warned by the Holy Spirit of trouble ahead. The tears and entreaties of friends could not dissuade him. Paul possessed an unshakable faith; he made an unconditional surrender; he set an unalterable course and would not be moved. Paul viewed himself as one crucified with Christ and dead to sin. Paul was sold out!

Such an unswerving commitment is rare in an age of comfort and compromise, and desperately needed. Modern cynicism has strangled the notion of a noble cause. Relativity has blanketed truth in a heavy fog. This generation will only believe in truth we are willing to back with our lives.

Be unmovable in your faith. If it's not worth dying for, it's probably not worth living for.

And he said to him, 'Well done, good servant;
because you were faithful in a very little,
have authority over ten cities.'
Luke 19:17 NKJV

Take care of the little things in life and the big things will fall into place.

The first attempt at creating the Panama Canal was made by the French in 1882. They hired the world's foremost engineer, Ferdinand de Lesseps, who had recently completed the Suez Canal. The work was abandoned, however, just six years after it began. The height of the mountains was nothing compared to the bite of the mosquito. Yellow fever and malaria savaged the work force. The mountains would not be conquered until the mosquito was controlled.

A lot of people try to tackle the mountains without first dealing with the mosquitoes. They take short cuts around character issues, thinking that a position will grant them the standing they should have gained through process. When trouble comes, they can't fight the fever and disaster soon follows. God always tests us first in the small things. King David had to learn how to lead sheep before he could lead people. Big dreams require great vision and great courage, but they are only achieved if we have taken the small steps first.

Be faithful in the little things today. They ultimately determine your tomorrow.

The hand of the diligent will rule,
But the lazy man will be put to forced labor.
Proverbs 12:24 NKJV

Find someplace to serve the Lord and get up some spiritual momentum. "Dead in the water" saints never get to the starting line on time. Saints in motion only require mid-course adjustments to hit their marks. Sitting saints can't even see the marks.

Momentum grants us power to crash through all obstacles. Lethargy can't overcome the smallest molehill. The man who is faithful in small things will one day step into a larger arena. The lazy man lives under a capped potential. God's laborers find joy in the most difficult places.

For the sitting saint, all places are difficult and joy is elusive. When the ship is under full sail, the rudder bites. Without wind and sail, no direction is found. Servants never lack for a purpose. The selfish have no capacity for vision. Workers insure a harvest. Whiners insure a drought. Those who run hard are conditioned to run harder yet. Those who fail to run diminish what strength they have. The sailor rides the wind. The slacker wastes in the doldrums.

You'll never be ready for the marathon if you don't start running the mile. Give yourself to the meeting of a need. All your bright tomorrows find their start in serving God today.

To everything there is a season.
Ecclesiastes 3:1 NKJV
Do your utmost to come before winter.
2 Timothy 4:21 NKJV

As a young man, he paid no attention to the seasons … too busy … too hurried. But with the passing years he found, like most older men, a greater interest in the weather and the seasons.

This morning he could smell that first breath of autumn, and it reminded him of Timothy. The boy always talked of the beauty of the autumn in Lystra, and as Paul looked out from his prison home, he longed to see him again. Demas was gone, the others were carrying out his bidding … only Luke remained. Paul knew what the others so fastidiously avoided: that his days were numbered … his season was passing. And so, he wrote: *"Come before winter."*

Eastern religions teach that life just keeps coming around again, and therein lies a shadow of truth. There are second chances in life, yet there are certain seasons that come and go but once. Life should be lived with a joyful sobriety, celebrating the moment and seizing God-given opportunities.

Tomorrow holds no guarantee. Paul knew that if he ever were to see Timothy again, it had to be before winter. Are there autumn issues blowing about in your heart? What needs be done, do it well, and do it now.

Brethren, be not children in mind: yet in malice be ye babes,
but in mind be men.
1 Corinthians 14:20 ASV

Five hundred years after Ponce de Leon, we are still in search of the fountain of youth. We have bought into a massive deception when we believe that love is lovelier, attraction is stronger, and life is better when we're young.

The American diet industry is now a twenty billion-dollar business ... and we're getting fatter! More than three million cosmetic surgical procedures were performed last year. At least half of these rebuilds were purchased by people between the ages of 35 and 50. These days every body part has a surgical specialist. It doesn't matter what it is, we can get it lifted, sanded, tightened, suctioned, enlarged, reduced, relocated, transplanted, or reconstructed. We live in a culture obsessed with abs of steel, organic peels, magic lotions, creams and potions; we're not far removed from sorcery. As a result we've got sixty-year-old Barbie dolls and midlife Rogaine Rickys acting like life's greatest lessons have been wasted on perpetual adolescents. Where will the madness end?

The stakes have never been higher for a Christian generation. The fields are truly white unto harvest. Oh that we would be young at heart, mature in spirit, and wise in our thinking.

Be very careful, then, how you live – not as unwise but as wise,
making the most of every opportunity.
Ephesians 5:15-16 NIV

Let me talk to men for a moment. I need to ask you a question: "What are you going to do with the extra half-life God has given you?" That's right ... an extra half-life.

The expected life span for a male in Zambia is thirty-six years. In Russia, life expectancy is fifty-nine years. Here in America, we can expect to live seventy-six years! What's more, if we avoid cancer and heart disease, that life expectancy rises to a staggering (or should I say shuffling) ninety-two years. We have an extra half-life that much of the world cannot possess. It's something to remember when we're inclined to grumble about taxes, hair loss, or work weeks. If I had been born here one century ago, at forty-three, I would be approaching the midnight of my life. As it is, I am enjoying an early afternoon. Life expectancy in 1900 was forty-seven years.

We have been given more time, more opportunity, and more resources to reach the world than any preceding generation. We can truly start over and start smarter than our fathers. We can give the next generation a gift they desperately need: a relevant, vigorous, and wise eldership.

Help Wanted: midlife needs a midwife; there's a new and vital half-life just waiting to be born.

Then Jesus went into the temple of God and drove out all those who bought and sold in the temple, and overturned the tables of the money changers and the seats of those who sold doves.
Matthew 21:12 NKJV

Judah winced as his wife washed his wounds. Two lashes had broken the skin and his forearms and shoulders were all bruises and welts. His marks were nothing compared to those worn by men who had been whipped at the post, but he hurt none the less and sleep would evade him tonight. This was crazy!

He wasn't a criminal, or a soldier; he was a money changer – a clerk. Pilgrims often arrived in Jerusalem in a spiritual frenzy. He provided a needed service. He exchanged currency, all for a tidy profit. He had been cursed and threatened but no one had ever raised a hand against him, let alone a whip. Ninety seconds, and not a table left standing ... animals running everywhere ... people shouting. That prophet, or teacher, or whatever he was ... looked right through him and said, "You have made my house a den of thieves." Judah shuddered at the memory. The look in his eye was like a gathering storm. The sound of his voice was like thunder. Maybe he would feel better in the morning?

Maybe his nerves would settle ... but Judah knew – he knew the moment he locked eyes with his attacker; it was time to find a new line of work.

*A woman came with an alabaster jar of very expensive perfume,
made of pure nard. She broke the jar and poured the
perfume on his head.*
Mark 14:3 NIV

I almost passed her by on this reading through the Gospels.

When I get close to her, I feel a little uncomfortable. She was quick to break with convention, and I'm a pretty orderly type. She was overly emotional, and I'm not given to great public displays of private feelings. She made others uncomfortable, and I've always shied away from people like that. She's just a footnote in the Easter week, and I would have passed her by except for a nagging question.

As I looked upon this woman pouring out her substance as she poured out her heart, the question rattled me a bit: "Have I ever done anything like that for Jesus?" Do I give my all and my best to demonstrate my love for Him? Have I ever evoked the criticism of others because of my ardent devotion to Jesus? Is my expression of worship excessive, or is it restrained, meager, and predictable?

She was criticized, possibly even shamed for her "wasteful" display of passion, but Jesus said that what she did would be remembered forever. I've learned that the great days in a life are lived outside the comfort zone. Look at this lady today and ask yourself, "Have I ever done anything like that for Jesus?"

"What are you willing to give me if I deliver Him to you?"
And they counted out to him thirty pieces of silver.
Matthew 26:15 NKJV

Of all the Bible characters, I must know Judas. I must know Judas because I fear I am like him. I carry a dark potential – we all do – and if one could walk so close to the light of the world and die in outer darkness – who then is immune?

He saw miracles, heard Jesus teaching, and witnessed resurrection. Every time his eyes fell on Jesus he beheld the Truth! And yet, he fell with incredible haste and violence. Judas calls me to vigilance. I must close doors left ajar in my heart. I must post a guard over my desires lest in moments of sheer madness, I too, am guilty of betrayal. He is history's most ridiculous gambler. He rolled the dice – and lost. There are some who argue that he was a victim of a cruel providence. How unfair that God would choose Judas to be the one to fulfill prophesy. Others argue that he was trying to force Jesus to seize power and reveal himself to the nations … but I can't buy that. There is nothing noble to be found in the story of Judas. He sold Jesus for thirty pieces of silver, and when it was done he couldn't live with himself. I must know this character, for he is a warning to all men.

God help us when our selfish allowances grow to maturity. God help us when unconfessed sins approach the finish line. God help us when thirty pieces of silver seems a reasonable price for integrity.

He sent his word, and healed them,
and delivered them from their destructions.
Psalm 107:20 KJV

KOSOVO: Affect Destiny Team: Skyler struggled to put it all on paper. Walking through the war-scarred towns, he writes of the depth of their suffering.

"It's not just the destruction of their homes and families; they have been stripped of their identities, their worth, and their freedom. Now they are attempting to regain the pieces of their lives that were broken and scattered. Some pieces will never be put back: killed fathers, mothers, and children will never come back; innocent girls that were raped will never have their virginity back." Other team members echoed the writer's poignant description of loss and suffering. At times, in personal danger, the team distributed books to wanting hands as threats were voiced and stones were thrown.

The team was undaunted. Skyler continued: *"So here we are in God's perfect timing, bringing them the only thing that can completely restore their lives; the only thing that can put all the broken pieces back together and heal the wounds. They are searching and striving for something to put their hope in; God has provided them with His Word."*

In the year 2000, Affect Destiny Teams distributed 150,000 copies of the *Book of Hope* in war torn Kosovo.

*I felt I had to write and urge you to contend for the faith
that was once for all entrusted to the saints.
Jude 1:3 NIV*

In April of 1985, "new Coca-Cola" arrived amidst great fanfare. Within twenty-four hours of its arrival, 81% of American homes had heard about the new taste of Coke. All was well for the first few weeks, and then the public reminded Coca-Cola that the market determines success of the product, not the company. Pockets of protest became an ad hoc committee to bring back "old" Coke. By June, it was increasingly obvious that "new Coke" wasn't going to make it. By August, new Coke was old news. The original Coca-Cola was coming back.

I contacted Coca-Cola in 1996 to see what happened to new Coke. They still sell the syrup, but they couldn't give me a single bottler in the Southeast who distributed it. Coca-Cola has no plans to change the recipe again. Some things just can't be improved.

This is Jude's contention concerning the faith his readers had embraced. He admonishes them to fight for the original. Compromise dilutes faith until it becomes a mere form.

How quietly and gently we are rocked to sleep by a culture that exalts compromise as a crowning virtue. Jude begins his letter with a warning shot across our bows. We must fight for the faith once entrusted to the saints. It's the real thing!

And I thank Christ Jesus our Lord who has enabled me,
because He counted me faithful, putting me into the ministry.
1 Timothy 1:12 NKJV

If you have a ministry, any ministry, be thankful that God has so blessed your life. Some places God sends us are fraught with difficulty. Others are for a short season. Few find themselves in a long-term life of ease in ministry, whether they are filling a pulpit or filing in the church office.

God uses the hard times to perfect us. He uses the short seasons to augment our experience. He uses pain to get our undivided attention. He uses a few unlikable characters to knock off our own rough edges. The fact of the matter is that God's hand is leading those He has called through the darkness, through the rain, through the trouble, through the pain, through the laughter, through the tears, through the hour or through the years. God is intimately involved in our lives. How can we fail to see the power and wonder of it all?

Ministry and mumbling are strange bedfellows. Our complaints undermine the very foundation that God wants to build through us. Whining is a sure sign that tawdry circumstances have drawn us away from His glory. Paul endured the prisons and stripes maintaining an attitude of gratitude.

You have been counted as faithful by God. You have been called to ministry. Don't stoop to be a king.

All we like sheep have gone astray;
we have turned every one to his own way.
Isaiah 53:6 KJV

Neitzche boldly proclaimed, "God is dead, God is dead, we have killed Him." Then Neitzche died.

Voltaire claimed that the Bible would be abandoned in his generation; then Voltaire died and was himself abandoned.

God-consciousness not only outlived its pallbearers, it increased in vitality. The funeral that is presently being conducted in the American arena commemorates the death of truth. "Truth is dead, truth is dead, we have killed it," says the secular humanist. In its place we have established tolerance, relativism, and individualism as crowning virtues.

We have witnessed the meltdown of right and wrong. The word "moral" has been cut adrift to find its own definition apart from law. A personal substitute for truth based on the person rather than the principle has us reeling like drunken sailors trying to find our way back to pier one.

When everybody is right and nobody is wrong, chaos reigns and we open ourselves to the most bizarre lunacy. Even as the funeral is drawing to a close, truth must show up in the church to expose the fraud. Relativism sets its course to destruction while the truth still sets men free.

Please Pray for India

Please Pray for India   Population under age 18: 398,306,000

India is home to hundreds of different religions, and spiritual warfare is intense. Pray for freedom from demonic oppression for the children and safety for the youngsters, new believers and Book of Hope distribution teams.

In India, Jaswant's Hope Helps Him Stand Strong for the Faith

In a city in India, Jaswant* had grown up in a strongly non-Christian household. At age 15, when he received the *Book of Hope*, there was no idea in anyone's mind that Jaswant would ever be anything but a follower of his religion ...

So his family was shocked – and appalled – when Jaswant announced that the book had shown him the way to salvation, and he would now follow Jesus Christ!

His angry family thought they would beat this new faith out of Jaswant, and they actually tortured him, trying to get him to renounce Jesus. Jaswant refused to turn his back on his new Savior, and when he saw the opportunity to escape from the torture, he ran away from home. From then on, Jaswant lived in the jungle, isolated from his family.

He still came to church, and soon the pastor found out what had happened to Jaswant. He went to the family home and intervened.

Although he could not win Jaswant's parents to Christ, he did make it possible for Jaswant to come home and live with his family, without being punished for his faith.

Says the pastor, "Despite his suffering, Jaswant has not turned his back on the Lord." Please pray with us for Jaswant, and for his family. God is at work in India!

*To protect those involved names have been changed

The precepts of the Lord are right, giving joy to the heart.
Psalm 19:8 NIV

Trying to create joy apart from the Bible is like trying to start up an ice hockey team in Key West – you're just a bit out of your element. In our mad pursuit of pleasure, we often find it only to suffer deep disappointment at our inability to possess it. Like a cocaine crash, we are left somewhat lower when the morning comes and the thrill is gone. We begin our pursuit all over again, needing a greater rush next time.

What we are missing is joy, and joy is a foundational element in life. Pleasure and happiness, without a foundation, are short-lived abstractions. The man who has joy can enjoy daily pleasures and happiness even in the midst of turmoil and suffering. A biblical foundation intensifies pleasure and re-interprets our happenings to create maximum happiness.

Missionary Alan Gardiner could write of being "overwhelmed by the goodness of God" even as he was dying of malnutrition on Pitcairn Island. He had a foundation of joy that supported the kind of contentment that Paul talks about.

Where can we find this joy? We find it in keeping the precepts of the Lord – God's instructions for daily living. When they are violated, we are joyless. Without God's precepts, we're just lacing up our skates in Key West.

"We should go up and take possession of the land,
for we can certainly do it."
Numbers 13:30 NIV

Twelve spies were sent into the land of Canaan. They all saw the same things but only two possessed vision.

Vision is spiritual awareness. Vision sees more than the size of a city or the strength of an adversary. Vision sees God at the center of the equation. Ten spies determined that the obstacles were immovable. Joshua and Caleb determined that the opportunities were inevitable. Ten spies said, "This is bad." Two spies said, "This is it!" Ten spies couldn't get past giant men, but Joshua and Caleb knew that God was greater than all the giants of Canaan. Their awareness of the greatness of God gave them confidence to speak boldly as others cowered in fear.

We would all benefit by a daily meditation on the attributes of God. We are surrounded by the limitations of the natural world; bombarded with godless philosophies; and assaulted with negativity. We need vision that reaches further than our eyes and faith that stands alone in God. When we have assessed the circumstances and taken the full measure of our abilities, we have done little to determine viability.

People of vision never forget that what really matters is what God thinks; what God wants; and who has the faith to embrace it!

For unto us a Child is born, Unto us a Son is given;
And the government will be upon His shoulder.
Isaiah 9:6 NKJV

A college professor calculated the probability of eight Old Testament prophecies concerning Jesus being fulfilled in any one person living down to the present time.

The probability was a staggering one in ten to the seventeenth power. That is one in ten followed by seventeen zeros ... incredibly long odds. Cover the state of Texas with silver dollars to a depth of two feet marking one silver dollar with a red dot turned face down. Then send a blindfolded stranger to walk across the state and randomly pick up just one silver dollar. If he happened to pick up the marked silver dollar he would have beaten the odds that Jesus met when he fulfilled eight Old Testament prophecies.

Of course, there are more than eight prophecies concerning Messiah, and Jesus fulfilled them all. Subsequent calculations based on forty-eight Old Testament prophecies revealed odds of one in ten to the one hundred fifty-seventh power!

People often say of a unique man, "He's one-in-a-million." When you're talking about Jesus, "one-in-a-million" doesn't even come close!

*"Beware of false prophets, who come to you in sheep's clothing,
but inwardly they are ravenous wolves."*
Matthew 7:15 NKJV

Some wolves employ superb tailors. Others are graduates of "The White Sheep Acting Academy." Still others possess blinding charm; but wolves are wolves and if you ever forget it ... you're dead. As one who has escaped a few "wolf" attacks, let me offer some help in spotting the wily critters. Wolves are cold, heartless predators.

Give a wide berth to anyone who shows a cruel streak – even if he's funny. A lack of mercy reveals a wolfish heart. Wolves are insatiable. Watch out for people who are always chewing on others – give them half a chance and they'll be chewing on you. Wolves are sneaky. Stay away from "cool" people who rely on subterfuge. Shifty saints always turn out to be trouble. Wolves work to isolate their prey before they attack. I think it stems from a basic lack of courage.

Stay in good fellowship with strong people. Wolves like to drive their prey to exhaustion. Watch out for people who draw your attention to a multiplicity of small matters. Wolves are notorious liars. Stay away from people who don't tell the truth. Wolves are best left on the open range. Don't open your heart and home to even the most well-mannered wolf, and above all else . . . stay close to the Shepherd.

*But we have this treasure in earthen vessels, that the exceeding
greatness of the power may be of God,
and not from ourselves.*
2 Corinthians 4:7 ASV

God never calls us to a task that fits. He always calls
us to something beyond our strength, imagination,
talent, and depth, because He wants us to trust him.

He also delights in pouring living water from well-worn clay pots. Look at the Bible record. Saul of Tarsus proved himself an able executioner, but as a life-giver, he was out of his depth. A missionary, you say? He was an angel of death! David didn't look much like kingly material writing whimsical songs and singing them to disinterested sheep. When God called Gideon a "man of valor," you could almost hear the angels snicker.

Remember Noah? We don't know that the man had ever built a rowboat, and God commanded him to build the Ark. And what did old Noah know about zoology? How about the Apostles? I wouldn't have expected them to be able to organize a church in Bethany, let alone Jerusalem, Judea, Samaria, and the uttermost parts of the earth.

God entrusts ordinary people with extraordinary tasks so that He might demonstrate His power through us. Does the task fit you perfectly? Cast it aside for a better challenge. God always calls us to something greater than ourselves.

The eye cannot say to the hand, "I don't need you!"
And the head cannot say to the feet, "I don't need you!"
1 Corinthians 12:21 NIV

I ran into a Lone Ranger the other day. He had been coming to my church for several months, hiding in an overflow section and ducking out during the final prayer.

When I finally cornered him, he admitted that he had been avoiding contact and guarding his anonymity. With a worried sigh, he gave me his name as I offered my hand. I suggested that he get involved in a class or small group to start developing relationships. He shrugged and smiled, and I knew he had already chosen to stay out on the range.

I couldn't make him see that there are no Lone Rangers in the Kingdom of God. We are all joined together; made better together; more effective together. I tried to help him see that the Body of Christ is diminished by every part that chooses not to integrate, but he was having none of it. Something keeps him out riding the fences alone. I know you're probably thinking this guy was hurt somewhere; burned by someone; wounded deeply.

The truth of the matter is that we've all been hurt and life is risky. The benefits of fellowship by far outweigh the occasional pains of strife. Get a life *kemo sabe* … join your church … stop hiding. Even a hero like the Lone Ranger needs a Tonto!

"But Lord," Gideon asked, "how can I save Israel?
My clan is the weakest in Manasseh,
and I am the least in my family."
Judges 6:15 NIV

Have you ever felt unqualified for God's work? Join the club. God-sized challenges leave us all feeling a little inadequate ... well, OK, make that *totally* inadequate.

Gideon was floored when God called him to save Israel. He was certain that God had dialed the wrong number, but you just can't hang up on God, so he swallowed hard and listened. His story teaches us that God knows more about us than we know about ourselves. He knows what we can become and accomplish by His power. It's not about where we've been or where we are, it's all about where God can take us. Gideon also reminds us that God always calls us to a task bigger than ourselves. If we can do it on our own, we don't need Him. When God says, "Get a life," we had better order an extra-large. He always gives us something to grow into, but He also promises to stay close and watch us grow. He never puts us in the field without support. He promised Gideon that He would be with him and that they would strike down the enemy together.

He has promised to be with you, too. Don't shrink from the big challenges. The enormity of the task invites the intervention of God.

This is my comfort in my affliction:
for thy word hath quickened me.
Psalm 119:50 KJV

Like many in the middle years, he had left his faith far behind. He admitted to being a failure as a husband and father. Alcohol dulled the pain. Adultery filled the void. His career soared in spite of his personal troubles.

He was a big time newsy ... the station chief for the Associated Press in Beirut. He covered all the big stories until, quite suddenly, he became a big story himself: Terry Anderson was kidnapped and held hostage for 2,454 days. Fearing for his life, shuffled between safe houses, blindfolded and chained to a wall, Anderson was suddenly and completely alone.

What do you do when the rug is jerked out from under you? Where does a man turn when he has nothing left but injustice, fear, anger, and despair? On his twenty-fifth day of captivity, Anderson asked for, and incredibly received, a Bible. It became his most precious possession. A revitalized faith grew out of his study and memorization of Scripture.

What incredible power God has invested in His Word! The combined works of history, fiction, poetry, and prose could never have pierced the hellish darkness of that hostage nightmare, yet God's Word held this shattered man together and brought him through the darkest night.

And Moses was content to dwell with the man:
and he gave Moses Zipporah his daughter.
Exodus 2:21 KJV

What has happened to Moses? What has happened to the brave young prince, intent on the deliverance of God's people? Where is the fiery passion that made him a fugitive?

Gone it seems ... gone in the warm afternoon of midlife. Here is a man pre-selected by God to deliver a nation enslaved. Here is a man quick with his words, or his fists, or the dagger. Here is the hope of Israel, content to herd sheep as Pharoah's lash continues to fall on the backs of his countrymen. What has happened to Moses? He tried, and he failed, and now he has settled for a common existence clothed in anonymity.

Don't sit down when you've failed ... get up and try again. If you settle in you might be out of the game for a long time. Moses sat for forty years. Settling for anything less than the "abundant life" Jesus promises is settling for a fool's inheritance. You might feel safe and content in your self-imposed exile, but you cannot enjoy the blessings of God when you're parted from His will.

It took a burning bush to get Moses moving again. Even then, Moses found his courage withered and his confidence shot. Don't embrace contentment until you are surely in the center of God's will.

*...because of your partnership in the gospel
from the first day until now.*
Philippians 1:5 NIV

Great relationships grow around what we choose to hold in common.

We may share the same goals, the same vision, the same Lord, the same stage in life. "Partnering" situations draw us together. Great relationships share responsibilities. It's not one person carrying the load, it's not one person contributing all the energy, it's a shared burden – a distributed load. The greater the sense of partnership, the greater the sense of shared vision. Friendships thrive in a cooperative endeavor.

Watch sailors in troubled seas; no one has to say a thing. Everybody works as one to get the job done. Friends will help you through the storm. Acquaintances will simply offer advice. Friends will give you their strength. Acquaintances will offer their insights. Friends don't hesitate to get their hands dirty. Acquaintances will point out how dirty your hands are. Paul enjoyed a growing relationship with the church in Philippi based on gratitude, joy, and partnership.

Maybe you are wasting your time trying to build a relationship with someone who does not share your vision. Maybe you are pursuing a potential mate who does not share your core values. Stop now! To proceed is to insure frustration.

He saved us, not because of righteous things we had done,
but because of his mercy.
Titus 3:5 NIV

DUBIN, POLAND: Dominika lives with her parents and one sister in a small farming community. A few months ago an Affect Destiny Team visited her school where she received a copy of the *Book of Hope.*

One of the young people on the team shared her address. Dominika wrote, *"When you were at my school, you spoke about God and about your change. I've never seen any person talking about belief so openly. You and your friends gave us an example of the real belief. I believe in God, but I'm still trying to accept Him to my heart. I go to church almost every day. I read and listen to the Bible. I pray to God in the morning and evening. I try to live properly and according to the Bible, but I feel that it is too little. Please give me any advice."*

Dominika is reaching out. She also asked for an e-mail address. Dominika is the reason behind Affect Destiny Teams and Hopenet.net. With a new friend in America, and through Hopenet.net, Dominika can find answers to the questions that matter most.

The ministry of the *Book of Hope* does not end when distributors leave the classroom. Technology is opening a new door of opportunity. Now, more than ever, we can reach the children of the world.

And he ran before, and climbed up into
a sycamore tree to see him.
Luke 19:4 KJV

There were a lot of people who wanted to see Jesus that day. The streets and courtyards were packed and anxious faces filled the upper windows. No one saved a place for the little man ... no one invited him inside.

Zacchaeus was a two-by-four man in a six-by-eight world. The Greek word used to describe him in Luke is "micros," from which we derive such words as microscopic or microprocessor. His stunted growth didn't stunt his ambition; as a matter of fact it probably fueled his desire to command a position of power. Firmly ensconced in the office of tax collector, Zacchaeus cast a long shadow. He wasn't popular but he was powerful and most men will make that trade.

I like what I see in the snapshot of Zaccheus that Luke displays. I like the fact that he was willing to make restitution above and beyond actual damages. I like the fact that he was singled out by Jesus and called by name. But most of all, I like the fact that Zacchaeus climbed the tree. When he reached his limit he refused to give up – he climbed up!

Therein lies the key to discovery and recovery. An "unclean" woman; a shouting blind man; a grieving father; a too-short tax collector. Determined people always find their way to Jesus.

*A stone was brought and placed over the mouth of the den,
and the king sealed it with his own signet ring and with the rings
of his nobles, so that Daniel's situation might not be changed.*
Daniel 6:17 NIV

The last dusty shaft of sunlight was extinguished as a stone was muscled into place. Outside they were sealing the opening with signet rings but Daniel would not have heard them if they had all been shouting his name and blowing trumpets – his ears were tuned to another sound.

Behind him, maybe a little bit to the left, he heard the velvet rumble of a lion. There was another to his right, he was sure of it, and then he froze as he felt hot breath on his neck. There was movement all around him, but Daniel dared not move a muscle. He stayed in the same spot where they had dropped him. His head turned slowly toward every new sound, straining to see through the darkness, his mind reciting the simplest of prayers: *"Oh God, oh God, help me God."*

He wanted to scream, but no sound escaped his open mouth. He heard a distant drumbeat and then recognized it as the racing of his own heart. He slowly rolled over onto his back – no response. He pulled himself into a sitting position – no response. And then it came like a sudden breath of wind – the realization that the lions weren't coming for him.

Amidst the rumble and roar of adversity, God never abandons His children.

But avoid foolish controversies.
Titus 3:9 NIV

The quiet was shattered when a bald tattoo in a low-riding Toyota pulled alongside to give me a few "vibrations" from his coffin-sized car stereo.

The thumping bass was so loud that I thought someone was kicking my quarter panels. The tattoo looked my way and sneered, making his nose ring flare outwards as he reached over to turn it up a little louder. The raging fury that spewed out the windows could best be described as two fools screaming at one another in a phone booth beside a slaughterhouse. The light changed, and we exchanged vital messages with parting glances. His look said "*wimp*" and my stare said "*punk*." For the first time in my life I found myself wanting just one stick of dynamite … just one! And then it hit me – how I used to love to pull up beside some "*square*" and give them a taste of *moderate metal*. I remembered my Dad pledging to never ride in my van again after I had tested his decibel tolerance and found it wanting. When I glared at the Toyota, I was glaring at myself.

Every generation struggles with the tastes and changes of the next. There are deeper matters than style and volume. We need to look hard at this fallen culture.

Rome is burning, and we concern ourselves with the faulty tuning of Nero's violin!

And this I pray, that your love may abound still more and
more in knowledge and all discernment.
Philippians 1:9 NKJV

Should a scholar become the most learned in the world – should he excel in the arts, a balanced combination of Michelangelo and Einstein – without love he is morally bankrupt, desperately lonely, and potentially dangerous.

Paul prays that knowledge would grow in the Philippians, but only in the context of abounding love. The wise sage might find a source of pride in knowledge, but there is no joy there. "Knowledge puffs up," said Paul. Without a doubt, he was drawing from his own life experience as a scholar. His brilliance was discovered early in life, gaining him entrance to Gamaliel's school. More than a scholar, Paul was a man of action. He was not content to make the Christian question an intellectual exercise. He coupled his deductions with destruction and set out to impose his "enlightened" world view on the misled and the ignorant. We find him in Acts 9 "breathing threats and murder" against the disciples. Who knows how many would have been killed, courtesy of Paul's great learning, had he not encountered Love on the Damascus road?

Some will argue for the intrinsic goodness of man, but even a cursory study of history reveals that a smart man without love is a dangerous man indeed.

*In those days when the number of disciples was increasing,
the Grecian Jews among them complained against the
Hebraic Jews because their widows were being overlooked in the
daily distribution of food.*
Acts 6:1 NIV

Some things never change.

The first church trouble we find recorded in the book of Acts centered on somebody being upset over neglect. I'm not saying that the problem was illegitimate, only that it seems to have survived the ages in spite of the appointment of deacons, committees, care teams, and associate pastors. If there is one thing I have learned in serving people, it is that you had better be fair and quick to make amends. Injustice and favoritism are fuel for the fires that consume our potential and scorch the fruit of a ministry.

The Apostles were quick to remedy the situation by appointing caregivers. When a slight is swept under the carpet, or a need neglected for a lack of compassion, bitterness grows. It seems that whatever is watered in tears outgrows everything else. The Apostles were wise men. They recognized that the need for ministry and reconciliation demanded that the caregivers be filled with the Spirit and with wisdom.

In an environment rife with hurt feelings and wounded hearts, we too must be full of the Spirit and wisdom. Anger, hurt and disappointment can only be conquered by the presence of a caregiver and the power of love.

And they immediately left the ship and their father,
and followed him.
Matthew 4:22 KJV

Have you come to a standstill in your spiritual walk? Do you feel as though you are standing in a box canyon, cut off from your future? You're not alone.

I've heard it a hundred times, "Pastor, I can't seem to find that place to which God is calling me." In some cases the issue is clear, such as disobedience, or immaturity. In some cases I must admit a total consternation as to why such a gifted brother or sister is not moving forward. Sometimes the answer is quite clear – we just don't want to face it. Andre Gide cut to the chase when he said, *"You cannot discover new lands unless you leave shore for a very long time."*

It is often our level of comfort and aversion to risk that binds us to mediocrity. When Jesus called the disciples, He did not offer them a guarantee of so many nights at home. To follow Christ was to leave shore for a very long time. Andrew left his work with John the Baptist. Peter left his nets. Matthew left his tax business. James left his activism. These men changed the world, but they would not have been heard of again if they had stayed safely in Galilee.

Could it be that the excitement you've lost in your spiritual quest lies just beyond the boundaries of your comfort zone?

It is finished.
John 19:30 KJV

The Bible is a book of words; words inspired by God – somehow invested with life-changing power. These words bring comfort in sorrow, hope in despair, and light in darkness. These words can change lives, break addictions, heal diseases, and offer direction. God's words correct, confirm, instruct, affirm, and reveal. They are likened to a sword, a light, bread, shelter. To search this book of words from cover to cover for its best word is a daunting task.

From Genesis to Revelation we find unparalleled brilliance, perfect wisdom and relevance. Were you to pin me down for the Bible's best word today, I would make a case for the word, "Finished." The English language requires three words to carry the essence of what Jesus spoke in one word from the cross: "It is finished." Charles Spurgeon called this text *"An ocean of meaning in a drop of language."* While we give proper attention to the resurrection, and rightfully so, we should linger a while at John 19:30. Christ is the "Lamb slain from the foundation of the world" (Rev. 13:8).

Everything He did to save us from our sins led to this singular moment in time when Jesus lifted up His voice as He lifted us to God and cried, "Finished!"

Arise, go down to meet Ahab king of Israel, who lives in Samaria.
There he is, in the vineyard of Naboth,
where he has gone down to take possession of it.
1 Kings 21:18 NKJV

Because of the evil means employed to take possession of Naboth's tiny vineyard, the satisfaction Ahab enjoyed was short-lived. God was already sending judgment on the lips of Elijah.

Ahab had just completed his first inspection when he heard the squeaking of the rusty gate. What followed was a prophecy so certain and devastating that it caused Ahab to humble his heart and beg God to relent. It can safely be said that Ahab never enjoyed his ill-gotten vineyard. Illegitimate gains are like an anchor dropped from inside a wooden ship; the anchor holds the bottom but holes the ship.

A middle-aged couple sat in my office pouring out their marital struggles. The more they revealed, the more I suspected a powerful undercurrent in their relationship. Finally, in tears she said, "Pastor, you need to know that we got together through an affair. We wrecked two homes in the process – I guess we're reaping what we have sown." I couldn't argue the point. In spite of a long line of counselors, books, and seminars – they are still struggling to make it work. The thrill of the chase has been replaced by the weariness of guilt.

If it's not right, getting what you want will leave you not wanting what you get.

The heavens declare the glory of God;
and the firmament sheweth his handywork.
Psalm 19:1 KJV

A prominent sociologist said, "There is nothing quite so entertaining as listening to a brilliant mind expound on a stupid idea."

Of such is the tortured logic of the atheist arguing for a random, godless universe. The intricacies of creation demand design. Not so, says a scientific community committed to a natural universe. In 1927, A.P. Eddington offered the monkey thesis to support the assumption that infinite time and chance could account for life. He held that, "Given time, an army of monkeys strumming on typewriters *might* write all the books in the English library." Imagine that you are the monkeys' supervisor reading the daily monkey transcripts. Every once in a while, a two or three letter word appears, or even a three-word phrase. Then one day, you pick up a transcript and begin to read, *"It was the best of times, it was the worst of times ... "*

What has happened – a perfect combination of chance and time? To believe so one would have to believe that a tornado in a junkyard could create a functioning jet liner. The Word of God reveals the truth concerning origin, meaning, morality, and destiny.

Without God's Word as a foundation, the rest is just a bunch of monkey business.

Who is like unto the LORD our God,
who dwelleth on high.
Psalm 113:5 KJV

To whom can you compare Him?

History cannot offer a single name. Empires have risen and fallen; great in their splendor and silent in their graves. Babylon forgotten, Aztecs erased, Mongols, Greeks, Egyptians, and Romans – gone. The Iron Curtain is rusted and trampled. Lenin's communism gasps for air in the grip of modern tyrants. Great philosophies are withered for lack of truth. Finding no god in the heavens, men search for gods in themselves. The tragic result is a lost man who *thinks* he is found.

Our sciences are morally bankrupt, our ethical foundations are gravel and dust, our constitution is pinned down in legal gridlock, the arts have become perverse even as perversions have become trendy. The great leaders of old are all dead, and no one scans the horizon for another hero. What meaning can we find in our grand monuments and well-chosen words? We don't believe in those things anymore. If we say we do, our actions betray our hypocrisy. I have lived my formative years amidst the chaos of a secular revolution. Yet there is One that will not be moved or shaken.

When all else is dust – He remains. My Redeemer, my hope, my Lord and my God … Jesus: Savior of the world.

Then he killed James the brother of
John with the sword.
Acts 12:2 NKJV

I wonder if John ever asked: *"Why was James taken and Peter delivered – why does my heart grieve even as Andrew rejoices in his brother's deliverance?"*

Peter was taken out of prison. James was simply taken out. Surely the disciples prayed for James as they did Peter? Surely their faith was as strong for one as for the other? Yet James was dead and Peter was free. Sometimes God says no. We don't want to hear it – we close our eyes to it – but it's true. Hezekiah pleaded for his own life, and God relented. David pleaded for the life of a newborn son, and God said no. What can we say when a missionary buries a life partner on a desolate field – and then a son? A frothy, sound-bite theology holds no answer when a faithful servant wonders, *"Did someone fail God?"* The eleventh chapter of Hebrews speaks in one verse of those who escaped the sword, and in the next of those who were martyred by it. Where can we find rest in the matter?

For everything there is a time and a season, and God never loses track of anybody's time. He does all things well. He never makes a mistake – and when He says no, it is ultimately for the best. While Peter was messing with people problems, James was resting at the Master's feet.

Commit your way to the LORD,
Trust also in Him, And He shall bring it to pass.
Psalm 37:5 NKJV

Can you imagine a wedding in which both celebrants committed themselves to fidelity at least seventy-five percent of the time? It sounds like an off-beat English comedy sketch. What if they promised to love and to cherish ninety percent of the time? We would still think it outrageous.

We know that covenants demand commitment. Commitment raises all things to a higher plane. It separates the journeyman from the genius; the gold from the bronze; the best seller from the unsold manuscript. Commitments hold when emotions falter; preserve when all else decays; determine when judgment grows cloudy. Commitments are costly and frightening, but they are also liberating. Without them no great advance is made, nor great cause embraced.

God calls us to an all or nothing proposition. We give him all of our heart and *all* of our soul – holding nothing in reserve. An outside observer may point out what we have lost, yet it is in the absolute commitment that we have gained freedom.

David Lloyd George spoke well when he said: *"Don't be afraid to take a big step if one is indicated. You can't cross a chasm in two small jumps."* Vibrant faith requires the utter commitment. Half a heart a tragic wedding makes.

And He said, "What have you done?
The voice of your brother's blood cries out to Me from the ground."
Genesis 4:10 NKJV

It was a misty, silent fall day. Yellow leaves from a cluster of white birch drifted on the slightest breeze.

I lifted my camera in an attempt to capture the barrenness of the enclosure that once held more than sixty thousand men. The fog blurred the distant perimeter as though it were trying to hide her shame. White towers looked down in a blind man's stare. I stood at the gates – the gates of hell – the rusting gates of Dachau. The pictures hinted at a story too horrible to tell; the starved; the tortured; brutalized beyond imagination. I walked through a mass gas chamber and turned away from red brick ovens in the crematorium. At first, few questioned the mysterious odors emanating from the compound.

Three chapels stand to offer a place of meditation for Catholics, Protestants, and Jews. This place makes you think. It seems the ground itself cries out for a justice that cannot be rendered in a courtroom. "It's been more than fifty years," you might say, "Time to put it all behind us and walk away."

But this place must never close her rusty gates lest another villain rise up to preach that God has lesser children; lest another fool dare stand in the place of God.

The one who calls you is faithful and he will do it.
1 Thessalonians 5:24 NIV

KRAZNOYARSK, SIBERIA, 1992: A twelve-year-old boy named Dima was given a copy of the *Book of Hope* by an American volunteer.

He accepted Jesus as his Lord and Savior. When I met him seven years later, he was serving as the Associate Pastor at the Christian Life Church in Kraznoyarsk and learning Chinese so that he might fulfill his missionary calling. During our 1999 crusade, Dima gave the altar call and hundreds of boys and girls responded, just as he had in 1992. When we returned to Siberia in September 2000, Dima joined our team in Chita, just one hundred miles from the Chinese border. Our hotel was filled with Chinese merchants, and Dima won his first Chinese convert in the lobby of the third floor. His eyes were dancing as we celebrated the grace of God so simply received by a little Chinese lady. The only thing keeping Dima from his mission field was a $600.00 plane ticket. Our team quietly collected an offering, and Dima was one step closer to his mission field.

Short-term missions are often criticized as "one shot" encounters, lacking any long term strategy. In this case we can read the rest of the story. A fully prepared Russian missionary is headed for China … and it all began with an Affect Destiny Team and one copy of the *Book of Hope*.

Lay not up for yourselves treasures upon earth,
where moth and rust doth corrupt,
and where thieves break through and steal:
But lay up for yourselves treasures in heaven.
Matthew 6:19-20 KJV

If you will leave behind anything lasting when you have departed this life, you had better start giving now. No monuments are raised to celebrate what a man took from life, or hoarded without pity. No day graces the calendar to pay homage the "wanna be" virtue of selfishness.

If you will be remembered, it will be for what you gave of your time, talent, passion, strength, and wisdom. If you'll not give, you'll be forgotten before the first obligatory flower wilts on your grave. What a man sacrifices these days to make his fortune. It's all about long hours, long distance, long shots, and long odds of keeping a family intact. When he has finally made it, he finds himself alone at the top. When he finally admits his error, his kids only want to know him like an uncle and his ex-wives only want the alimony.

Be careful in the mad rush to possess – you'll one day miss the hungry years. It is estimated that over his lifetime, John Wesley gave away nearly $150,000.00. When he died he left behind a well-worn frock coat, two silver teaspoons and the Methodist Church.

Don't worry so much now that your net worth demands respect. Net worth is never really determined until we are weighed on heaven's scales.

The end of a matter is better than its beginning,
and patience is better than pride.
Ecclesiastes 7:8 NIV

Amby made his high school jayvee basketball team but he didn't get to play, except for the last few seconds in blow-out games.

He was a poor player on a poor team coached by a frustrated man. One day in practice the coach lost it. *"You guys aren't accomplishing anything on the court today. Get out there and run the cross-country course!"* Nobody wanted to run the three mile course behind the school, but when the coach says run – you had better run. Amby's life changed that day. A mile into the run he realized that he was a better runner than the rest of the guys. He literally left them in his dust. The next year he went out for the track team. In 1968, Amby Burfoot won the Boston Marathon.

I wonder what would have happened to Amby, were it not for a frustrated coach and a run that came packaged as punishment? The coach didn't know what he was doing when he sent the boys out to run, but God knows what He's doing with every beat of our hearts.

The very thing you're grumbling about may be God's way of revealing your destiny. Amby Burfoot is now the executive editor of Runner's World magazine and a successful author to boot. God knows who you will be. Trust Him in all ways to guide your steps.

Thy word is a lamp unto my feet,
and a light unto my path.
Psalm 119:105 KJV

The blueprints number more than sixty pages. The book of specifications is thicker than a phone book. One building; millions of dollars; thousands of decisions; it's hard for me to believe that this mess will ultimately become a new church building.

I wouldn't dare build without a plan, and yet people in astonishing numbers live their lives without a blueprint. Aiming at nothing, they hit it every time. Failing to make up their minds, their unmade minds unmake them. Drifting through life, the rudder never bites, the sails never fill, no oceans crossed, no grand discovery. Our lack of purpose is captured in the lyrics of our music. *"I can't get no satisfaction – All we are is dust in the wind – I still haven't found what I'm looking for – All in all you're just another brick in the wall."*

We live in the age of synthetic religion. You can put together your own faith from bits and pieces of world religions and believe in anything that you want. This new synthetic faith doesn't have to answer to logic, reason, or truth. As long as it works for you, who cares?

It all leaves me to wonder what kind of house would result from mixing random pages from fifty different sets of blueprints. I wouldn't live there – would you?

*If you then, being evil, know how to give good gifts to your children,
how much more will your Father who is in heaven give
good things to those who ask Him!*
Matthew 7:11 NKJV

We didn't catch many fish. As a matter of fact, I don't have too many memories of reeling in the big ones. Our fishing trips were mildly successful, but they stand tall among my fondest memories.

Dad took time to spend with me in a leaky boat or tramping up an icy trout stream, and that made all the difference. I usually fell asleep on the drive up country and then again on the way back. I snarled my line, hooked my finger, and complained about the bugs. I dropped my pole over the side and dumped the worm can a few times. I can't remember having any deep conversations as we waited for the fish to bite. These moments weren't scripted – they were lived. I was spending time with the hero of my life, and he seemed to want to be there. That was enough.

Dad and I didn't share a team sport heritage like some. We just enjoyed being together; we still do. I'm past forty now and he's seventy. We get together every year for four days alone. Now he falls asleep while I drive and the conversations have gone a little bit deeper, but the greatest gift my Dad ever gave me keeps on giving.

Dad gave me his love, his life, and his time. Should I never earn another dollar, I am a rich, rich, man.

Be self-controlled and alert.
Your enemy the devil prowls around like a roaring
lion looking for someone to devour.
1 Peter 5:8 NIV

The lion is a master stalker. He doesn't dash in for a quick kill. The very balance of nature gives the hunted and the hunter a fair chance, so the lion watches and waits.

Once the herd is consolidated, he creeps into the strike zone. Suddenly, he rises up and lopes easily toward his prey. The herd is immediately alerted and moves, almost as one, away from the threat. The lion is watching, still watching for the weak one that lags behind, or the arrogant young speedster that separates himself from the herd. This roaming, seeking, killing machine is programmed to single out prey rather than charge the herd.

Peter chose the lion to give believers a visual fix on how the devil works. He is moving, plotting, and always watching. He waits, he roars, he intimidates, all for the purpose of singling out the weak or the prideful. His great and simple strategy is to separate brothers and sisters – to drive a wedge between friends. When we are isolated we are vulnerable. When we've been cut off, or cut out, we're about to be cut down. Jesus' prayer for the church is that they would be one – kept in perfect unity.

Jesus was praying for our safety. Stay in fellowship by all means. There's a stalker on the loose.

For which of you, intending to build a tower,
does not sit down first and count the cost,
whether he has enough to finish it.
Luke 14:28 NKJV

I love dogs ... I really do. Or should I say, I love the idea of a dog. The thought of a sweet-natured, quiet, clean, Golden Retriever laying at my feet-on a snowy night as I page my way through a great book ... that's a picture for the photo album (add a steaming cup of coffee).

That same loyal dog awaiting me at the door every night with a disciplined show of joy ... that one goes in the same album. But someone has to train the dog, bathe the dog, exercise the dog, treat the sick dog, and deal with the dog when the family goes on vacation. I know what puppies do to carpets; what Labradors do to millwork; what the smell of dog food does to my stomach; and what impact Bowser is going to have on my checkbook.

In short, I want the blessings, but I don't want to pay the price. When the girls ask, *"How much is that doggie in the window?"* I offer them new jeans and a cool CD. Dog lovers have called me cruel. Kid lovers have called me heartless. I've almost given in a time or two, but I'm holding steady.

Most things in life carry a price. Every believer should count the cost. Somebody got it right when they said, "If it's too good to be true, it must be Jesus!"

Please Pray for Indonesia

Indonesia has experienced civil war and religious strife. Pray for the children who accept Christ and for the local believers, that they would be spared persecution.

A Gift of New Life for Marji!

A Book of Hope volunteer named Cindy was on her way home from a full day of distribution when she stopped by the drugstore, and was immediately drawn to a young woman who looked very depressed and had purchased a small bag full of pills.

When Cindy asked what was wrong, the girl, Marji*, poured out a heart full of pain and anguish: she had come from a broken home, her friends had deserted her. "I hate this life," she declared. She was ready to end it all, with the pills she had bought.

"Wait, I have something for you," Cindy told her, and gave her the *Book of Hope*. Together they looked through it, and Cindy explained the love of Jesus. "It can't be," Marji said. "Nobody loves me!"

But through the words of the book, and with Cindy's help, she accepted Christ's love and made a commitment to live for Jesus right there! The *Book of Hope* helped to save her life, on the very day she had decided to commit suicide.

* Marji's name has been changed for confidentiality in Indonesia, the largest Muslim nation in the world.

In the beginning ...
Genesis 1:1 NIV
In the beginning ...
John 1:1 NIV

I don't think it's by chance that John begins his gospel narrative with words that echo the first thought in Genesis. It is John's conviction that Jesus brought all things to a new beginning. He records the dialog between Jesus and Nicodemus, dialog that centers on a man's new birth in Christ (John 3:3-7). Genesis records the creation of the world. John records the creation of a new person in Christ. The first creation is a world in sharp decline. The new creation is a life without end.

Genesis records the ordering of cosmos out of chaos. John records the issuing of life from death. Genesis sets redemption's center stage. John records the play. Genesis begins with God and Adam. John begins with God in Christ. Genesis is paradise lost. John is paradise regained. Genesis is history. John is good news. Genesis is light to darkness. John is darkness to light. Genesis is truth that paints the backdrop. John is the Truth that makes men free. Genesis records Satan's theft. John records heaven's recovery. Genesis is the pollution of sin. John records the cleansing of Jesus' blood.

God breathed into Adam and he rose to a temporary life. Christ died for Adam's race and we now rise to eternal life, abundant and free.

For they sow the wind, and they shall
reap the whirlwind.
Hosea 8:7 ASV

Whatsoever a man sows ... accelerates!

How often I have listened to the sad tales of unintended consequence. It started with a couple of beers and ended in vehicular manslaughter. It started with flirtation and ended with two broken homes and five shattered children. It started with peaked curiosity and ended in an addiction to pornography. It started with a shred of gossip and ended with a shredded friendship. It started with a cigarette and ended with lung cancer. It started with slight of hand and ended with a prosecutable fraud. It started with a need for leisure and ended with loss of fellowship.

It started with compromise and ended with a loss of integrity. It started with a fantasy and ended with a nightmare. It started with prejudice and ended in genocide. It started with a careless word and ended with estrangement. It started with a freshening breeze and ended with a hurricane. When you cross moral and ethical boundaries you will find yourself on a slippery slope that ends in the valley of regret.

The seed we sow generates a windfall of blessing or a whirlwind of sorrow. Be careful what you sow. When it's out of your hands, it's out of your control.

Therefore submit to God. Resist the devil and
he will flee from you.
James 4:7 NKJV

Have you ever noticed that things often get worse when you commit yourself to fasting and prayer?

I don't say that to discourage you, but rather, to draw attention to the effectiveness of a prayer priority. Your adversary, the devil, is especially contented with a lukewarm variety of Christianity. He has discovered that prayer-less churches and prayer-less Christians do him no harm. In fact, the prayer-less church does much to foster an environment in which the great deceiver can work his dark arts. When we pray, we should not be surprised by increased troubles. James says that we are to resist. Resistance is offered in the face of attack. In times of leisure and rest, no resistance is required. When troubles are greatly increased, anchor deep in the Word of God and hold on. It won't be long before a victory is won.

Immature Christians make the grave error of thinking that their trial is evidence that they are doing something wrong, when, in fact, that very trial is evidence that they are doing something right. Keep holding out, even when it seems that your prayers are stirring up more trouble.

Satan wants us to believe that he is inexhaustible, when, in truth, he suffers a crippling lack of endurance. Hold on!

At Gibeon the LORD appeared to Solomon in a dream by night;
and God said, "Ask! What shall I give you?"
1 Kings 3:5 NKJV

"If you need anything, just ask." I don't doubt the sincerity of my host, but I know that the offer has limitations.

What if I were to say, "Well, now that you ask, I need a thousand dollars." Or what if I were to ask for a car, or maybe a few selections from the family jewelry box? How rude! Most of us offer the polite answer, "Oh, I think I have everything I need" – but what if the offer were unlimited in its scope and offered with perfect sincerity?

What if your host was a mega-billionaire with a generous reputation? What if he could deliver anything from a fur coat to a Ferrari? What if he pushed the issue by saying, "Ask! Please ask! What shall I give you?" It happened, you know. It happened to a king named Solomon at Gibeon. The offer came from God Himself, and Solomon found Himself staring down the barrel of a loaded pro-mise. "Lucky Solomon," you say? How about "Lucky you ... and lucky me?"

God wants us to ask Him for blessings. The Old Testament reveals the giving nature of God. The New Testament commands us to ask great things. God wants us to approach Him as a beneficent Father. Walk with me for a few days and learn more of a God who loves to be asked.

"But woe to you, scribes and Pharisees, hypocrites!"
Matthew 23:13 NKJV

Remember the big Earth Summit in Rio a few years ago? Do you think the delegates were eco-sensitive? Harpers Magazine reported that the Earth Summit crowd generated seven tons of trash . . . per day!

Hypocrisy can really sneak up on you. I'll always remember Coach Hogan preaching the four virtues of physical conditioning to our sophomore class. I just couldn't "receive the truth" for coach's beach-ball belly and overstressed coaching pants. It looked to me like the four virtues would wreck your health, if coach was any indicator.

Hypocrites do a lot of damage in the church. While a nitpicker can find some inconsistency in almost any situation, sincere seekers are often put off their search by compromised church-goers.

Jesus was gentle and kind when it came to broken down prostitutes and top-skimming tax collectors, but he was relentless with hypocritical spiritual leaders. He called them snakes, hypocrites, blind guides and fools.

Spiritual leadership requires integrity. Be certain that your "talk" and your "walk" are more than distant cousins. They need to be twins if we will have a "one-faced" witness in a "two-faced" world.

Every good and perfect gift is from above,
coming down from the Father.
James 1:17 NIV

A ninety-nine percent service rating is generally considered an exceptional achievement, but in some cases ninety-nine percent isn't good enough. At ninety-nine percent, doctors and nurses would drop over 15,000 newborns every year. At ninety-nine percent, pharmacies would send 20,000 people out the door with the wrong medications. At ninety-nine percent, we would suffer more than 500 incorrect surgical procedures per week.

Ninety-nine percent might be an outstanding achievement if we're talking about Happy Meals or coffee filters, but when it comes to life issues it's not enough, especially if you find yourself in that doomed one percent.

Quality assurance will never find perfection. The human element shadows every process and product with a reasonable doubt. Recalls, re-design, re-engineering, and replacement are all part of our striving for unreachable perfection.

Yet, there is one Provider who never falls short of one hundred percent. His promises are absolute. His gifts are perfect. His delivery is timely. His track record is impeccable, and He only stocks the best. With God, ninety-nine is never enough.

I rise before the dawning of the morning,
and cry for help; I hope in Your word.
Psalm 119:147 NKJV

My new day is as blank as the white screen on my notebook. The sun is rising. What will today's blank page hold?

Will it be interruption, cancellation, inspiration, vanilla or all thirty-three flavors? Where will my emotions take me today – anger, joy, compassion, disgust, frustration or hope? What will I witness, dismiss or embrace? What will I miss? Will I give or receive, rest or strive, reap or sow, like or love – or hate? Will I lift up or let down; look up or despair; rise up or fall short; step up or put off? How will I do in the daddy department today? Will my husbanding make the grade?

I'll make hundreds of little decisions; choose attitudes and reactions. I'll prioritize my emotions and grant them an excellent or lousy expression. What will this blank page hold at day's end? I need to decide what I can and what I will because it's time to leave this corner table in the coffee shop and drive the last mile to the office.

Life is so complicated. I need a simple ethos to overwrite it all. That's where God's Word is to be richly applied. Today, I'll clothe myself in a Psalm, tomorrow – in a Proverb. From Genesis to Revelation, God's wisdom, strength, and comfort awaits application to the white page of a brand new day.

For the word of God is living and active.
Sharper than any double-edged sword.
Hebrews 4:12 NIV

KRAZNOYARSK, SIBERIA, 1999: The young man sitting across the table told us of his missionary calling to China.

His eyes flashed with that determined excitement that marks people of strong passion. At twenty-two years of age, he was already a leader in his church. He was preparing himself, waiting for God's open door. I couldn't help but wonder if I was looking at the next Taylor or Livingstone, so great was his passion. "How did you come to know Jesus?" I asked. He pointed to the copy of the *Book of Hope* on the table. "I received that book from Americans in 1992 when they came to our school," he said. "I read the book, came to the meetings and accepted Jesus Christ as my Savior." I shook my head in awe and wonder. This young man was just one of dozens of converts I had met from that first Siberian distribution. In the classrooms they were just beautiful, dark-eyed children, anxious to receive a gift from their visitors. Now they were leaders, pastors, and missionaries.

The leaders of tomorrow sit in the schoolrooms of the world today. They need to know that there is a God who loves them and that there is hope for tomorrow. They need God's Word. If we will reach them, we can change the world.

Who has measured the waters in the hollow of His hand,
Measured heaven with span And calculated the dust of
the earth in a measure? Weighed the mountains
in scales and the hills in a balance?
Isaiah 40:12 NKJV

How great is our God? The oceans cannot fill the hollow of His hand. The heavens are measured by the span between His fingers. The quantity of the dust of the earth; the weight of the mountains; the depths of the seas; the volume of the atmosphere; the intricacies of microbiology – He holds it all in a perfect accounting without apparent effort.

"How Big is God?" asks the old Gospel song. The answer, in a word, is "Bigger." He is greater than any measure applied. When we have praised Him until all strength is gone and intellectual capacity exhausted, we have not even begun to satisfy His worthiness of praise.

When we extend grace that goes beyond all cause or reason, giving ourselves up to extend love to another, we have only offered the barest reflection of the grace He offers to all, whether saint or sinner. When we have loved to complete consummation, we are shadowed by transcendent love demonstrated on a Roman cross. When we boast in our knowledge, parade our successes, gloat over our technologies, or take pride in our wisdom, creation must stifle its laughter for we are but dust.

How great is God? If you have a measured answer, you don't know God.

"To whom will you compare me?
Or who is my equal?" says the Holy One.
Isaiah 40:25 NIV

How can you compare what cannot be measured? The comparison of religions is quite easily drawn, but God is not religion. He is above all, in all, and over all. Isaiah's fortieth chapter draws one indisputable conclusion: God is incomparable. All adjectives fail to describe Him. All superlatives fail to grasp Him. He exceeds the most excellent. He succeeds all measure of greatness.

When we study our great God in the Scriptures, we find immeasurable love, unspeakable joy, amazing grace, surpassing peace, irrational mercy, incredible hope, incorruptible power, unshakable covenant, inscrutable wisdom, unwavering faith, and abundant life. When feeble comparisons are drawn, He remains unmatched, unbeatable, incomprehensible, and untouchable. He is perfectly supreme.

It is no wonder that the Jews found it impossible to describe Him in a single name. All who oppose Him are soon withered and gone. All who deny Him join the company of fools. All who ignore Him are destined to bow. All who reject Him reject life itself.

Yet to those who will seek Him, He becomes a Father and a friend. The only concept more staggering than His colossal greatness is His knowledge and love of you and me.

In the day of my trouble I will call to you,
for you will answer me.
Psalm 86:7 NIV

Danny Cox was in big trouble. He was riding 79,000 horsepower at 60,000 feet, 1200 miles per hour, upside-down . . . on fire! The cockpit was smoky. The control panel was lit up like a Christmas tree. This was the kind of morning that puts the "test" in "test pilot." Cox toggled his radio and called control central. "May-Day, May-Day, May-Day. I'm at 60,000 feet, upside-down, and on fire. Request landing instructions."

Put me in that situation and I would have been babbling away like Barney Fife on speed. I marvel that Danny was able to do anything but scream.

How do you respond when life is one supersonic fireball? Some people bail out, others "augur" in, yet some find the courage, strength, and guidance to land safely and live to fly another day.

Danny's call tells the story. First of all, he admitted his problem. I know people who are crashing fast, but they won't admit it. Then he asked for guidance. "Request landing instructions" has become a prayer for me since I read Danny's story.

When life is out of control, He's not. When you don't know what to do, He does. Make the call, but don't delay. Burning up is one step removed from blowing up.

*"But everyone who hears these sayings of Mine, and does
not do them, will be like a foolish man who
built his house on the sand."*
Matthew 7:26 NKJV

A world without moral law is a scary proposition. The abandonment of absolutism for relativism raises monstrous implications for the future. Can we trust an undefined morality to keep us safe amidst the fierce global competition?

Tread-shedding tires and flipping SUVs should give us pause. A few years ago, Ford Pintos exploded in a certain kind of collision. In a lawsuit brought against Ford over Pinto's safety, the prosecutors introduced a Ford study that estimated the placement of the fuel tanks would result in 180 burn deaths and a little over 2000 burned vehicles. It was further estimated that the costs in court judgments would be in the $50 million range. The cost of a design change would exceed $125 million. A deadly decision was made based on dollars.

Without a moral law, who is to say whether the decision was right or wrong? Who can argue the value of a human life? Some boldly assert that man is bettering himself as knowledge increases and globalism emerges to save the day.

As the light fades on the bloodiest century the world has ever known, the inherent goodness of man is anything but a foregone conclusion. Without God, mankind builds a pretentious house on sinking sand.

Why are you downcast, O my soul?
Why so disturbed within me?
Put your hope in God.
Psalm 43:5 NIV

Janis Ian's haunting song touched the hearts and told the stories of many born with imperfect features and perceived handicaps: *"I learned the truth at seventeen that love was meant for beauty queens and high school girls with clear-skinned smiles who married young and then retired."*

The song was more than a ballad to teenage angst. It reached people who were well past their teen years, living with a debilitating sense of inadequacy. *"To those of us who knew the pain of valentines that never came..."* Gayle was driving alone, heard the song, and burst into tears. Gayle is fifty-two-years old.

Teen peer pressure and targeted advertising features rail-thin bodies and sculpted frames. But feelings of "not quite measuring up" pursue us to mid-life and beyond. The need to be valued, loved, and wanted drives the human soul – sometimes to disaster. How tragic to find love and invest trust, only to have it stripped away through divorce or deceit.

There is One Whose love is forever true; Whose grace is always extended; Whose door is always opened; and through Whose eyes, we are beautiful. I too, *"learned the truth at seventeen"* that ultimate security is ours for the taking in relationship with Christ.

*So all the days of Methuselah were nine hundred
and sixty-nine years; and he died.*
Genesis 5:27 NKJV

I wonder if Methuselah ever got tired of living? Do you think he ever rolled over in his seven hundredth year and said, "I'm just too tired to get up?" I wonder if he had trouble bridging the generation gap? In a life that spanned the better part of a millennium, a lot of questions are raised. How long was his mid-life crisis? How did he keep up with his great, great, great grandchildren? How many wives did he bury? Did he feel that the world was changing too fast?

If life were measured only by length, Methuselah would be the most important figure in human history. As it is, he's a biblical curiosity. Standing against Methuselah's mind-boggling longevity, the life of Jesus is a comparative snapshot. Yet in His thirty-three years, He not only changed the course of human history, He fused it all – from the garden to the gates of the New Jerusalem – with meaning. In Revelation, He is both the Lamb slain from the foundation of the world, and the King crowned world without end.

When a life is measured by its length alone, that life is truly unmeasured. Be careful that your life is not reduced to the marking of time. Every day should count for more than its passing.

But mark this: There will be terrible times in the last days.
People will be lovers of themselves.
2 Timothy 3:1-2 NIV

Yesterday I caught about ten minutes of "reality television." At first I found it rather funny that essentially dull and stupid living had become a marketable product. My laughter was soon stifled by the tedium of this pointless brand of entertainment. It took all of five minutes to get a full dose of low people and low living.

It used to be that life was reality and television provided a fantastic escape. Now it seems that "reality" TV is the rage and we cannot escape the dullness of self-absorption. It used to be that heroes set a high standard and others were inspired by their daring feats. Now it seems that modern heroes resemble thugs and the lowest things are paraded in public to unite us around our lowest common denominators.

We used to be shocked at adultery. Now the culture is surprised by virginity. It used to be that vulgarity was confined to the fringes of society. Now, it seems that vulgarity guarantees ratings and virtue is marginalized. It used to be that the soap opera plumbed the depths of sleaze and hedonism.

We have now become the soap opera and we're enthralled with our own depravity. Look out world, somebody in Hollywood is working on a new fall series to take us even lower.

*Instead, speaking the truth in love, we will in all things
grow up into him who is the Head, that is, Christ.*
Ephesians 4:15 NIV

Life is measured by its length, breadth, depth, and finally – height. Have you any stature, or are you a spiritual pygmy?

Pygmy babies are born of normal size and weight, but in early childhood something in the genetic code interrupts their growth. The analogy is all too clear among the Christian populace. Where we should be standing tall, we are laying low. Where we should be looking ahead, we are looking around. Where we should be strong, we are weak.

The disadvantage to vertically challenged Christians is great. They cannot see things from a lofty perspective. Rather than soaring with eagles, they strut among the turkeys. They fail to see both opportunity and obstacle. Without a clear look at the horizon, they wander indecisive pathways. Without warning, they are always in a state of surprise, even consternation.

Christians must get up, and lift up, and look up, but above all, they must grow up. Like a fifteen-year-old boy with a big body to grow into, we are called to grow in Christ. Our potential cannot be measured by human factors; it must be measured by God's divine plan. Perilous times are upon us requiring men and women of stature. Stand firm, stand strong, stand together, and stand tall.

Yet who knows whether you have come to the
kingdom for such a time as this?
Esther 4:14 NKJV

I am constantly amazed at how God gets His work done. Somehow He makes ordinary people achieve extraordinary results. He delights in the most unlikely characters and circumstances. He confounds the wisdom of men with ironies and longshots.

For example, if I were seated on a committee to raise up a leader for the purpose of thwarting the genocide of the Jewish race, I would probably be looking for a man. This man would have to possess great natural and learned leadership skills. He would have to be both diplomat and warrior, strategist and orator. The process would take years and the selection committee would probably render a split decision.

When God wanted to prevent the annihilation of the Jews, He started with a beauty contest! That's right – a beauty pageant that truly crowned a winner. Esther became the Queen of an empire by virtue of her beauty. No committee could ever have conceived such a bizarre plan. God was positioning a courageous woman in a place of great influence for a particular and peculiar moment in history.

Do you consider your circumstances somewhat strange? Who knows but that you have been divinely placed for such a time as this?

*They took Jesus therefore: and he went out, bearing the cross for himself,
unto the place called The place of a skull, which is called in
Hebrew, Golgotha: where they crucified him.*
John 19:17-18 ASV

The world that crucified Jesus was a barbaric world; a world wherein the life of a commoner held no value.

One born in a stable, the Romans concluded, could only be an animal. As the cross was raised and tamped into place it was just like a thousand other crucifixions on a thousand other hills. The mighty Roman Empire was just taking out its trash – nothing more, nothing less. Pilate was troubled, but surely his misgivings would fade with a good meal and a bit more wine. Herod was pleased with his legal and political maneuvering. They called him "the fox" with good reason. The Jewish leaders preserved their power and the illusion that they were the keepers of God's law. Even as nature gathered herself to roar in defiance, this cold, dark world ridded itself of one: Jesus of Nazareth. What would it matter; one peasant Jew; a bit of dust in the wind. Yet today, the crucifixion will be remembered on every continent and in every nation.

On this chosen Friday, all of time looks back to a moment immediately forgotten by its executioners and forever remembered by its benefactors; the moment of ultimate grace.

*This is why it says: "When he ascended on high, he led
captives in his train and gave gifts to men."
Ephesians 4:8 NIV*

From an earthly point of view it was the deadest day in history. All creation was looking for Jesus from the foundation of the world (Rev. 13:8). They longed for him; God's Anointed One; Messiah.

Now Messiah was taken down from a cross, dead. They wanted to put him on a throne, but now they put him in a borrowed tomb. Hope wailed in mourning as its light was extinguished. Jesus is dead. The tomb is sealed. His prediction of resurrection is forgotten. His disciples are devastated. It's the deadest day in history, but only from an earthly point of view.

In Hades, that place where the rich man lifted up his eyes and called across a gulf to a beggar named Lazarus … in Hades a voice is heard proclaiming victory. To those tormented, it is the sealing of their doom, and to the righteous dead, it is graduation day. Jesus said, "It is finished" on the cross.

Jesus proclaimed His victory in Hades, taking the righteous dead into his presence forever. Now, on the deadest day in history, Jesus awaits the Father's appointed hour to play out the greatest moment in all history past and yet to come. An empty cross and an emptied Hell are about to be joined by an empty tomb (1 Peter 3:19, 4:6).

Even though you have ten thousand guardians in Christ, you do not have many fathers, for in Christ Jesus I became your father through the gospel. Therefore I urge you to imitate me.
1 Corinthians 4:15-16 NIV

Lot had Abraham. Moses had Jethro. Joshua had Moses. Ruth had Naomi. Samuel had Eli. David had Samuel. Elisha had Elijah. Hezekiah had Isaiah. Paul had Barnabas. Timothy had Paul. Apollos had Aquila and Priscilla. The twelve apostles had Jesus.

Who do you have in your life to guide you through the narrows and take you to the heights? Who can hold you accountable? Who can speak with authority in the foggy confusion of conflicting desires? Who do you look up to? Who looks out for you? Have you a mentor?

Spiritual poverty in the modern American church can be attributed to the depreciation of eldership in our culture. A generation awash in clever technology and scientific arrogance casts aside its fathers, and in so doing, discards true wisdom. The Corinthians were proud of their intellectualism and modernism. They felt that they had outgrown their mentor, like the student who rises to instruct his instructors. Paul's letter points up their foolishness and sin.

We would do well to learn from their errors. The faster we race into the future, the more apt we are to leave behind the wisdom of the aged. The young and wise captain places youth at the lookout, but experience at the helm.

And if Christ has not been raised,
our preaching is useless and so is your faith.
1 Corinthians 15:14 NIV

The most important question in the world is asked at an empty tomb: "Did Jesus Christ rise from the dead?"

If it is not true, Jesus was a liar or a lunatic; anything but a good man. If it is not true, the church is a predatory fraud. If it is not true, man is the product of incalculable chance, a cosmic accident. If it is not true, there is no meaning, no transcendent purpose in our existence. If it is not true, we must agree with the atheist Bertrand Russell who issued the following joint statement with Albert Einstein just two days before the latter died: *"Those of us who know the most are the gloomiest about the future."*

Human history argues convincingly for our ultimate self-annihilation. If the empty tomb is an empty lie then we are to be pitied. But if it is true that Jesus rose from the dead ... then He was, and is, God; and we were, and are, His crowning creation. And a man must be ignorant, arrogant, misinformed or just plain crazy to reject Him.

What happened in a Jerusalem graveyard some two thousand years ago continues to be the most important question, and most liberating answer the world has ever known.

So shall my word be that goeth forth out of my mouth: it shall not return unto me void, but it shall accomplish that which I please, and it shall prosper in the thing whereto I sent it.
Isaiah 55:11 KJV

ZACUALPA, GUATEMALA: The teacher treasured the worn and tattered book above all others. To her, it was the "most important book in the school."

She had received it years ago at another school in another town. Every day she carried her treasured book to class and read aloud to her students for ten minutes. How many times had she read through that book with her students over the years? How many seeds were planted in the hearts of the little ones? Only heaven will tell.

Recently, an American Affect Destiny Team stumbled across this teacher, and her remarkable story in a remote mountain village. She watched with tears as every student in the school was given a copy of the book she deemed most important in any school – the *Book of Hope*.

I'm sure that there will be millions of people in heaven because of mass evangelism, mercy ministries, and pulpit preaching. But somewhere over there I think we'll find a surprising number of brothers and sisters who came to Christ because of a loving teacher who read aloud for ten minutes every day from the most important book in the school.

But they did not understand what he meant and
were afraid to ask him about it.
Mark 9:32 NIV

Something's wrong! You just haven't felt good. Your family has a history of cancer, but you won't let your mind dwell on it. Something says you should go see the doctor but there's another voice telling you it will go away. Fear keeps you from seeking the truth. Fear keeps you from the very one who may be able to effect a cure. Fear locks down your future – you're afraid to ask.

You're not alone. Some of us are afraid to ask what happened. What happened to our relationship? Where did things go wrong? We live with acid suspicions because we're afraid of the truth that might be revealed – afraid to ask.

Jesus made it very clear that truth is liberating. Sometimes the truth hurts. Sometimes the truth reveals what we would have preferred to keep hidden. Sometimes the truth is expensive. Sometimes the truth is convicting. But always, the truth liberates where ignorance imprisons.

The disciples were worried over the radical, inscrutable nature of Jesus' teaching. He was predicting His own death, and death didn't figure into their plans. In the final analysis, fear cost them a glorious revelation. Think about it. He was talking about God's marvelous plan of redemption, and they were afraid to ask.

And Hezekiah received the letter from the hand of the messengers,
and read it; and Hezekiah went up to the house of the LORD,
and spread it before the LORD.
2 Kings 19:14 NKJV

Bad news often comes in the form of a letter. I remember the nausea I felt a few years ago when I received a special letter from the Internal Revenue Service. I read, I wept, I prayed, I appealed, and I won. That letter was a snap when I compare it to a few poison letters I've received from angry parishioners. I needed someone to sound a bell between paragraphs so that I could run to my corner and clear my head.

I really shouldn't complain. I know men and women who have opened letters from their spouses; letters that amounted to final notice on a marriage and a family. I've walked into homes where a doctor's letter lay isolated on a table. The test results were positive . . . options for treatment were limited. Not so long ago in America, mothers and fathers dreaded that government letter that began, "We regret to inform you . . ."

The letter Hezekiah received was just as devastating, but Hezekiah shows us how to deal with bad news. Rather than spread it around the kingdom, he spread it out before the Lord. Before he called a staff meeting, he called upon the Lord.

God knows our troubles before the letters are posted. How it must please Him when we come alone to seek Him first.

. . . that I may win Christ, And be found in him.
Philippians 3:8-9 KJV

God's first question for man was, "Where are you?" When Adam failed to show up, and own up to his actions, man's quest for identity and purpose moved outside of God and the garden.

We're still struggling with the question, "Where are we?" Outside of Christ we don't know who we are, why we are, or where we are going. Man's search for meaning is ultimately frustrated in a world of irony, hypocrisy, and paradox. One claims to have found meaning in meditation. Another claims to have found meaning in medication. Still another asserts that life's ultimate meaning is meaninglessness. The search goes on amidst false hopes and frothy ideologies. Possessions fail to satisfy. Pleasure fails to sustain itself. Power breeds corruption. Philosophies drill dry holes around the question.

It's really not so complicated. When you don't know where you are, you're lost. That's how the Bible characterizes us apart from Christ . . . lost. Most of us are very slow to admit it – Adam's final legacy. There is only one sure answer to God's first question; one sure and certain address for the lost and wretched soul. In Christ, my soul takes refuge. In Christ, the lost are found. In Christ, my quest is over.

Finally, brethren, pray for us, that the
word of the Lord may run swiftly.
2 Thessalonians 3:1 NKJV

Something of the essence of our faith is forfeited when we lose our sense of urgency!

Imagine a football team that had no concern for time. The quarterback tells jokes at every huddle. The wide receiver wants consensus before he dares cross the middle in front of the line-backers. The quarterback only throws high looping passes because throwing hard could hurt his arm. Nobody looks at the clock or stresses over delay-of-game penalties. The coach sits on a stool sipping hot chocolate and discussing the merits of the last play with his assistants before he sends in the next play.

With this team, you can't really tell the difference between a drive and a timeout. The other team is up by ninety-two points, but nobody on our team keeps score. They will all stand up and tell you they are real players. They will all be deeply offended if you point out how poorly they play the game. Truth be known, they enjoy the huddle more than the game itself.

My ridiculous imagining displays a lethargic church. Our message and mission were born of blood. Our calling is forged in the fires of urgency. We are now living deep into the two-minute warning. We have received the ultimate hand off. Now we must run!

*Having many things to write to you, I did not wish to do so with
paper and ink; but I hope to come to you and
speak face to face, that our joy may be full.*
2 John 1:12 NKJV

A pop star recently asked his wife for a divorce – by fax!

We live in the impersonal world of beepers, digital messaging, voice mail, e-mail, snail mail, phone tag, mail-o-grams, and message boards. Though we work in the same office, we communicate over the Internet. We leave messages in response to left messages.

Often, the pen covers our lack of courage or class. A greeting card company puts out a line of cards that offer "morning hugs" and apologies to the kids for not being there to see them off to school. The line is marketed to guilt-ridden traveling parents. John recognized the value of face-to-face fellowship. His letter is brief because he is waiting until they can get together to share his heart.

Some things shouldn't be committed to paper and ink. Husbands and wives, parents and children, brothers and sisters, old friends and new friends, should operate in the arena of the human touch, lest in great volumes of information we lose the incredible magic of relationship.

God sent His Son to walk among us; gave His written Word to guide us, but He also sent His Spirit to abide with us. We're close to running out of fuel on the information super-highway. Face-to-face makes the empty heart full.

I am doing a great work, so that I cannot come down:
why should the work cease, whilst I leave it,
and come down to you?
Nehemiah 6:3 ASV

(O)ne of Satan's great strategies against us is distraction.

Nehemiah was rebuilding the broken walls of Jerusalem; restoring national identity and security to the nation of Israel. Sanballat and Tobiah were regional leaders opposed to Israel's re-emergence. They conspired throughout the project to isolate, intimidate, and delegitimize Nehemiah. When it seemed that the work would be completed, their last conspiracy involved getting Nehemiah to leave the project for a special meeting on a remote site. Nehemiah saw through their plan and responded as we should respond to our adversary: *"I'm doing a great work, so that I cannot come down."*

We should never come down from God's work to entertain gossip, intimidation, or petty arguments. When Christian leaders are embroiled in small and carnal squabbles, the work of the Lord suffers. There will always be cold-hearted people attempting to set your spiritual temperature. Don't let them! The courts of the land don't have to accept every appeal that demands attention ... neither do you.

Stay focused on building a life that pleases God. Set high standards and don't come down no matter what they say. You cannot marry high calling to low living.

But you, keep your head in all situations.
2 Timothy 4:5 NIV

I know why Paul told Timothy to keep his head in all situations: Because he was going into the people business, and the people business will stretch you to the breaking point.

Timothy was going to face cantankerous deacons, contentious women, squabbling saints, shameless gossips, pompous preachers, emotional pygmies, God robbers, arrogant teachers; and that's just the Sunday morning crowd. Timothy would know the sting of slander, the disappointment of abandonment, the loneliness of leadership, the paralysis of insecurity, the wounds of criticism, and the unreal demands of unreasonable people.

Paul wanted Timothy to bear the good fruit of self-control. "Keep your head, Timothy!" he pleaded. Shepherds aren't supposed to bite the sheep, even when the sheep act like wolverines. We could all take a lesson from Paul. We are far too easily provoked, in and out of the church. We react rather than respond. We take vengeance rather than wait on God (Romans 12:19). We disqualify ourselves from ministry in thoughtless moments of frustration.

For the steady laborer there is always a harvest, so long as he works in the fields and stays out of the mud.

I thank my God upon every remembrance of you.
Philippians 1:3 NKJV

1976: The toughest man in politics was crying . . . in front of a crowd . . . in front of the president . . . on the courthouse lawn in Russell, Kansas.

After fifteen years in Washington, everyone knew he was a fighter. Some called him hatchet man. His party called him when they needed someone to fight hard. Bob was an "extra rounds" fighter.

Terribly wounded in the waning days of World War II, Bob had battled against the odds to survive. He had risen to prominence through the House of Representatives and the Senate. Now he stood as a candidate for the vice-presidency. What makes a tough man cry? What breaks through the iron bulwark of a veteran campaigner? All it took that day was a memory of the good people of his tiny hometown collecting money in a cigar box at the drug store so that Bob could have a needed surgery. When tears interrupted Bob's speech, the president stood and led the applause. Bob Dole's vice-presidential quest failed by two percentage points. The fighter fought on for another two decades.

We should all look back with grateful hearts for the good people and good blessings that have marked our way. Cicero was right when he said, "Gratitude is the parent of all virtues."

Please Pray for Nicaragua

Population under age 18: 2,490,000

Nicaragua has experienced social and political upheaval and still suffers economically. Pray that the children will have enough to eat and that the local believers will be able to keep reaching out in Jesus' name with the *Book of Hope.*

Maria and Her Brothers Choose Life!

Living in one of the poorest sections of Nicaragua, 11-year-old Maria was trying to raise her three little brothers on her own. She woke up early every morning to make tortillas to sell on the street and to get her brothers ready for school. Then she spent most of her day trying to make enough money for them to survive.

She was tired, hungry and despairing, like many people in her neighborhood, and the latest rash of suicides gave Maria an idea. She decided to end the family's misery by killing her little brothers; then she would kill herself.

That same day, Maria's little brothers came home from school with the *Book of Hope*. After they begged Maria to read it to them, Maria began to read out loud about Jesus, who loved them so much that He had already paid the price for their sins!

Right then, the whole family prayed to receive Christ as Savior.

They went to the church that had sent volunteers to their school with the *Book of Hope*, and they told the pastor of their decision to follow Jesus – and about their dire circumstances.

Today, that little girl and her brothers are receiving the support of their local church, and they are all vibrant new Christians.

In everything set them an example by doing what is good.
In your teaching show integrity.
Titus 2:7 NIV

There is a voyeuristic aspect of seventy-channel surfing. We click through the stations, glancing into windows until something grabs our attention. Because we have a short attention span, we soon move down the block to see what's happening between CNN and the Home Shopping Network.

While channel surfing, I caught the final few minutes of a paid seminar by a lady who really seemed to understand relationships. I wasn't surprised that her books called her a relationship expert. She was really making sense. People were laughing and pondering and hugging and smiling as she wove a bit of "get real" therapy together with a healthy dose of "love yourself" philosophy topped with just a bit of psycho-babble. When she finished with a bell-ringer love story, the people applauded.

I was intrigued. People don't usually applaud when I'm finished. I hoped she was in print. I wanted her pithy stories; her clever sayings; her sterling insights. I couldn't find her book but, quite by accident, I found her mentioned in another book. Here, I discovered the basis of her expertise. My new relationship guru was working on marriage number five! Funny . . . nobody seemed to think that it mattered.

*. . . "but when you are old, you will stretch out your hands, and another
will gird you and carry you where you do not wish." This He spoke,
signifying by what death he would glorify God.*
John 21:18-19 NKJV

Peter died as Jesus said he would, stretched out on a
Roman cross. Tradition holds that Peter insisted on
being crucified upside-down because he did not feel worthy to be crucified in the same manner as our Lord. The
details of his death, and of the martyrdom of the other
disciples, are not nearly so important to the Christian
faith as is the fact that they all willingly gave up their
lives.

Nobody dies for a lie. These eyewitnesses to the resurrection believed unflinchingly to their last breath.
Lawyers put pressure on witnesses to see how far they will
go with their story. When the price gets high, the truth is
irrepressible. A witness breaks down, an alibi is dissolved,
a case collapses as truth illuminates a courtroom.

In the disciples, we find witnesses that could not be
broken. They stood by the truth though it cost them their
lives. What they saw and heard following Jesus' resurrection was absolute truth. These did not die together in the
mutual support of a lie in a bunker or fortress. They died
somewhat isolated, spread throughout the nations of the
earth. They died proclaiming the resurrected Lord.

There was only one reason for men to act as they did;
it was all true – any other explanation defies logic.

*" . . . and that You would keep me from evil, that I may not cause
pain!" So God granted him what he requested.*
1 Chronicles 4:10 NKJV

As I read the Old Testament, I am fascinated by the
names that were chosen. Parents didn't choose a
name because it was trendy or pleasant to the ear. They
chose names based on their hopes, circumstances, or
prophetic impulses.

Sometimes the name was a blessing. The name David
was an easy name to live with, meaning *Beloved.*

But some didn't get off so easy. Hosea had a son he
named Lo-Ammi, meaning *Not my people.* Hosea's wife
had a history of prostitution. Can you imagine what extra
baggage Lo-Ammi carried through life? He might as well
have carried a sign that said: *Illegitimate!* Jacob was a
deceiver until God offered to change his name to Israel,
Prince with God. God didn't have to make the offer twice.

Then we have the interesting case of Jabez, whose
name means *Causes pain.* Now there's a name I could
have lived up to. But Jabez prayed a remarkable prayer
that he "might not cause pain," and God granted his
request.

Jabez prayed as we should all pray that we might live
beyond the limited expectations of others; that we might
break free of family histories, bad beginnings, and poor
parenting. Jabez was determined that input would not
determine his outcome.

*How lonely sits the city that was full of people! How like a
widow is she, who was great among the nations!*
Lamentations 1:1 NKJV

The colors that flow from Jeremiah's rich brush are dark; the canvas deeply shadowed. Jerusalem is conquered. Her people deported. Her broken walls and burned gates lend the appearance of an aged prostitute, unable to properly cover herself. In this first chapter of sorrow, Jeremiah describes a city that describes a wayward and broken life.

When our sins finally break us, the glory is gone and a fragile, blackened shell remains. Enslaved, betrayed, abandoned, restless, vulnerable, desolate, embittered, afflicted, helpless, naked, unclean, violated, reproached, deceived, distressed – that is how Jeremiah views Jerusalem. She was once full of people. She was once great among the nations. Now the skeletal remains cause the prophet to mourn. Jerusalem has become a city of beggars and thieves.

The price of arrogance bankrupts a nation. Willful sin impoverishes the soul. The lonely widow calls a warning across the ages. Have we ears to hear?

Guarding the heart against pride and bitterness guards a life against destruction. Keeping the gates of the soul under the Spirit's control keeps the adversary from his ultimate goal. How lonely sits the city, once envied – now mocked.

> *"... for man looks at the outward appearance,*
> *but the LORD looks at the heart."*
> *1 Samuel 16:7 NKJV*

A female voice in line behind me cursed the three high tech companies she held stock in. She had followed the legion of Americans trying to cash in on the stock market rocket ride.

She cursed again, and I glanced over my shoulder expecting to see a thirty-something banker type tapping away at her palm pilot. Instead, I saw a gray-headed granny with a cane and an attitude. Two elderly friends listened as her assault on money managers continued. I winced as a set of red-hot expletives caused a chuckle down the line. She looked like a saint and cussed like a sailor. I dared another glance. She caught my eye and raised an eyebrow as if to say, "What's your problem, boy?"

I've been cussed at a few times – and good. Somehow I knew that "granny" could surpass all the cussers I had ever known. I looked away and moved up to the register to pay for my groceries. When I left she was cussing a popular banking stock. It just goes to show you that outward appearances can be very deceiving.

When God looks at us, He sees us as we truly are. We had better be real when we seek His blessings or sing His praise. No amount of Sunday posturing or put-up piety can hide a dirty heart.

And the earth was without form, and void ...
And God said, Let there be light.
Genesis 1:2-3 KJV

PORTEVIEJO, EQUADOR: The city struggles amidst economic meltdown. Inflation tops 100% per month! All foundations are shaking. Local school teachers go out on strike as an Affect Destiny Team touches down to distribute the *Book of Hope* to school children.

It would seem, to the outside observer, the most inopportune time to carry out a distribution. But God isn't limited by calamity. He sees and moves with a perfect understanding. He capitalizes on confusion that His glory might be seen. The repeated teachers' strikes have caused many parents to enroll their children in private schools. Since the public schools are closed, the teams concentrate on private schools that are bursting at the seams. Results: 11,000 children receive copies of the *Book of Hope.* A local film crew is interviewing university professors for commentary on the strike. They notice that American volunteers are distributing a book to the university students. Results: A local pastor is interviewed prime time about the *Book of Hope* and doors open all over the city.

God doesn't need our scripted plans and five-step wonders. He is forever the God who calls cosmos out of chaos.

*For His merciful kindness is great toward us, and
the truth of the LORD endures forever.
Psalm 117:2 NKJV*

Just when we think that science has conquered all, somebody tells the truth. Time magazine wrote of astrophysics: "The experts don't know for sure how old or how big the universe is. They don't know what most of it is made of. They don't know in any detail how it began or how it will end." That statement casts a long shadow on scientific certainty.

On October 19, 1987, the stock market crashed. Long-time Federal Reserve chairman Alan Greenspan was on his way to Dallas. When he landed, he found that the securities climate had changed from summer to Siberia in four hours. Greenspan has had a decade to figure out what happened, but Bob Woodward reports, "Even ten years later, he could still find no credible explanation for the abrupt one-day decline in stock values that had built up over the years." Last week I heard the vocal agnostic Alan Dershowitz say that he could not tell anybody what was right or wrong . . . quite a statement from a defense attorney.

In truth, we are living in an "I don't know" world. No wonder the Christian is out of step. We believe in the absolute surety of God's eternal Word. Stand fast for the truth of Scripture. It seems to me that the world's only certainty is uncertainty.

He asked me, "Son of man, can these bones live?"
Ezekiel 37:3 NIV

The question would have never crossed my mind. *"Can these bones live?"* Dry, bleached, dismembered, and scattered bones are a testimony to fatality and finality, not regeneration. In human terms, when breathing, heartbeat, and brain activity have ceased, all hope is gone.

In Ezekiel's vision, that hopelessness is heightened by the statement, "The bones were *very* dry." God could not have given Ezekiel a more graphic vision of the human impossibility of Israel's restoration. Jerusalem was destroyed. A generation was growing up disconnected from her homeland. It was like Egypt all over again.

Have you a valley of dry bones? Do the promises of God seem impossible? Maybe you should spend a week searching out the impossible settings in the Old Testament. Spend some time with Noah filling the ark with matched pairs. Drop in on Moses in Pharoah's waiting room. Stand beside Joshua for a while and size up the walls of Jericho. Stand tall at the campfire as Goliath roars and say, "My money's on David!"

Noah filled the ark. Pharoah let the people go. Jericho fell at Israel's shout. David could have made you a rich man. Can these bones live? How will you answer the question?

. . . who maketh the clouds his chariot: who walketh
upon the wings of the wind.
Psalm 104:3 KJV

"Why is this happening to me? What's going on, Lord? How can I find Your will in this mess?" Have you ever asked God those questions when the clouds blocked out the light? Have you ever lost heart in the face of a mounting gale? If you haven't, then you haven't really lived.

Deep troubles come, and it looks like faith might blow away with the storm. Questions rise up with the tempest. Is God good and not powerful; or, is He powerful and not good, that troubles have multiplied, and sorrows deepened? Have I made God angry? What did I do to deserve this? The greatest question of them all is, "Where are you, Lord?"

The good news is: God is there in the midst of the storm. The bad news is: God sometimes rides on dark clouds and walks amidst mayhem. In these moments of divine calamity, we make the mistake of focusing on what we don't know, rather than what we do. We can't see His will, so we doubt His love. We can't see purpose, so we lose faith. We can't understand, so we assume that there is no answer.

But, don't we know that He is forever faithful? Don't we know that He will deliver us? Don't we know that He loved us all the way to Calvary? Can't we yet trust Him, even when He thunders?

"Stand at the crossroads and look; ask for the ancient paths,
ask where the good way is, and walk in it,
and you will find rest for your souls."
Jeremiah 6:16 NIV

There's a serial killer loose on the road to completion. He has littered the roadside with dead dreams, shattered visions, and broken trust. His common appearance enables him to approach without notice, and just when some traveler begins to see the light of hope, he strikes a blow to the heart. He leaves mourning and bitterness in his wake. If the victim yet lives, he's been known to return to the scene of the crime to strike a deathblow.

His name is Disappointment and most of us have felt his dark and bitter touch at one time or another. Disappointment usually hangs out with Loneliness and Hopelessness; two killers of equal distinction. You had better watch out for this dark trio. They have killed before, and they will kill again. They hide along the shadowy corridors of pride. They slip, unnoticed, among unreasonable expectations. They're waiting for that moment of darkness; that moment the complacent traveler looks away from the light. The dagger is sharpened; the moment well chosen; dark clouds gather, and Disappointment strikes at the soul.

Stay on the "ancient paths." There is safety in walking close to the Lord. Keep your eyes on Jesus and deprive the killer of every opportunity.

> *The Spirit himself testifies with our spirit*
> *that we are God's children.*
> *Romans 8:16 NIV*

Comedian George Goebels asks the question, *"Have you ever felt that the world was a tuxedo and you were a pair of brown shoes?"* Well, have you?

While in high school, I was hired as a stock boy at Sears. I was responsible for rolling out new merchandise for five departments – ladies' departments! I didn't mind rolling racks around, but one day the boss put me behind a register to cover coffee breaks. After that, I was often asked to fill in here or there. I hated it. When one of the girls I liked from school came through with her mother, and I was running the register in the purse section, it was just too much. I found another job.

When I get that "I don't belong here" feeling, I'm usually looking for a door. People will not stay in churches where they cannot find a sense of belonging. Put a brown pair of shoes with a black tuxedo and the brown shoes will walk. Do you live your life in such a way that people around you feel welcomed? Have you bordered your life with wide entry lanes or barbed wire?

The Holy Spirit works without ceasing among us to affirm God's welcome. Today we have an opportunity to live in harmony with the Spirit. Be God's inclusive welcome to somebody standing on the border.

. . . do good to them that hate you.
Matthew 5:44 KJV

The old spinster loved us as though we were her own grandchildren. Her pantry always smelled of cookies and her parlor was filled with missionary memorabilia.

Her house was a spooky-looking monstrosity, sitting alone on a rocky hill. For a wide-eyed seven-year-old boy, going over to her house was an adventure. Mom would take us two or three times per year. We were warned to be on our best behavior. I didn't listen. I just wanted to see the dagger from Liberia again.

Years later, I learned the rest of the story. There had been a conflict between the old lady and my parents. Bitter words were spoken. My parents suffered deeply from reckless rumors. Though Mom and Dad were open, there was no reciprocal desire for reconciliation. The old lady held a deep bitterness, but she missed our visits. Through a friend, she let it be known that she would like to see "the children," and, for years, my mother took us for regular visits.

Mom knew how much those visits meant to an aged, embittered, lonely lady. She put her feelings on the shelf and offered kindness to an adversary. That lesson has endured while others have been forgotten. Adversity is a prime opportunity to show the world God's grace.

... for he knows how we are formed,
he remembers that we are dust.
Psalm 103:14 NIV

Adam got a second chance, as did Eve. Jonah got a second chance; so did Peter. David got a second chance, as did Elijah, John-Mark, and Onesimus. The children of Israel were given repeated chances.

Mary Magdalene lived a terrible life. She got a second chance. Zacchaeus was a notorious cheat, and he was given a second chance. How about the brothers of Joseph? Those evil sons of Jacob should have been hung in Egypt, but they were given a second chance. Through Noah, a whole world was given a second chance.

The truth is, we need a second chance, because we are all sinners. We all fall short of the mark. We all walk outside the lines. From the mighty to the small, we're cut from the same cloth; sons of Adam; all "bent" towards sin. Yet God forgives, restores, and renews when we repent. The patience of God stretches beyond our horizons.

By my sense of justice, He should have closed the books on the human experiment long ago. The key to God's patience is His love. He never forgets that we are children. He is the Perfect Parent, exercising restraint born of love. He knows that we will fail. He expects that we will stumble, but He also expects that in the process, His children will grow.

Elijah was a man just like us. He prayed earnestly that it
would not rain, and it did not rain on the land for
three and a half years.
James 5:17 NIV

How do great men pray? Wouldn't you like to be able to tap into the prayers of Hudson Taylor for China? Wouldn't it be fascinating to know what Martyn Luther prayed just moments before his trial? I would like to know what Paul prayed just five minutes after Luke told him that Demas had disappeared. What did John pray on his second lonely day on Patmos?

I certainly won't know any of the answers this side of heaven, but the Scripture is filled with recorded prayers offered by heroic saints. Paul's recorded prayers are models for instruction. David's prayers drip with human emotion. Solomon's prayer, invoking God's presence in the temple, should be a daily touchstone for all who love His presence. Elijah's prayer shut up the heavens. Jesus' instruction on prayer gives us a protocol for approaching God's throne.

We have quite a library of prayer in the Scripture. Why, then, do we pray such lame and anemic prayers? Why do we ask for trinkets and baubles? It seems to me that we often pray without thinking. Could it be that we grow lazy in prayer? A college term paper receives our earnest attention and careful ordering. Should we not order our prayers? After all, we have an audience before Heaven's King.

*"The princes of Judah are like those who remove a landmark;
I will pour out My wrath on them like water."
Hosea 5:10 NKJV*

Question: What invites God's wrath like a waterfall? Answer: Removing historical landmarks so that a generation slips her moral anchors.

Israel had forgotten God. Her leadership was culpable. Having thrown off moral restraint, the nation tottered on the edge of destruction.

Leadership is responsible for more than its visionary reach. Leadership is responsible to maintain the moral landmarks – reminders of who we are and how we got here. In recent years, a concerted effort has been made to remove the Christian landmarks from America's history. The rise of pluralism has been marked by a downgrading of Christianity, from a dominant and driving force, to an insignificant historical footnote. Some would have us forget that the majority of our founding fathers felt that our form of government was untenable except for its Christian underpinning. Should we now ignore the God that they so freely invoked, we shall cease to know His blessing and hasten to invite His wrath.

Without landmarks, we are lost. Without moral precepts, we have no basis for justice. Without truth, we have no rudder, nor compass. Without remembrance, we invite the repetition of barbaric atrocity.

*"You looked for much, but indeed it came to little; and
when you brought it home, I blew it away."*
Haggai 1:9 NKJV

Haggai's view of Israel's landscape is one of naked honesty. God claims absolute responsibility for the blighting of personal and national prosperity. Read the word of the Lord to a people who lack priority: *"I blew it away."*

Some people fail to achieve because they are lazy. Others fail to achieve because they are foolish. Still others languish in mediocrity for a lack of vision. In this situation, God has taken initiative to blow away the pitiful wages paid out during Israel's recession. Why would He do that? After seventy years of captivity in Babylon, the people returned to a destroyed Jerusalem. The initial enthusiasm to build God's temple and re-establish worship was displaced by a passion to restore personal properties. The people were working hard, but in self-interest. The temple lay in ruins while the people were paneling their homes and rebuilding their boundary walls. Their hearts were revealed.

Unless God is given His rightful place in the heart, we live lives of frustrated expectation. Disappointment shadows us and the path grows dark. God wants to bless us and infuse our lives with purpose, but until we give Him first place, our lives may rightly be titled: *"Gone With the Wind."*

. . . they received the word with all readiness, and searched the
Scriptures daily to find out whether these things were so.
Acts 17:11 NKJV

Bedford, England houses a wonderful museum to the life and work of John Bunyan, author of *Pilgrim's Progress*. With the exception of the Bible, Bunyan's great work has been translated into more languages than any other book in history.

Dr. Ravi Zacharias was visiting the museum and made the following comment to the lady at the front desk: "Isn't it amazing that a simple little book from the hands of a mender of pots and pans has won such world-wide acclaim?" Zacharias was floored when she confessed that she had never read *Pilgrim's Progress*. She was directing people through a museum built to remember a book she had not read.

I don't find it so shocking as did Dr. Zacharias. I am surrounded by Christians who gladly point others to the general goodness and veracity of Christianity, only to admit that they haven't read all of the Book. The percentage of Christians who could not walk a seeker through a Biblical path to salvation is embarrassing; even tragic.

Our Biblical illiteracy limits our effectiveness and invites the scorn of bankrupt ideologies. God has placed a Sword in our hands, unrivaled in its power, beauty, and craftsmanship. Should we not learn to wield it well?

"Forget the former things; do not dwell on the past.
See, I am doing a new thing!"
Isaiah 43:18-19 NIV

Dinnertime has passed and my three girls are whirling around the kitchen sealing leftovers, loading the dishwasher, and cleaning up the mess I made with the coffee maker. From where I watch, I see them hemmed in by their pictures. There's at least one trio shot from every year. The "munchkin" picture by the sliding glass door makes me remember the wide-eyed looks we would get with three strollers at the shopping mall. The "hay bale" picture was the calm before the teenage storm. The "pencil sketch" on the coffee table is our latest three-teen picture.

There are others, but I won't bore you. Snapshots stir up warm and wonderful memories, but there is no life in them. Life is whirling around my kitchen, teasing, laughing at me, hugging Mom, and chattering non-stop about "stuff."

Life is not a snapshot. It will not wait, not even for a moment. It is constantly moving, growing, searching, and grasping. From the cradle to the grave, God has us in constant motion. We are in process, or at least we should be, until we die.

Are you still growing or are you freeze-framed? Are you moving on, or do you look like all your old pictures? Enjoy the memory . . . but embrace the moment!

During the night Paul had a vision of a man of
Macedonia standing and begging him,
"Come over to Macedonia and help us."
Acts 16:9 NIV

Short-term missions have changed my life. From Southeast Asia, to the rocky shores of Panama, to the depths of Siberia, I've touched fields my grandfather thought untouchable. I've climbed empty pedestals to stand where Lenin's great monoliths looked blindly upon a crumbling empire.

The statues are gone, but the darkness remains. My world view has been sharpened with each short-term encounter so that I now consider myself a "world Christian" – one who sees all of the world as a single great harvest field.

Western perspectives have been stiffly challenged by needs that can't be met with an American program or offering. A child's smile and hug has undermined my cultural prejudices. I can no longer despise a people because of their political ideologies or religious persuasions. I have lost my sense of "us" and "them." Politics dissolve in the tears of a hungry child. Racial barriers are swept away in the cleansing flood of redemption. Cultural distinctions flow into a common pool of need. For all that is being done, the need just keeps growing. Help us!

Begin to pray daily for a nation; a people; a city. Go, or make it possible for someone else to carry God's light. There's not much time.

For we are labourers together with God.
1 Corinthians 3:9 KJV

CHITA, SIBERIA: A container with forty thousand copies of the *Book of Hope* sat on the back of a flat-bed truck outside a warehouse. There were no palates or forklifts to be seen. One thousand packages had to be unloaded and stacked forty yards down a hallway – by hand. One person could get the job done in a day, if they kept at it. By days end, that lonely worker would have made five hundred trips down the long hallway.

Affect Destiny Teams have learned the power of unity in diversity. It's a lesson learned "bucking books." When it was time to unload, we showed up with forty team members. It took about five minutes to get a human chain organized. It took an hour to unload, move, and stack forty thousand books. A twenty-one-year-old saxophone player from Perm anchored one end of the line. A pre-teen girl from Greensboro, North Carolina took her place. A bishop's wife from Ukraine stood alongside an interpreter from Kraznoyarsk. Russian, Ukrainian, Siberian, and American all worked together – and had great fun in the process.

Wouldn't it be great if the church discovered the power and beauty of unity in diversity? We make short work of tall orders when connectivity is job one.

If we endure, we shall also reign with Him.
2 Timothy 2:12 NKJV

I'll never forget the midpoint in my first marathon. Everything was slowing down. I didn't see how I could possibly run another thirteen miles. In those moments I wanted to quit.

The middle miles are often the toughest, whether we're talking about a marathon, a marriage, an education, or life itself. The start creates its own excitement. Beginning and hope run lockstep. It's in the middle miles that we suddenly question our resolve. It's in the middle miles that many a marriage is lost. In the bright blush of the honeymoon or the afterglow of the diamond anniversary, we find a stability that disappears in the middle miles. In the middle miles, it's tough to see where we started, and tougher to see where we might finish.

It's a good thing I had a running partner through the middle miles. We reminded each other of all the hard training miles. In the middle miles you have to generate a little excitement. In the middle miles you have to work up your own enthusiasms. In the middle miles you need to remember the calling, the quest, the goals, the dream.

Keep going, whatever you do, keep going through the middle miles. There's a celebration waiting, just around the corner.

He that observeth the wind shall not sow; and he that
regardeth the clouds shall not reap.
Ecclesiastes 11:4 ASV

It's a gray, rainy, cold, wet morning. I'm fighting a hard battle between what I should and what I will. I should run. I have the right gear for rain. I always enjoy having run in the rain. I have the time set aside. I need the exercise, yet the battle rages.

The first mile is hard. The cold slaps me in the face. My back feels a little bit tight. My feet will probably get wet. What if the drizzle turns into a downpour? I know I'll regret it if I don't run, so . . . where did I put that Gore-tex jacket?

Life is filled with easy "put-offs." "I'll do it later," we say. "There's plenty of time," we tell ourselves, so our days end unfulfilled; the culmination of seven decades of putting off the little things.

The daily "put-offs" feed a growing monster called procrastination. This "big boy" ultimately devours our future, our hopes, our dreams, our destinies. We are left with pocket change when we should have been set for life. We live at the bottom when we should have scaled the heights. We live cluttered and inefficient lives, flustered by our inability to help, or lead, or influence.

Go back to school! Finish off your list! Settle an issue! Organize a mess! As for me, I'm going running in the rain.

*Then Peter came to Him and said, "Lord, how often
shall my brother sin against me, and I forgive him?"
Matthew 18:21 NKJV*

Lock them up, those who have hurt you. Lock them up and hold them responsible. Never forget a slight, never forgive an indiscretion, never write off a debt . . . make them pay. You are justified by suffering. You are understood in your anger. So build a prison to hold all offenders. Build it large and strong. Craft airtight cases and ironclad indictments. Don't let anyone escape. They don't deserve parole. Lock them up and keep the only key in a very safe place.

Only one thing you should remember – you must stay at the jail to guard your prisoners. You can't move on. You can't rise above. You can't pursue your noble dreams. You built the jail; now you're a jailor.

It's dawning on you now, isn't it? There's not much difference between being in or out. Walls are walls. What's that I hear you say? You don't want to be a jailor? Well, then let them out! Open all the cells and offer complete pardons. Choose to forget and forgive and dismiss the charges. Let them out and let God work His justice. Let them out and tear down the jail. That jail was a real eyesore anyway.

Every Christian needs to decide whether they will spend their lives looking at stark prison walls, or mighty oceans of mercy.

*So do not worry, saying, 'What shall we eat?' or 'What shall we drink?'
or 'What shall we wear?' For the pagans run after all these things,
and your heavenly Father knows that you need them.*
Matthew 6:31-32 NIV

If we were to heed all warnings, the American consumer would be a frightened breed.

Cholesterol is lurking in every tasty morsel. Diet Coke is killing brain cells. I'm limiting the use of my cell phone for fear of a tumor. I'm choking on fossil fuel byproducts, yet I'm afraid I'll run out of gas for my SUV. The sun is going to kill me because of ozone depletion. If I stay inside, I have to worry about radon gas. When it rains, I worry about the acid content. The polar caps are melting. I'm eating apples to keep healthy, but the skin might harbor pesticides. Coffee is drying out my tissues while caffeine is jacking up my heart rate. Irradiated beef and chickens on steroids have turned me on to tuna, but tuna carries the risk of mercury contamination.

I fear my clothes might have originated in an Asian sweatshop. I'm worried about human cloning, nuclear terrorism, vast left-wing conspiracies, vast right-wing ignorance, gross taxation, and road rage. Yesterday, I read a newspaper article about killer stress. I don't think the paper was using recycled newsprint. I've written enough today . . . worried about radiation from the computer screen.

We waste our days when worries reign. Illegitimate concerns distract the soul.

O LORD, how long shall I cry, and You will not hear?
Even cry out to You, "Violence!" And You will not save.
Habakkuk 1:2 NKJV

The first prayer of Habakkuk reveals his heart with a stark honesty. "How long?" Have you ever prayed that prayer? Have you wept as you've cried out to God over a lost loved one, stubbornly resistant to the Gospel?

Can you relate to the prophet with the strange name? His frustration with injustice and violence is heightened by the seeming absence of God. It's the cry of the falsely accused; the question that haunts us when dying is painful and slow; a longing that aches in silence: "O Lord, how long?"

In times like these we need to be reminded that Jehovah never sleeps nor slumbers. He is never idle, absent, ignorant, ambivalent, or insensitive. The veil of mystery that shrouds His way is often unlifted. His purposes, though perfect, are often obscured and impervious; they are also glorious.

Nobody understood the cross when Jesus died. Yet in that dark hour, the greatest gift was given; the greatest love displayed. God answers Habakkuk (v.5): "Look among the nations and watch – Be utterly astonished! For I will work a work in your days which you would not believe, though it were told you."

What is God doing in the midst of your suffering? You probably wouldn't believe it if He told you.

Finally, all of you be of one mind, having compassion for one another;
love as brothers, be tenderhearted, be courteous.
1 Peter 3:8 NKJV

Like rushing water, conversation bubbles around me. Two ladies sit hunched over for privacy. Their brows are furrowed, their words are whispered with malicious intensity; looks to me like somebody did somebody wrong.

A loud-mouthed businessman proudly runs his numbers, loud enough for all to hear; alcohol and arrogance conspiring to reveal a fool. A round table full of office workers erupts in frequent laughter. They're all represented at the table: the joker, the climber, the flirt, the watcher, the princess and the ghoul. A moonstruck couple plays footsie in the booth across the way; hands touch, words glide, eyes convey what best goes unsaid. There's a constant clanging in the kitchen; the clatter of silverware bouncing off tile.

A dull roar covers music no one listens for, and I sit here in the middle of my favorite restaurant, pecking on my laptop and nursing a cup of coffee. Though I'm surrounded, I might as well be alone. We've all come to be fed, but we never connect.

It's like a lot of Sunday mornings: Christians gather; fed but lonely; assembled yet disconnected. It's almost time to go to church. Don't feed and flee. Make a real connection where you worship this Sunday morning.

Let your gentleness be evident to all.
Philippians 4:5 NIV

Building a family is the greatest building project of all. Sticks, bricks, steel, glass, and concrete are all child's play when compared to the complex nature of molding and shaping a child.

God is the Master Builder, but He has entrusted fathers with a lot of the "rough-in" work. Builder Dads need to use high quality oil. Oil represents gentleness, kindness, and patience. Don't settle for a pint, you're going to need a barrel, especially if you have daughters. Dads are naturally equipped to apply muscle and pressure, but that manly strength can sheer off vital connections. Some Dads have gummed up the works with the best of intentions. A little bit of oil in preparation and maintenance lowers the muscle quotient and keeps us from doing long-term damage. Oil can do what brute force can't!

Most Dads don't need bigger hammers or tighter grips – just more oil. Raising children requires that we take them apart, clean them up, and apply some fine-tuning from time to time. Don't try to take them apart without plenty of oil. You'll never get them back together. Before you try to give your kid a big adjustment, make sure you apply the oil of gentleness and moderation.

Arise, go to Nineveh.
Jonah 1:2 ASV
But Jonah rose up to flee unto Tarshish.
Jonah 1:3 ASV

What was going through Jonah's mind? Was he intimidated by the evil reputation of Nineveh? Was he afraid that he wasn't ready for the "big time?" Did he fear for his life on the mean streets of sin city?

There can be no doubt that Jonah knew that God was calling. If not, then why not just stay home? Jonah ran. Nineveh lay 600 miles to the east, and Jonah set his course 2400 miles due west. Tarshish, the modern day city of Tartessus in Spain, was just about as far away as a man could get from Nineveh.

The story has a familiar and contemporary ring to it. How often do we sense the prodding of the Holy Spirit to some course of action, only to run off and do the exact opposite? Why do we run from God's calling? Is it because we feel inadequate, ill-prepared, afraid of rejection, or are we just lazy?

We need to remember this: God doesn't lose track of fearful fugitives. He tracks us down. He may not send a fish to swallow us up. We may get all the way to our Tarshish, but we can be sure of this – we're not hidden at all. At any moment God might whisper, *"What are you doing here?"*

Maybe today you're a fugitive from God's call. The telephone is ringing – will you answer?

Then the word of the LORD came to Jonah a second time.
Jonah 3:1 NIV

Thank God for second chances. If life were a *"one shot"* affair, we would all be out of the game. When Jonah ran from God's call, God's call found him again. But God's generous invitation was not issued until Jonah had repented of his sin.

Paul makes it clear that we have all sinned and fallen short of God's glory (Romans 3:23). Therefore, we are all in need of repentance that our ears might be opened to hear God's call once again.

If it were up to me, I would probably have washed my hands of Jonah. The stakes in Nineveh were measured in human lives, and I wouldn't have thought Jonah a good risk. But God runs to mercy like we run to judgment. "Arise, go to Nineveh." This word from the Lord finds Jonah spit up on a beach without so much as a change of clothes. He has been through the most harrowing ordeal of his life. He is alone and displaced when God speaks the second time. He looked a lot better on the docks at Joppa. He had a plan. He had money then. He was in control. But now, he has nothing. Sitting alone on a desolate shoreline, Jonah hears the familiar voice of God calling again: "Arise."

Oh, that we would learn from Jonah – when you have God's call, you have it all.

This is love, that we walk according to His commandments.
2 John 1:6 NKJV

Love keeps the rules. Somewhere in the seventies, a pop song hit the charts, showing surprising staying power. It was a pretty melody wrapped around a ridiculous proposition. The story line centered on a girl explaining to one love that she has another lover – *"but that doesn't mean I love you any less."* While the song admitted that having two lovers broke all the rules, it defended the illicit involvement based on felt needs.

"Torn Between Two Lovers" played out as my high school days ran out. In my naivety, I laughed the song off as a silly writer's fantasy. Imagine my surprise when I started hearing that song played over and over again in counseling situations. "Pastor, I know this is wrong, but it feels right" – "I love my wife and kids, but I love her too, pastor."

They should have titled that song: "Tearing Up Your Loved Ones."

Even an atheist admits that true love is shrouded in mystery. King Solomon couldn't figure it out with all his experimentation. Love requires a framework of truth and commitment. For the mysteries of love to find their purest expression, we must love within the rules. Don't tell people, *"Down deep I really love the Lord,"* unless you walk according to His Word.

So he said to me, "This is the word of the LORD to Zerubbabel:
'Not by might nor by power, but by my Spirit,'
says the LORD Almighty."
Zechariah 4:6 NIV

There is not a great deal of difference between a broken-down city, and a broken-down life. In both cases, the defense mechanisms have been compromised. In both cases, the devastation is catastrophic. In both cases, a sense of hopelessness descends like the night to suffocate the last embers of a dream.

Whether looking upon a razed city or a ruined heart, the word "impossible," whispers like a cold wind. Zerubbabel felt its chill as he surveyed the mountains of debris; charred timbers; impassable streets and ungated archways. Once a glorious temple stood here – but now, a blackened ruin. Once a priesthood led worship here – but now, the only sound is the sound of weeping followed by an anguished silence. Once there was gold. Now there is garbage. Once there was incense. Now there is insult. Once there was honor. Now there is horror.

But God is working in the midst of the rubble. The great promise keeper is making promises again. The temple will be rebuilt. The glory will be restored. The city will be strong again. None of this is humanly possible, but by God, it shall be done.

Does the wind whisper, "impossible" over your broken life? God has come to rebuild His shattered temple in you.

Please Pray for Philippines

Population under age 18: 32,371,000

Islam has made great inroads in the Philippines, and we need to pray for safety for local believers and missionaries, and for the power of God's Word to reach children and their families and bring them to Jesus.

Finding Hope in a Cyber-café!

Joseph* came from a broken home in the Philippines, but he tried not to think about the trauma of the divorce and its impact on him.

In fact, the day he received the *Book of Hope* at school, he only had one thing on his mind, really. His favorite video game was now available for anyone to play at the local cyber-café! So although he didn't have a computer of his own, he could still play after school.

He dumped his books beside the computer in the café and made an internet connection to get to the game. Then the woman who owns the cyber-café, a believer, noticed the *Book of Hope* among his school things. She invited him to take a break from the video game and access www.hopenet.net, the Book of Hope interactive website for teenagers.

Joseph went to the site and began to read the web page about family. It talked about broken homes and failed marriages, and Joseph felt the website was speaking directly to him!

He read through the entire website and committed his life to Christ, right there at the cyber-café.

*Joseph's name has been changed for confidentiality.

But he himself went a day's journey into the wilderness, and came and
sat down under a juniper-tree: and he requested for himself that
he might die, and said, It is enough; now, O Jehovah, take
away my life; for I am not better than my fathers.
1 Kings 19:4 ASV

Frustration is like an unheard scream in the night. Depression follows close behind. There is something about impossibility wrapped up in inertia that moves us to anger and tears.

I know what I'm talking about. I'm living there right now. I'm white-knuckled and weary. I am faced with a limitation I cannot exceed. I'm like a pyromaniac in a petrified forest. I strike the match, but there's nothing to burn. One minute I want to charge – the next minute I want to leave.

Knowing the right answer doesn't always make the pain go away – and the pain of frustration spreads to the joints and marrow of life. Elijah's frustration cut so deep, he wanted to die. That helps me gain a bit of perspective. He had been to the mountaintop and called down fire and rain. He had pronounced judgment and carried out executions. He had sent a message to the very core of Ahab and Jezebel's dynasty – and for what? The same people stayed in office and Jezebel conspired to send out a posse. "Kill me Lord!" he cried.

I guess I'm not so bad off after all. God was faithful to Elijah, and God will be faithful to me, and you. We would do well to stop looking at our troubles and start listening for His voice.

But others fell on good ground and yielded a crop:
some a hundredfold, some sixty, some thirty.
Matthew 13:8 NKJV

BISHOPVILLE, MARYLAND: Julie Turpin is a missionary to the eighth grade. She heard of the *Book of Hope* and thought it might provide a good opportunity to share Christ with her friends. Julie raised funds to purchase a full case of Campus Packs (Books in packages of five for "Five Friend Focus").

We are often limited in distributions of the *Book of Hope* here at home, but Julie has complete freedom. She has already won five friends to Christ, and plans to distribute the rest of her Campus Packs by year's end.

Through the years I've seen, first hand, the stunning results when the seed of God's written Word is planted. Discarded books have been found in ditches and trash bins. What some cast aside, others found in dark moments of the soul. Some might call it chance; we call it miraculous. Stolen books, resold on the black market in Russia, have proven the power of the Word.

In a diversity of cultures, the effect of God's Word has been uniform and life-changing. It really doesn't matter whether it's given by a church worker in Brazil, an Affect Destiny volunteer in Ukraine, or an eighth grader in Maryland – the Word of God changes people.

Help us shake our world!

We are bound to thank God always for you, brethren, as it is fitting, because your faith grows exceedingly, and the love of every one of you all abounds toward each other.
2 Thessalonians 1:3 NKJV

When faith grows, and love abounds, the environment is ripe for great spiritual progress. It is obvious that God blessed the Thessalonian church. The language implies a human element also. For anything to grow it must be exercised. Every body builder knows the mantra, "no pain – no gain."

A study of the Thessalonian church reveals real pain and struggle. They endured trial. They were being forged in the fires of persecution. They knew what it was to face great adversity, but in the heart of the storm they were packing on spiritual muscle. They stood firm, and God made them stronger. Their love was abounding as their faith was growing.

To abound is to thrive; to break the barriers; to spread rapidly. How can love abound? It only happens by design. Abounding love is not an accidental convergence of amiable personalities. Abounding love flows out of right choices. The Thessalonians had decided to reach beyond their church cell. They had decided to bear persecution with love, rather than resentment. They didn't let trial push them apart; they pulled together. This filled Paul's heart with thanks.

Today, let your faith grow by exercising it. Let your love abound to all around.

There shall not any man be able to stand before thee all the days of
thy life: as I was with Moses, so I will be with thee;
I will not fail thee, nor forsake thee.
Joshua 1:5 ASV

What an incredible promise God made Joshua – and what a wonderful life Joshua lived in response to God's promise.

Talk about your *"Renaissance Man!"* Here is a guy who seems to have the whole package. He is a warrior, a servant, a protégé, a leader, a lover of God's presence, a portrait of integrity, an administrator, a wise judge, and a conqueror. Joshua's life was not marred by eruptions of egomania, or abuse of power. His flaws are not revealed in the Scriptures.

I've thought a lot about Joshua. I've wondered how God chooses men for certain tasks. Billy Graham has often said that the first question he wants answered in heaven is, "Lord, why me?" This much is certain: Joshua was entrusted with the leadership of Israel during a most critical time. Once across the Jordan, Israel could have easily been pinned against her banks. A weak or corrupted leader might have spelled early disaster and frustration to a plan that God set in motion while Israel was captive in Egypt.

If I want God to use me as He did Joshua, I should seek to be like the *"Renaissance Man"* in character and surrender. Sterling character, a humble heart, a surrendered will, and the touch of God make a man capable of any task.

Thou hast beset me behind and before,
And laid thy hand upon me.
Psalm 139:5 ASV

I'm a fourth-generation preacher. You might presume that the ministry was a foregone conclusion for me; a pre-ordained pathway.

It wasn't like that at all. For a time, I just wanted to be a drummer. Having received the call to preach at seventeen, I finally followed in the footsteps of my forefathers. I've never regretted that decision. Almost twenty years ago, I stood before the elders; a candidate for ordination. The superintendent granted my father the privilege of laying hands on me, and praying the ordination prayer.

A Sunday does not pass that I don't feel my father's hand. He has always been there. He was the "larger-than-life" superhero of my boyhood. I remember him squeezing my shoulder when I took the keys to my first used car on the lot at Crescent Chevrolet. Often, in the afterglow of the Sunday night service, I would feel his hand on my shoulder and his prayers in my heart. His hand has faithfully corrected me, directed me, encouraged and comforted me.

That's the kind of influence and intimacy God wants with us. His hand will guide, shelter, chasten, and lift up – if we so desire. Don't resist your heavenly Father. The very best you could know is in His hand.

Then Pharaoh gave this order to all his people:
"Every boy that is born you must throw into the Nile."
Exodus 1:22 NIV

The sentence falls; a common decision; the verdict is final; the order is executed; and life goes on for everyone but the aborted child.

All too often, the courtroom is beyond the reach of those who wish to stop the horrors. The judge's chambers are locked away deep within a mother's heart. The sentence imposed is a crime against nature. The defendant pleads "choice," and a baby is voided.

Where God is forgotten, the innocent suffer. A self-absorbed culture cannot see the truth. The child, though unwanted, is God's child, too. In my generation, we've slaughtered by millions, sons and daughters beloved by the Father. In my generation, judicial barbarians sentence the unborn as Pharoah did Moses. In my generation, we're numbed to the violence, but heaven takes note of the killed and the killer.

Pharaoh's madness resulted in unspeakable horrors. He rose to the level of Hitler and Stalin. We've done Pharoah "one better" with doctor's approval. We've washed out the blood by judicial decree. In four thousand years, darkened hearts still prevail.

Moses was blessed to be born in old Egypt. He may not have survived in the "land of the free."

*Moses thought that his own people would realize that God was
using him to rescue them, but they did not.*
Acts 7:25 NIV

He was born a slave and raised a prince, walking in two worlds. A Hebrew woman gave him life, but an Egyptian princess game him a name: Moses. His birth mother linked him to his true identity and calling. Pharaoh's daughter gave him the education and position to make his calling possible.

From an early age he understood his mission. His miraculous rescue and placement in the house of Pharaoh were sure signs of destiny. From the bulrushes of the Nile to the household of Rameses II; a slave disguised as a prince. He waited for that moment when he would step out from behind the royal curtain to break the yoke of slavery from the necks of his kinsmen. He would lead his people back to the land promised to Father Abraham.

Who could have scripted such a story except God? The whole set-up was perfect. But Moses made a fundamental blunder. He tried to do God's will his way. He acted on the assumption that God would follow his lead. He carried off a sloppy murder. Within a few days, everybody knew the story. Moses took the only option available – he ran.

When the pressure is on, you need more prayer and more Bible. Disaster lurks behind false assumptions.

Now Moses was keeping the flock of Jethro his
father-in-law, the priest of Midian.
Exodus 3:1 ASV

From a large rock on a small rise, the shepherd welcomed the dawn. This was the time he loved the most – when darkness receded, leaving a blanket of dew.

The sheep were quiet now, having drunk their fill. The shepherd took the morning census as the sheep worked the ground in earnest for sparse green shoots.

Only the strong survived the untamed plains of Midian. Most who tried to settle here were soon broken by silent isolation. But isolation was a friend to the shepherd. A man could just disappear into these rocky heights – and that was his intent. The shepherd's wanderings made him difficult to trace. He doubted that anyone was looking for him anymore, but his troubled past made him a cautious man. He had wandered into this desert seeking temporary shelter. Had it not been for a kindly priest, he would have kept moving. Now, the valley was his home and the sheep his livelihood. Moses – a man born to lead men, was now content to lead sheep for forty years!

Fugitives from God's will live diminished lives. They settle for far less than second best. Don't ever make your failures a dwelling place. Were it not for a burning bush, Moses might have lived out his life in a desert – leading sheep.

"Destroy this temple, and in three days I will raise it up. "
John 2:19 NKJV
But at last two false witnesses came forward and said, "This fellow said,
'I am able to destroy the temple of God and to build it in three days.'"
Matthew 26:60-62 NKJV

Some people use words to paint pictures. We call them poets. Others use words to build foundations. We call them statesmen. And then there are those sorry souls who twist words into verbal pretzels. I call them "pretzel kings."

Have you ever run into a pretzel king? Words have hardly passed by your lips when the pretzel king twists them into a noose with which to hang you high. Pretzel kings have been with us since time began. It all started in the Garden of Eden when Satan approached Eve with a question, "Did God really say, 'You must not eat from any tree in the garden'?" (Genesis 3:1). Pretzel kings take their cues from the father of lies and wreak havoc through exaggerated language and innuendo. They rewrite your script, recast your motives, and leave you with discredits. They fix out a lie with a truthful exterior and dance with glee when discord is sown.

By John's account, the first words Jesus spoke to those who would seek His death were ultimately twisted into a charge to be made at his trial. Crooked people put a corkscrew into everything they touch. Watch out for pretzel kings. I've learned, when in their presence, it's best not to speak at all.

And he led the flock to the back of the desert, and came to Horeb, the mountain of God. And the Angel of the LORD appeared to him in a flame of fire from the midst of a bush. So he looked, and behold, the bush was burning with fire, but the bush was not consumed.
Exodus 3:1-2 NKJV

The morning sun lit the eastern slopes of Horeb. The sheep seemed restless, and the shepherd scanned the perimeter for predators. Nothing.

He laid out his mat and reached into his satchel for a little cheese and bread. A tremor ran through the flock, and he stood to search the horizon again. Something was out there. A jackal, a wolf – what was that? Something caught his eye to the left at the base of the mountain . . . a shepherd's fire? No, this fire was bigger . . . brighter somehow.

He strained to see if anyone was standing near, but he was quite alone. He reached for his staff, and began picking his way across the valley floor. The fire glowed brighter as the shepherd drew near. It was a bush somehow set aflame. He had seen smoke and fire on the slopes of Horeb before. He had watched the lightning ignite dry brush. From a distance he had viewed the campfires of shepherds, robbers, fugitives and traders. But he had never seen fire behave like this. He stepped closer when a voice called out of the bush, "Moses! Moses!" His strength left him and Moses whispered, "Here I am."

After forty years, God breathed new life into a dead dream. He still does that you know – if He can only get our attention.

But Moses said to God,
"Who am I, that I should go to Pharaoh and bring
the Israelites out of Egypt?"
Exodus 3:11 NIV

The bush was burning bright with God's presence and promise, but Moses' confidence was up in smoke. *"Who am I, that I should go ... "*

Forty years in the wilderness can sure take its toll on a failed revolutionary. Forget that young guy who strutted through Pharoah's palace – he's dead. Forget that radical who iced the taskmaster – he's gone. The great emancipator has become a shepherd. His dreams are dead and buried. Moses knew he had taken his best shot, and blown it. In forty years of desert dwelling, he had done nothing to ready himself for another attempt. He was past his prime. He was grasping at straws. God's command reduces him to a blubbering child. *"What if they won't listen . . . what if they won't believe?"* he cries. *"I don't talk so good, Lord – Oh please, please, send somebody else."*

Moses hasn't learned much in the wilderness. He still thinks it's all about him. He still believes that God needs more than a willing vessel. He catalogs his weaknesses, as though human strengths and weaknesses limit God.

None of us bring anything special to the table. Our talents and abilities are God-given. Our knowledge cannot begin to be compared to His wisdom. It's not about you – it's Christ, in you!

Therefore, as God's chosen people, holy and dearly loved, clothe yourselves
with compassion, kindness, humility, gentleness and patience.
Colossians 3:12 NIV

It's seven a.m. at the Orange Blossom Café, in a town so small it could never hide a stranger. The morning crowd shuffles in for a blue-collar breakfast and small town banter.

"Carol is getting a brand new double-wide!" says the red-faced woman as she steps through the door. The girl behind the register is already punching numbers; the cook puts on the "regular." An old man steps in from the cold. Everyone is happy to see him. It takes about thirty seconds to learn that the old widower just finished his last radiation treatment. His breakfast is free, and everyone stops by his table to offer best wishes.

As I finish up a three-egg omelet, the buzz around me centers on stray dogs, ills and aches, kids and grandkids, storm fronts and front porches. Every once in a while someone cuts me a look that says, "You're not from 'round here, are ya?," but I feel quite welcome here.

We've given up a lot to live in the metro world. Civility and community are exceptions, not rules. Caring and tenderness died before we drove the last nail into the privacy fence. I'm not sure how to fix what's broken in the metro world, but love and laughter seem to go a long, long way at the Orange Blossom Café.

(All the Athenians and the foreigners who lived there spent their time doing nothing but talking about and listening to the latest ideas.)
Acts 17:21 NIV

No wonder ancient Greece went to ruins. Sitting around, shooting the breeze, or listening to the nightly lineup of talking heads will surely wreck you – body, soul, and spirit.

Geraldo, Oprah, Montel, Sally, and the whole afternoon lineup make massive contributions to the blubbering of our brains, not to mention our bodies (You can't watch Oprah without a snack pak!). Get up! Get off that couch! Turn off the TV before "clicker-mortis" sets in (I've seen it too often, and it's not a pretty picture).

The sedentary lifestyle saps creativity as it ruins health and limits interaction. Henry David Thoreau said, "Methinks that the moment my legs begin to move, my thoughts begin to flow." Thoreau was right. My best ideas come to me when I run. Movement is a common gift we most often take for granted. To walk, to run, to dance, to grasp – how precious and neglected is this ambulatory blessing. You were made to move; intended for travel; rigged to run.

Get away from that trivial pursuit that clogs the airwaves, even as it chains us to the Lazyboy. Stay away from gossip and rumor. Care for the body that it might enhance the mind. What are you waiting for? Move it!

The eye cannot say to the hand, "I don't need you!"
And the head cannot say to the feet, "I don't need you!"
1 Corinthians 12:21 NIV

When the neuro-pathways of the brain shut down, confusion marks the onset of dementia. At first, a person can look so healthy, so strong – but soon this cruel disease begins to leave its mark. When vital thought-connections are broken, the body suffers accelerated decline. With frightful speed, vitality is replaced by vacancy.

The body of Christ suffers in the same manner when vital connections are broken. When respect is drained away; when trust is trampled; when the wagons are circled, the resilient glow of fellowship is lost to a stone-cold indifference.

Paul clearly states that we are all different; we are supposed to be different; our glory and giftings shine through our differences. But rather than withdraw in the face of our diversity, we must all become keepers of the pathways; men and women who connect. The more "connectors" a church has, the more healthy her fellowship. If we were to suddenly pull the "connectors" from churches, the doors would swing shut from coast to coast.

Are you a "connector?" Do you draw people together, or push them apart? Keep connecting! Establish and maintain vital pathways to insure unity in diversity. Ignore connectivity and spiritual dementia is sure to follow.

Be patient, then, brothers, until the Lord's coming.
James 5:7 NIV

It's a cold, wet morning – looks like the sky has settled on gun-metal gray. The bright, striped waiting room offers a stark contrast to the people who have gathered here. An old gentleman flips through an outdated magazine. His wife clutches an overstuffed medical folder. It looks as though her days are numbered. I wonder how many waiting rooms they have seen this year.

A little girl has that feverish look that guarantees a few days off from school. She takes a few slurps from the water fountain, and shuffles over to sit next to me. Mom is hammering away on her cell phone. The kid's flu has thrown a big wrench into her real estate business. The receptionist greets everyone with the same cold disinterest. Paperwork seems to have taken priority over people-work.

An inner door opens, but nobody calls my name. The little girl lets go with three gale-force sneezes. I decide to hold my breath for two minutes. I'd rather be having a picnic lunch at Chernobyl. Oh, I wish I were somewhere else – anywhere but here.

Patience is surely an unwanted virtue, but I'll wait a little longer. It took me three full days to develop this fever. I guess it's worth an hour or two to try to find a cure.

*So Peter was kept in prison, but the church was
earnestly praying to God for him.*
Acts 12:5 NIV

RIO DE JANEIRO, BRAZIL: On a Friday afternoon, everything was ready for the long anticipated Book of Hope distribution in the massive Brazilian
city. Teams and leaders were in place. Schools were sched-
uled, transportation was provided, and the governor's
approval was secured. Saturday distribution would begin
through a local church in a slum area called the Rocinha.

As is so often the case with Book of Hope distributions, a few miracles are needed along the way to get
things rolling. The miracle needed in Rio centered on the
books; they were still held in customs as teams were
preparing for distribution to start the next morning.

At four o'clock in the afternoon, the books had not
been released, and Book of Hope representatives were
unable to get an appointment to see the proper customs
official.

José Bernardo remembers that stressful afternoon:
*"We were near despair, but then we remembered that this
ministry belongs to the Lord and we are just His helpers. We
started to pray and within one hour we had the customs official on the phone!"* José couldn't believe what he was hearing: *"If you come now, I'll go to liberate your books."*

When we pray, God unlocks prison doors.

Let your moderation be known unto all men.
Philippians 4:5 KJV

It's 6:30 a.m. and I'm enjoying my daily indulgence at the coffee café (sip, ahhhhh). The cost of my triple-venti, one Sweet and Low, no foam latte is indefensible. I know, I know – I should quit! I've read the articles, heard the stories, and been condemned for a lack of self-control (sip, ahhhhhh).

I've found an ally in the annals of church history – and with this I comfort myself. In 1746 he made a brave attempt to give up his tea, but writes, "... *my flesh protested against it. I was but half awake and half alive all day, and my headache so increased toward noon that I could neither speak nor think. This so weakened me that I could hardly sit my horse.*" – Charles Wesley (sip, ahhhhhh).

I'm reluctant to give it up. Just about the time I quit, some new study will surface lauding the healing qualities of black expresso beans. I don't know what consumer reports to believe anymore (sip, ahhhhhh). I think I'll take my cue from ole' Charlie and practice java moderation – don't want to get a headache and fall off my horse.

Extremists sacrifice joy for legalism. Carnivore and vegetarian, caffeinated and decaf will, one day, stand side by side in the new Jerusalem. I'll meet you at the corner café – the coffee's on me (sip, ahhhhhh).

In the day that thou stoodest on the other side.
Obadiah 1:11 KJV

The courtroom fills. You sit at the defendant's table, falsely accused. Though you find the court intimidating, you're not worried. Your friends are loyal, and you know that they will testify on your behalf. The bailiff cries, "All rise," and the judge takes his seat. As the court comes to order, your hopes soar. Your friends, like brothers, have gathered in support.

The opening statements by the prosecution are baseless. You sit back and wait for your friends to come to your aid. The prosecutor calls his first witness. There must be some mistake. You spin around in your chair to see your best friend walking to the witness stand. Your best friend is a witness for the prosecution! You're speechless, wide-eyed, terrified, confused. One by one, your friends testify against you. Mercifully, you wake up from this nightmare.

For Israel, this nightmare was a living reality. Edom should have come to her rescue. Blood should have bound these two nations against a common enemy, but Edom delighted in the destruction of Jerusalem. God destroyed Edom for her treachery.

The tiny book of Obadiah, and the empty ruins of Edom, stand as an eternal reminder – it is a fearful thing to stand *on the other side* of God.

And I, if I be lifted up from the earth,
will draw all men unto me.
John 12:32 KJV

Om bifler funsel qimlett oufer stonstil. Having trouble with that first sentence? Can't quite grasp the meaning? It's the first sentence of a new language I'm writing. It sounds almost as foreign as "church language" sounds to the un-churched.

We often speak as though everybody understands. When we tell un-churched people that they need to be *"saved"* or that they must be *"washed in the blood,"* we should not assume that they know what we mean. Every Christian should write out their story in plain language, and then read it back to see if it is clear of theological jargon. Can you tell of encountering God without lapsing into "clichés?"

At thirteen, I was accosted by a "street preacher" on a busy sidewalk. She rattled on about judgment and sin, hardly giving me an opportunity to speak. She closed her swirling sermon with the warning: *"It's a long chilly swim over Jordan."* I was raised in church, so I knew where she was coming from. An un-churched person would have labeled her a "nut-ball."

"Church-ese" is a very confusing language for those outside the community of faith. Try English, and make it clear. Jesus is drawing men and women into relationship. Are we helping, or hindering?

Then he (Peter) began to curse and swear, saying,
"I do not know the Man!"
Matthew 26:74 NKJV
But go, tell His disciples — and Peter.
Mark 16:7 NKJV

Abraham Lincoln's life was marked by multiple failures and remembered for success. Lincoln stands
out as an exaggerated example of what we often see in
great achievers: An unwillingness to abandon the stage to
failure.

I learned to walk through a process we all know as
"trial and error." I tottered, I tumbled, I bruised, I
bawled, but I kept getting up and I hardly fall down anymore. Babe Ruth is remembered for his home runs, but
he also led the league in strike-outs! The greatest baseball
players fail to get a hit two out of three times at bat — but
they don't quit. The great quarterbacks only get a few
touchdowns, when you compare their throws to comple-
tions. Thomas Edison saw each failed experiment as an
opportunity to begin again, "more intelligently." High-
flying entrepreneurs have experienced an average of 3.8
catastrophic failures on the way to success.

It seems that you have to sort through a few turkeys
to find the golden goose. Michael Jordan was cut from his
high school team in his sophomore year. It's probably one
of the best things that ever happened to the sport of basketball.

Nobody lives a failsafe life. Learn from your losses.
You'll be hard-pressed to find a better teacher.

LORD, what is man, that You take knowledge of him?
Or the son of man, that You are mindful of him?
Man is like a breath; His days are like a passing shadow.
Psalm 144:3-4 NKJV

The years pass too quickly. Wasn't it just yesterday that I was wrestling my way out the door with two car seats, a booster, and a tandem stroller? Wasn't it just yesterday that life was play, and play was cheap? Wasn't it just yesterday that a boy caller was a wrong number, and all three girls could fit in my lap, and bedtime was 8:30 with lights out?

Now, I'm a taxi driver, answering service, and a twenty-dollar bill dispenser. We need a revolving door, a full-time scheduler, a clothing consultant, and driver's ed. It seems that I never see a quiet Friday, a night with everyone home, or change from that twenty.

It's the suddenness of it all that unnerves me. I don't think I've missed a thing, and yet I feel that something's sneaking up on me. It's a big truck with a bumper sticker up front that says, "Get Out of the Way, Baldy!" I used to be able to leave that truck in my dust, but lately, he seems to be gaining a little.

Life is a vapor, and time never pauses to catch a breath. Kids grow up and out and you wake up one morning wishing you had taken more pictures, and appreciated the exquisite joy of having your baby fall asleep in your arms. We need to live and love now, lest tomorrow holds regret instead of joy.

*Keep on loving each other as brothers. Do not forget
to entertain strangers, for by so doing some people
have entertained angels without knowing it.*
Hebrews 13:1-2 NIV

I was stuck in an airport – delayed by a storm. Fast food kiosks and chains were doing a brisk business, but I couldn't stomach another "cardboard fiesta." I searched the commons and found *"Cheers."* The restaurant was fashioned after the television comedy. The menu beat McTacos hands down.

I took a table, humming the catchy theme from the show: *"Sometimes you want to go where everybody knows your name – and they're always glad you came."* The cast of characters stepped out of my memory and took a bow. I looked around to see if this *"Cheers"* had captured the flavor of the long-running comedy.

My waitress was grumpy. "Don't you want to know my name?" I asked. She wasn't amused. I didn't dare ask if she was glad I came. There were no happy patrons at the bar; no laughing staffers; and unfortunately, no fine restaurant upstairs. I ordered the grilled chicken salad and hoped for the best – it turns out my hopes were in vain.

A "look-alike" restaurant couldn't live up to the *"Cheers"* theme. Maybe the church should give it a try. People really do want to go where everybody knows their name – and they know you're glad they came.

And he sent them to Bethlehem and said, "Go and search carefully for the young Child, and when you have found Him, bring back word to me, that I may come and worship Him also."
Matthew 2:8 NKJV

If dictionaries featured pictures to illustrate every word, we might find a picture of Judas beside the word, "greedy." The word, "doubt" might be illustrated by a sketch of Thomas. The word, "missionary" would undoubtedly be flanked by a picture of Paul. King Herod's picture would grace a number of words: brutal, crafty, murderer, wicked, assassin, deceiver, and fiend.

Herod was a ruthless king. His pursuit of enemies, real and perceived, was unrelenting. He married for power, then murdered the allies he gained through marriage. He murdered his own wives and sons with relish. The bloodletting continued to his deathbed. Just five days before his death he ordered the murder of his son, Antipater, whom he perceived to be a threat to take his throne.

This same Herod ordered the deaths of all Jewish children under the age of two in hopes of preventing the Promised One from rising to power. It would be difficult to identify a greater embodiment of evil than Herod and his household. It's hard to believe that a king could get away with such a murderous campaign of terror, but then, an honest reading of the history of our last century should cause us to pray with passion: "Deliver us from evil."

"Woe to you, scribes and Pharisees, hypocrites! For you are like white-washed tombs which indeed appear beautiful outwardly, but inside are full of dead men's bones and all uncleanness."
Matthew 23:27 NKJV

They numbered six thousand strong, walking the corridors of power with unveiled conceit. They prided themselves in their vain knowledge of the intricacies of the Law and traditions of the Jews. They watched each other, like hungry vultures, for any violation of the written code . . . ready in a moment to devour one another to increase their stature among the elite.

They held absolute sway at the synagogues, sat in the best seats for weddings and feasts, and recited long prayers from rote to impress the lesser lights. Their pockets were lined with policemen and lawyers. Their hearts were filled with bitterness and greed. They could dispense truth and judgment, but their expansive knowledge of God had no light or heat . . . it had turned stone cold in the graveyard of their own injustices.

John rightly called them vipers. Jesus called them fools. They called themselves Pharisees; the separate ones. They lived by a code; an exacting measure of personal piety. They held contempt for all but their own. Living so close to their laws and traditions, they couldn't see a horrible paradox.

In separating themselves from people, they ultimately separated themselves from God.

Forgetting what is behind and straining toward what is ahead.
Philippians 3:13 NIV

I was plodding down the trail, happy to be jogging again – grieved that I had gotten so out of shape. I wasn't running for time – I was just trying to finish four miles without injury.

I saw them coming down the trail at about a half mile; three runners in single file. They were flying. I estimated that they were running a low six-minute mile pace. The distance between us melted away, and I picked up the pace and sucked in my gut. I didn't want to look too bad when we passed. The first runner nodded. The second runner waved. The third runner said, "How's it going?" He was one of my old training partners. When our eyes met, I could see a question forming as he blew by: *"What happened to you, son?"*

There was a time I could have held their pace, but that was several years and injuries ago.

I glanced over my shoulder to see them disappear around the bend, stumbling over a root and landing in a heap. I sat there for a moment, but thoughts of my faster days got me back on my feet. Was I going to grovel in regret or run my way back to fitness? I got back into my fat-boy shuffle and remembered the joy of running hard. I ran like a mad man – I relished the future, and I left my regrets in a heap on the Starmount trail.

*. . . for He causes His sun to rise on the evil and the good, and sends
rain on the righteous and the unrighteous.*
Matthew 5:45 NASB

Why is all the good stuff fattening, and the bland stuff healthy? Why does it take two hours to run off what I ate in ten minutes? Why does it always rain on my day off? Why does the government tax people when they die? How come some people have ten talents, and I have two? Why does an honest soldier die on the last day of the war, and a scoundrel survive to amount to nothing? Why do the rich get richer while the poor struggle to get by? Why does the lowest seed play the highest seed in the first round of a tournament?

I'll tell you why . . . because life is unfair! I was born into a Christian household in a prosperous nation. I have had access to education and multiplied opportunities. I have enjoyed good health. I look to the future with bright hopes. The inequities of the western way of life are glaring, when compared to the third world.

One day, the great Judge will settle all accounts. With perfect justice, He will examine us all. Having received the lion's share of earthly blessing, will we be praised for our stewardship, or rebuked for our selfishness?

God placed you and me in an unfair world to display His mercy, grace and generosity. Are we living up to our responsibilities?

An angry man stirs up dissension, and a hot-tempered one
commits many sins. A man's pride brings him low,
but a man of lowly spirit gains honor.
Proverbs 29:22-23 NIV

"Get out," I said. "Walk home if that's how you feel."
My friend stared in disbelief. He got out and slammed the door. "Jerk!" he yelled. I burned rubber and muttered a few choice words I hadn't learned at choir practice. I didn't look back. We didn't talk for years. "A guy has to draw the line somewhere," I thought. "You don't just sit there and take it." So I kicked him out on a country road in Iowa and left him in the corn.

I was seventeen, and my ex-best friend had just insulted my . . . car. Yeah, I know, how juvenile. But that '69 Camaro was my life. I had never insulted his "piece-a-junk" Chevelle. Just where did he get off – well, we know where he got off . . . five miles north of Des Moines in a cornfield.

Eighteen years later I took a seat on a little commuter plane. Guess who sat down beside me? I'm glad he didn't throw me off the plane – he owed me one. Conversation was cordial. We caught up on family and careers, but the conversation soon died. My Camaro was rotting in a Polk City junkyard and his Chevelle was probably paper clips. Nothing was gained – much was lost.

Anger elevates your heart rate as it robs your soul. Have you let a "small" matter rob you of a friend?

But when all goes well with you, remember me and show me kindness.
Genesis 40:14 NIV
The chief cupbearer, however, did not remember Joseph; he forgot him.
Genesis 40:23 NIV

When my first daughter turned sixteen, I developed amnesia: I forgot what it was like to be a teenage boy. I forgot what it was like to fall under the gaze of a date's father. I forgot what it was like to have to wait for fifteen minutes with "Dad" while she finished painting and primping. I forgot the unspoken hostility I felt when I showed up in a van with a two-foot afro.

Now the roles are reversed, and I'm the guy who's trying to intimidate all unworthy candidates (and they really are unworthy). Now I'm the guy who thinks double-dating with grandparents is a good idea. Now I'm the guy who loves to make 'em sweat! I think that glass-top jeep that the Pope uses would make a great *"datemobile."*

We all develop amnesia, it seems, when the shoe is on the other foot. In affluence, we forget what it was like to have need. After the wedding, we forget what single loneliness was like. When we've become mature Christians, we forget what it was like to be a "newborn." We need to remember, because somebody needs a break.

I've decided to back off a bit. I've simplified the "date application" and only requested a fifty-year family history and a criminal record check. Sometimes memories make you wise.

Get your FREE subscription to the GLOBAL REPORT newsletter

and see how God is using your Book of Hope ministry!

Just fill out this card and drop it into any mailbox today, and you'll receive a free subscription to the *Global Report* newsletter, full of testimonies of how God is changing the children and youth of the world by the power of His Word! Write for it TODAY.

Return the card below or write to:

Book of Hope
3111 SW 10th St.• Pompano, Florida 33069
1.800.GIV.BIBL (448.2425)
www.bookofhope.net

❑ **Sign me up for a FREE subscription!**

Name

Address

City   State   Zip

(   )   —

Phone

@

Email

Send for your FREE
Global Report Subscription!

BUSINESS REPLY MAIL
FIRST-CLASS MAIL   PERMIT NO. 46   POMPANO BEACH, FL

POSTAGE WILL BE PAID BY ADDRESSEE

Book of Hope
3111 S.W. 10th Street
Pompano, FL 33069-9903

"Moses My servant is dead. Now therefore, arise, go over this Jordan."
Joshua 1:2 NKJV

No blues go so deep as country blues. Sad country songs are really, *really* tragic. Some poor guy loses his job, loses his girl, crashes his pickup, his dog dies, and he gets dandruff – all in the same week. Add drinking and cheating and you've got a real country blues classic.

Sometimes the truth gives fiction a run for its money. It all began when the foundry closed down. "I lost my job in 1986," said Joe. But that wasn't all. His wife divorced him. He was audited by the I.R.S., gained a lot of weight, and totaled his pickup truck.

Joe concentrated on the one thing he still had: weekend jobs singing country music. He left Duncan, Oklahoma to take his shot in Nashville. His first album, released in 1990, held four number one country hits. "If the foundry hadn't shut down, I'd probably still be there today," said Joe Diffie – a country star, for all the hard knocks.

We've all had days, even weeks, that could find their way into a sad country ballad. Misery has no uncharted waters. You can be sure somebody's been there before you. Why not concentrate on what you can do, rather than moan and whine over what is lost? A little country wisdom goes a long way. If the horse is dead – dismount!

Now to him who is able to do immeasurably more
than all we ask or imagine.
Ephesians 3:20 NIV

DOMINICAN REPUBLIC: Jennifer Dalton, a Book of Hope Intern writes: *"After we finished one of our school distributions, we stopped at the store to get a few snacks. One of the girls working at the store had a copy of the* Book of Hope *with her. I asked her if she had read the book and if she was enjoying it. She said that she was and pointed to a section of the book that talks about prayer. She told me that her teacher had made an assignment for her class to read from the book. The next day they would discuss it in class." "We went into the schools of the Dominican Republic praying that God would touch lives with the* Book of Hope; *that God would motivate people to read the book. He went way beyond our expectations. He used teachers to insure that students were reading His Word."*

God always goes *"way beyond our expectations."* A god defined by our plans and strategies would be a god confined to our puny limitations. The cross makes the point with stunning emphasis.

It never occurred to the Jews (nor to anyone) that God would come in flesh and offer Himself as the perfect sacrifice for the sins of man. Who could have imagined such a strategy? Only the One who loves us beyond all expectations.

Population under age 18: 9,798,000

Poland is a progressive European nation and the youth struggle with many of the same challenges as the kids in the USA: drugs, alcohol, immorality and crime. Pray that we will reach the children and youth and that God's Word will transform them.

In Poland, You Brought the Good News of Forgiveness and Hope to Kasia.

In Pila, Poland, Kasia was filled with anger and regret. Her dear father had killed himself – and why? Because her mother was unfaithful to him, and not just once. She'd had many affairs which had ultimately destroyed her father's will to live.

It filled Kasia's heart with despair for her father and anger toward her mother. She began seeking solace for her aching heart in relationships with boys.

Then she received the *Book of Hope* and learned about the unconditional love of Jesus. She decided to commit her life to Christ, and see if He could bring her the joy her circumstances had destroyed. She even joined a Hope Club Bible study group, a club based on the *Book of Hope*.

Kasia found that her anger began to ebb away. At a crusade service, she went forward to ask for emotional healing, and today her Hope Club leader says, "I believe God is working in what was once a barren heart to make it a blooming garden."

Thank you for sending the good news of Jesus' love to Kasia, and thousands like her in Poland and around the world!

Ask of me, and I will make the nations your inheritance,
the ends of the earth your possession.
Psalm 2:8 NIV

Few have ever taken God up on this astonishing proposition, but those daring few changed their world.

Africa had David Livingstone. China had Hudson Taylor. India had William Carey. Tibet had Victor Plymire. The results were not always seen within the lifetimes of these missionary pioneers, but what has grown from the seed they planted is a direct answer to their requests: "Lord, give us the nations." Because evil seems so prevalent in this twilight of the age, we make a grave error when we assume that God is not working on the world stage. Revival could break out at any moment in Cuba, Iran, Sri Lanka, or Vietnam.

God doesn't have to initiate great movements from the west. As the day of the Lord draws near, we will watch in awe as nations we evangelize send missionaries to America to evangelize us. Are we praying that God would flood these nations with His Spirit? We often ask for things we don't really need, but we don't ask for great things! If heaven will allow us regret, we will all regret that we didn't ask largely of God.

If we ever see what we settled for, compared to what He held in store for us, I think heaven will have at least one cloudy day – one sorrowful moment.

If you abide in Me, and My words abide in you,
you will ask what you desire, and it shall be done for you.
John 15:7 NKJV

I cannot fully enjoy the benefits of American citizenship if I choose to dwell in Peru. I cannot fish the oceans if I stay in Arizona. I cannot know the joy of the summit if I choose to remain in the shadows of the valley. I cannot have the abundance of His blessing if I wander from His presence.

Some would argue that the Christian cannot wander, but this idea does violence to the simple words of Jesus. The "if" that accompanies this great promise of God's provision stands out as the great qualifier from the human side of the equation. A plain reading of the promise leads me to an inescapable conclusion: If I am to enjoy the supernatural providence of God, I must abide in Him, and His words must abide in me. Reason, then, would dictate that I must make a first priority of dwelling in Christ, and hiding His Word deep in my heart. When I am hidden in Christ, and His Word is hidden in me, I am welcome to ask God for anything. What then will I ask?

Dwelling with Christ has a profound impact on my desires. The more I abide in Him, the more I find myself wanting what He wants and loving as He loves. In His presence, my wants and 'greeds' are supplanted by another's need.

We are hard-pressed on every side, yet not crushed;
we are perplexed, but not in despair; persecuted,
but not forsaken; struck down, but not destroyed.
2 Corinthians 4:8-9 NKJV

John Maxwell made a sobering point when he said, "Every genius could have been a failure."

We can all get a free ticket for the "loser" train. All we have to do is quit. Persistence has often been mistaken for genius. Faithfulness has often been mistaken for giftedness. Determination is often disguised as brilliance. Greatness is birthed out of a refusal to give up. In 1922, Harry was thirty-eight-years-old, in debt, and out of work. By 1945, he was the most powerful leader in the free world. Harry S. Truman refused to quit. His story numbers with thousands of others who achieved greatness through persistence. Their stars burn bright to guide generations. Far beneath those stars, the landscape is littered with the husks of burned out dreams and "could have beens." Excuses here are chiseled in the gravestones of regret. Blame hugs the ground like a toxic mist. Time might as well stand still – nobody's going anywhere, or doing anything.

We each must make our decision, to reach for the stars or ramble about the graveyard. Life is hard. People fail. Dreams die. Fights are lost. If you've lived at all, you've been knocked down. Get up – get smart – gain wisdom – trust God. You're not a loser until you quit!

Saved? By Bob Hoskins

Our ministry executive director, my son Rob, was speaking in a church about the importance of getting God's Word to the children of the world, because only faith in Jesus can save them for eternity.

Afterward, a deacon's wife came to him and said, "You don't really believe that my Jewish doctor, who is one of the finest men I've ever met, is going to hell just because he has never confessed faith in Jesus?"

"Yes, I do," Rob answered truthfully, "for the Bible makes it clear that only those who accept Christ as Savior can be saved." The woman was stunned!

Her bewilderment demonstrates the tendency in many American churches today to accept the kind of universalism that assures the anxious that somehow God will save every nice person, whether or not they have been cleansed in the blood of Jesus.

Although this may be a comforting thought to some, it is simply a comforting lie ... and I am wondering how this deception has worked its way into the Christian churches of our land.

Christians are still willing to evangelize the lost – and for this I am so grateful – but many are even more enthusiastic, it seems, about clothing the naked and feeding the hungry than they are about saving the lost.

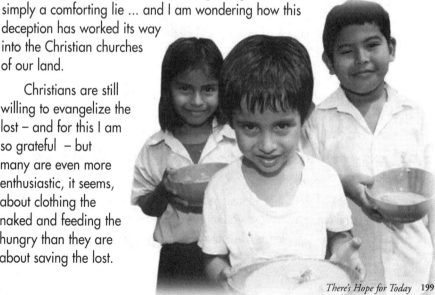

I endorse and support compassionate ministry. In fact, Book of Hope volunteer team members bring suitcases and containers full of food, blankets, and medicine for the needy in the former republics of the USSR and the poor countries, and we encourage it. We have also sent these shipments ourselves.

But somehow it seems that many Christians have forgotten Jesus' words: "For what is a man profited, if he shall gain the whole world, and lose his own soul? or what shall a man give in exchange for his soul?" (Matthew 16:26).

> *"But somehow it seems that many Christians have forgotten Jesus' words: 'For what is a man profited, if he shall gain the whole world, and lose his own soul? or what shall a man give in exchange for his soul?'" (Matthew 16:26).*

We can feed every hungry child in Africa, and yet if we do not lead these little ones to Jesus, they will be physically satisfied in this life and doomed to all eternity in hell!

Jesus fed the hungry. But did He come to this earth to feed the hungry? No. He came to die on the cross as a perfect sacrifice for the sins of all mankind. If we only take His teaching that calls for us to feed and clothe those in need, and ignore the true purpose for which He came, then we have failed the Master.

The non-religious world is eager to feed the hungry and provide compassionate aid for the poor and needy, and God bless them for it. But Jesus gave His people an even more important command when He said, "For the Son of man is come to seek and to save that which was lost" (Luke 19:10).

Jesus came to save the lost. Have we forgotten that? Have we forgotten that there is a heaven to gain and a hell to shun?

In the book of Acts, the disciples Peter and John boldly declared that Jesus "was the stone which was set at nought of you builders, which is become the head of the corner. Neither is there salvation in any other: for there is none other name under heaven given among men, whereby we must be saved" (Acts 4:11-12).

There is no other way to salvation, and to pretend otherwise is to doom those who might be saved because of our own foolish wishes and lack of motivation to reach them with the Gospel.

There is only one thing mentioned in the Bible that brings joy to heaven: the salvation of a lost soul. We cannot forget that fact. For what could be more dramatic and intense than a man or woman – or boy or girl – saved from eternal damnation, rescued into the loving arms of Jesus?

I remember the story I heard from one of our missionaries of a young man in Poland who was lying in the hospital, dying of cancer. He had received a *Book of Hope*, and the volunteer team came to pray with him. They led this young man to the Lord ... and then he asked them if they would come back when he died, and preach his funeral.

That day came soon, and the team returned. After the funeral message, 21 other young people made commitments to Jesus Christ.

That young man is safe, at home, in heaven today because someone gave the 33¢ to place the *Book of Hope* into his hands. If he had never received it, his death would have meant his entry into eternal hell, and those 21 other youth would still be on the road to hell, too.

The Bible says, "Whosoever shall call on the name of the Lord shall be saved" (Acts 2:21). That's all it takes to avoid the flames of hell and attain eternity with God in heaven.

The plan of salvation is so simple ... "That if thou shalt confess with thy mouth the Lord Jesus, and shalt believe in thine heart that God hath raised him from the dead, thou shalt be saved" (Romans 10:9).

But what about those who have never heard the Word? No matter how

"The plan of salvation is so simple ... 'That if thou shalt confess with thy mouth the Lord Jesus, and shalt believe in thine heart that God hath raised him from the dead, thou shalt be saved'" (Romans 10:9).

simple the plan of salvation is, if they do not know about it, they cannot accept it. "How then shall they call on him in whom they have not believed? and how shall they believe in him of whom they have not heard?" (Romans 10:14).

The modern culture in America tends to gloss over the religious differences between faiths and stress instead that whatever you happen to believe – if you believe it sincerely and try to be a good person – will save you.

But this is untrue, according to the Scriptures, and the Book of Hope ministry simply will not give in to this pressure from the modern culture. Rather we will continue to base our faith on the Word of God and preach to children, youth and their families that only Jesus saves.

"For I am not ashamed of the gospel of Christ: for it is the power of God unto salvation to every one that believeth" (Romans 1:16).

Some people will criticize us for clinging to this truth. They will take us to task for bringing Scriptures to children and youth instead of bringing food, clothing and medicine to the needy. These are good people, called by God to be His channels of compassionate aid to those in need.

But we have been called, too. We have been called to support compassionate ministries ... but when it comes to our own ministry, we have been called to place the destiny-changing, life-saving Word of God into the hands of all the children and youth of the world.

I thank God that you have been called, too, to carry the light to the world. Thank you for your prayers and partnership. •

If the Son therefore shall make you free,
ye shall be free indeed.
John 8:36 KJV

"I know not what course others may take; but as for me, give me liberty, or give me death!" said Patrick Henry. His words have retained their brilliant luster amidst the tarnished relics of a post-Christian culture.

There is, in the heart of every man, a yearning to be free. To take away one's freedom is our favored mode of punishment. Its threat is the greatest deterrent since our moral base went on life support. We brace ourselves against all attempts to fence us in.

Some consider the punch clock to be their warden. Others see their marriage covenant as a ball and chain. Libertarians seek the dissolution of all laws except those that keep us from violating the rights of others. Modernists within the church argue for an updating of all Biblical themes to loosen restrictions and better reflect a permissive culture. Limits and restrictions are under attack on every quarter.

We want to be free! But can we be free without limits? Can we truly have liberty without law? Can we have law without absolutes? Within the framework of our faith we have both law and liberty; commandment and creativity; boundaries and bounty. Unframed liberty gives way to uncontainable chaos.

. . .always be ready to give a defense to everyone who asks you a reason for the hope that is in you.
1 Peter 3:15 NKJV

A lack of preparation diminishes returns. A preacher who does not prepare is like a baker who offers ingredients rather than hot bread. That bakery soon closes.

Peter admonishes us to "always be ready to give a defense" of the gospel. Here, we fall woefully short of effectiveness. Have you ever written out your testimony? Have you ever taken a few minutes to consider the most concise way you might share Christ with someone who opens a door of opportunity? We should be prepared! Our world is marked by a raging spiritual hunger. People are looking for answers. Only the gospel can truly satisfy the yearning soul. We have the message, and we are surrounded with need. Shouldn't we then prepare ourselves for those opportunities? Shouldn't we be prepared in prayer; prepared in response; prepared in the Word; prepared to lead?

On one side of a table I assemble all of the ingredients that go into a loaf of homemade bread. On the other side, a golden loaf, forty minutes out of the oven, awaits a bit of butter and strawberry preserves. Only a fool would prefer the ingredients to the prepared loaf.

Every valued achievement comes by preparation. Shouldn't we prepare ourselves to be used of God?

And it came to pass in those days,
that he went out into a mountain to pray,
and continued all night in prayer to God.
Luke 6:12 KJV

Some people get more out of their days than others.

One man might organize his time and tasking down to the minute. Another may rise at 5:00 a.m. to steal an extra hour or two while the rest of the office sleeps.

Martin Luther had a time-tested method for squeezing the most out of every day. *"Work, work from early till late. In fact I have so much work to do that I shall spend the first three hours in prayer."* Luther's approach revealed what he believed about the effectiveness of prayer. It all comes down to where you think creative power is found. I have found that my creative reservoir runs pretty shallow – a couple hot days and alarms start sounding. Drought makes my emotions brittle, my vision blurred, and my relationships strained. Prayer brings the rain that fills the reservoir. When I take time to pray, I work smarter, run longer, see clearer, lead better, love more, and cover more ground than when I'm too busy to pray.

Prayer is sharpening the saw – establishing a day's foundation – investing in the harvest – priming the pump – logging on – powering up – tapping in. No one has been able to accomplish anything for God without it. Start with prayer that you would not finish in frustration.

". . . but you have saved the best till now."
John 2:10 NIV

The law of thermodynamics declares that our world is in the grip of terminal entropy. In other words – everything is in the process of decay. I am well aware of this depressing law as my body ages and bifocals become a necessity. Nothing in this world gets better on its own.

Sorry to be such a downer, but laws are laws. Incredibly, God is not subject to the law of thermodynamics, or any other law, for that matter. With God, things can actually get better. In Christ, a marriage can go from good to great, and from great to golden, and from gold to platinum. God's creative power can re-invent us, over and over again, making us more and more like Jesus. While all of the joys and pleasures of this life have their limitations, there is no cap on the goodness of God.

Beyond human joy, we can have *"joy unspeakable and full of glory"* (1 Peter 1:8). Beyond the depth of earthly peace we can have *"the peace of God that passeth all understanding"* (Philippians 4:7).

In Christ, there is always a better tomorrow; a greater understanding; a richer reward; a higher call; a deeper love; and hope unlimited. Jesus demonstrated this principle in the first miracle. He always saves the best for last.

Charm is deceitful and beauty is passing, But a woman who fears the LORD, she shall be praised.
Proverbs 31:30 NKJV

Susannah took one hour each Thursday for "Jackie." She had eighteen other children to care for and no modern conveniences to help, but she held one hour every Thursday for Jack.

Susannah was no ordinary woman. Should she have been born in our times, who knows what contribution this brilliant woman could make to the world. But as it was, she came in the wretched conditions of the seventeenth century. By her teen years, she knew Latin, Greek, and French. Her theological knowledge rivaled that of her preacher-husband. She could have written textbooks. She could have poured her life into academics, but she chose to pour her life into her children, and on Thursdays, she kept one hour aside for Jack.

In that hour she saw to his education, as well as his spiritual disciplines. In that hour, she taught what mattered most and cared for the emotional needs of her second son. We may have enjoyed the notes and sermons of Susannah today, were it not for a fire in 1709.

No lives were lost, but a life of writing had gone to flame. Susannah did, however, give the world a gift: One hour invested every Thursday in the son she called Jackie. Dad called him Jack. We know him as John – John Wesley.

*Saying, This man began to build,
and was not able to finish.
Luke 14:30 KJV*

For five years the great stone church was silent on Sunday mornings. A caretaker kept enough heat in the old building to preserve the massive pipe organ that had once called a vibrant congregation to worship.

In the last years of the 50's, the church had embraced a liberal theology, and suffered staggering losses in attendance. Her only recourse was to merge with another dwindling congregation, leaving the massive and beautiful building empty – a casualty of compromise.

The granite church had been rebuilt in 1917 following a fire. Dr. Burns offered a prophetic warning at her re-de-dication: *"If certain disturbing conditions existing now in the church are allowed to continue, and should we forget that the Church is not this edifice made with hands ... then, the day will come when your great pipe organ will fall silent and these windows will cast their sad eyes upon your empty pews ... and as the ghosts of yesterday haunt this sanctuary, all who pass by will shake their heads and say, 'They began to build, but they could not finish.'"*

When our message is compromised, the gospel is emptied of its power. When the Gospel is emptied of its power, the church is soon to suffer – silent Sunday mornings.

... Andrew, Philip, Bartholomew ...
Mark 3:18 NKJV

Tell me everything you know about Bartholomew. You could write it on a three-by-five index card, couldn't you? Not much to go on, is there?

He was numbered among the twelve apostles. The historical record is thin and tainted with legend. The Scripture focuses primarily on Peter, John, and Paul. At best, we have a thumbnail sketch of the most important men in the first century. How could characters, so illusive and misty, survive for two millennia? What defines them, apart from three-and-a-half years with Jesus? I think it comes down to the way they died. Only John died of "natural" causes – after attempts had been made on his life. The rest died for what they believed in – a resurrec-ted Christ.

People won't die to sustain a legend or myth. Death is the ultimate moment of truth – the revealer of what is truly believed. The Apostles did not die in the company of friends; they died alone, and dispersed across Asia and Africa. The less notable among the Apostles retain their importance after all these years for their testimony. They were eyewitness to the greatest event, and proof of the greatest claim to ever be recorded in human history: Jesus Christ rose from the dead!

For that truth, they died. For that truth, we live.

Come unto me, all ye that labour and are heavy laden,
and I will give you rest.
Matthew 11:28 KJV

We live in a chaotic world. Our culture runs hard on a mix of adrenalin, affluence, power, and lust. Our senses are under constant assault. Inventors hurry to create the next generation of entertainment technology to fill up our senses with virtual reality.

"Real" life just doesn't move fast enough anymore. Advertising hits hard and fast – a story line and a sales pitch in thirty seconds. Yesterday's marvel is today's antique. Today's breakthrough is tomorrow's old news. Tomorrow's big hit has ninety days to succeed. We're living in the fast lane, building on the fault lines, and blurring all the boundaries that once defined our values. It's easy to get lost in these uncharted waters. The stars won't stand still and the compass is spinning. We can't take in sail and we can't find the anchor. The rudder won't answer and the wind screams, "Run faster!" We pick up the pace as we race to disaster. Meditation? Contemplation? Deliberation? These are antiquated concepts from the black and white TV days.

Against the backdrop of this raging storm, Jesus walks the tempest to lead us to a safe and quiet place. Slow down – say no – enjoy a sunset – be quiet – unplug! Rest a while – you'll run better tomorrow.

Let not the wise man glory in his wisdom,
Let not the mighty man glory in his might.
Jeremiah 9:23 NKJV

ᒪᒪ *We have modeled our educational system after the United States, so we cannot allow religious materials to be distributed in our schools,"* said a regional minister of education in the Philippines. What a tragic irony!

It is conveniently forgotten by modern administrators, that religion was once the soul education in America. The first eight American colleges – Harvard, William and Mary, Yale, Princeton, Brown, Rutgers, Dartmouth, Columbia and the University of Pennsylvania – held religious affiliation. Four were birthed out of the "Great Awakening." The following sentence is found in the original charter of Princeton: *"Cursed is all learning that does not point to the cross of Jesus Christ."* Malcolm Muggeridge summed up our present state when he said, *"We have educated ourselves into imbecility."*

Has education improved since religion was jettisoned? Hardly! William Bennett points out, *"Today, there are greater, more certain, and more immediate penalties in this country for serving up a single rotten hamburger than for furnishing a thousand schoolchildren with a rotten education."*

If nations flounder when Christ is rejected, should educational systems fare any better?

Peace I leave with you, My peace I give to you; not as the world gives do I give to you. Let not your heart be troubled, neither let it be afraid.
John 14:27 NKJV

Michael left the lawyer's office after the reading of the will.

He was too stunned to speak when the lawyer walked him to the door. The receptionist said something as he cut across the lobby, but Michael didn't hear. A courier jumped to get out of his way as he pushed through the double doors – Michael never saw him. On an empty sidewalk, he turned to stare at the office, then at the papers clutched in his hand. A frown wrinkled his brow. He had listened to every word at the reading, but the words deepened his confusion. Everything was wrong. For a moment, the clouds parted, and then he knew. There was only one explanation – only one reasonable conclusion. He sat down on the steps and rifled through the papers. *"This can't be right. This doesn't make sense. This can't be my father's will."*

The name was right, but the address was wrong. How could it happen? He hurried back in to the law office. Michael had found the right lawyer, but received the wrong legacy. Impossible? It happens all the time.

The legacy that Christ left the church is peace, but it seems as though we've opened up the wrong will. Anxiety and fear are written on every page. Whose legacy are you living under?

And whatever you do in word or deed, do all in the name of the Lord Jesus, giving thanks to God the Father through Him.
Colossians 3:17 NKJV

BICOL REGION, PHILIPPINES: The gym is alive with the sound of basketball. A cheering crowd; the thump of the dribble; the swish of the jumper; the referee's whistle; the hometown heroes are taking on the Book of Hope All-Stars.

Twenty-two games, fourteen clinics, nineteen cities, thirty thousand spectators, twenty thousand *Books of Hope*, countless school assemblies; this is Affect Destiny Distribution taken to a whole new level.

At half-time, the All-Star team members powerfully and clearly presented the Gospel. At one of these events, a regional basketball commissioner and his wife stood along with many high school and elementary students to invite Jesus into their lives. All over America, young men and women are sharpening their athletic skills as they seek God's direction for their lives. Who could imagine that their love of sport could open the doors of a schoolhouse to the Gospel? In these last days God is going to use the sports arena for His glory.

The love of team sport is universal and Book of Hope All-Star Teams are opening new avenues for evangelism. What talent has God given you? What do you hold in your hands? Maybe God will use you as the key to open a new door.

That he would grant you, according to the riches of his glory,
to be strengthened with might by his Spirit in the inner man.
Ephesians 3:16 KJV

How can we stand under the weight of evil in our world? How can we bear up when circumstances turn mean and markets tumble? What remedy can be found to alleviate the pressure that mounts when life goes crazy?

The answer is found in the strengthening of the inner man. We fly in comfort in a frigid and inhospitable stratosphere because of the pressurized environment of the cabin. We can journey by submarine to the crushing depths of the ocean by creating pressure inside that equals the pressure outside. If the inner man is compromised, the soul is crushed under the weight of the world.

John tested the strength of the inner man against crush of external circumstances. His conclusion: *"Greater is He that is in you than He that is in the world"* (1 John 4:4). Paul said that he was *"hard pressed on every side, but not crushed"* (2 Cor. 4:8). The increase of evil and stress in our culture must be met by the ever-increasing strength of God in us. By strengthening the inner man, the heroes of faith were able to prevail against the very "gates of hell."

Before today's sunset, you will probably encounter some kind of pressure to compromise. Christ, in you, overcomes the world.

I have set you an example that you should do
as I have done for you.
John 13:15 NIV

"Dad came home every day, popped open a beer, and turned on the television," said the weary engineer. "I hated him for it, but I find myself doing the same thing with my kids – strange how that happens, isn't it?"

He went on with a confession, of sorts, at 33,000 ft. He rambled on a bit, and my mind drifted to my own childhood. What a parent values will make its mark on a child – for good or bad. I grew up in the company of a thousand books. Television was an amusement. Books were treasured. My father cherished his preaching library. My mother filled the house with biographies and novels. My earliest book memories center on the bizarre creations of Dr. Seuss. Golden Books and pirates' tales accompanied the Bible stories from the big blue ten-volume series.

A love of reading is a part of the continuing legacy of my mom and dad. I married a book lover, and we cherish shelving over crystal. My kids have caught the bug, too. My youngest prefers a library to a game arcade.

What will your children say that you valued thirty years from yesterday? Would you want them to pass it on? What you model – they will follow. Watch out Daddy – the kids are watching you.

I tell you the truth, anyone who will not receive
the kingdom of God like a little child will never enter it.
Mark 10:15 NIV

Complexity has found a new showplace – the coffee shop.

It used to be that you ordered coffee black, or with sugar and cream. Decaffeinated coffee brought the first major subdivision in "Javaland." Now, we are awash in options. Large or small has been replaced with tall, grande, venti, double-cupped, triple-shotted art forms. Expresso, Latte, Machiato, Mocha, and Americano have broadened the field. "What will it be this morning?" asks the girl with twelve tattoos. "I'll have a triple-venti-half-caf-skim-vanilla-sweet-n-low-wet-latte," I say. My morning creation gurgles and sputters to life – all steam and foam. "Three-fifty," she says. "Would you like to try soy instead of milk?" I shake my head as I pay the ransom demanded for my caffeine fix.

Soy! What next – designer colors? God could have made redemption a complex maze of prerequisites, but He made it simple enough for a child to grasp. False religions take their pilgrims through intricate levels and stages.

God points us to the cross. Christianity is not complex. Come as a child. Take what is freely offered. Trust God. Follow the plan. When in doubt – be like Jesus.

Let the words of my mouth and the meditation of my heart
Be acceptable in Your sight,
O LORD, my strength and my Redeemer.
Psalm 19:14 NKJV

It took surgically-enforced silence to drive home the value of the spoken word. Doctor's orders – not a peep for three weeks.

It's been three days, and I'm showing all the signs of cracking up. I wasn't built for silence. Our vocal cords vibrate more than two million times per day. What do we have to show for the effort? Much of what we say is frivolous. Sometimes our words are reckless – more often, benign. In the silence, I'm reassessing the value of words … encouraging words, uplifting words, thankful words, loving words. We should make words count. We should load them with meaning. We should use them with grace. We should soak them in tenderness. We should craft them with care, until our intentions are unmistakably clear. We should use them for the highest and best. To one suddenly silent, offensive words are doubly so. To waste a word to curse or gossip is like throwing gold coins into a bottomless well.

Something precious is irretrievably lost when foolish words flow out of empty heads. Words reveal what the heart conceals. Is the vault of our heart filled with gold or scattered pennies? Consider the value of the spoken word – a common luxury so sadly devalued.

"For I know the plans I have for you,"
declares the LORD, "plans to prosper you and not to harm you,
plans to give you hope and a future."
Jeremiah 29:11 NIV

Uncertainty gives rise to our darkest fears. Will global warming create an ecological disaster? Will some new virus exploit our tenuous grip on mortality? Will overpopulation overtax our resources? Will old age find us a dollar short and physically wasted? Will our families stay together? Will our children break our hearts? The questions echo in a nervous void. Hope must have an object, and we've little left in our jaded world to trust anymore.

Against the darkness a light shines brightly, and hope springs eternal in the hearts of those who embrace it. This hope comes from God alone, and He offers it to all who believe Him. He sent us a message through a prophet named Jeremiah – a message of hope. Jeremiah wasn't prattling on with untested platitudes. He was a man who knew deep trouble. His nation was about to experience exile and destruction. He had stared wide-eyed at what others had ignored.

God's judgment was falling, and Jeremiah became known as the weeping prophet. But beneath the tears and futility, God gave Jeremiah hope in the darkest hours. He still does that, you know. God always looks upon you with a heart full of hope.

Jesus looked at them and said,
"With man this is impossible, but with God all things are possible."
Matthew 19:26 NIV

Henry Ford went broke five times before he succeeded in business. Albert Einstein didn't speak until he was four, didn't read until he was seven, and was considered "mentally slow" by his teacher.

The famous sculptor, Rodin, was thought an idiot by his father. Walt Disney was fired for a lack of creativity. Lombardi was accused of lacking motivation. Winston Churchill failed the sixth grade. Abraham Lincoln's resume is one long trail of failure and disappointment. Fred Astaire was considered an average dancer and a screen test failure. Rocky Marciano couldn't make it in baseball.

IBM decided to pass when first offered the photocopier (so did Kodak and RCA). Cheese, penicillin, paper towels, and aspirin were all the by-products of mistakes. History proves time and time again that the number one qualifier for outstanding achievement – is failure.

We all fall down, but we mustn't stay down. Every failure is the opportunity to begin again in a wiser fashion. We have more going for us than the formidable human spirit. We have the help of the Holy Spirit.

Get up! Get moving! Quit whining! Seek guidance, and live your life in Christ to exceed everybody's expectations.

Then I sent to him, saying,
"No such things as you say are being done,
but you invent them in your own heart."
Nehemiah 6:8 NKJV

Rumors are as deadly as guns. Gossips make snakes look noble. Liars destroy relationships like fire in a forest. Rumors, gossip, and lies share the same destructive family traits. They're all part of the Busybody Clan and there's no a shred of decency to be found among them.

Have you ever had a run-in with the Busybody Clan? Have you ever had someone attempt to assassinate your character, poison your mind, or burn up your friendships? Get to know Nehemiah. He did his best to do what God commanded. He worked hard and brought people together around a noble cause. He took precautions against a frontal attack, but his enemies changed tack and assaulted him with false charges and threats. Nehemiah refused to stoop to their level (Nehemiah 6:3).

Unless you're careful, responding to gossip can make you guilty of gossip yourself. Rumormongers revel in the discord they sow. They live in the shadows and hide like cowards. They always seem to have a scapegoat tethered nearby, just in case they need a diversion to enable their escape.

Bite your tongue rather than spread a rumor. Better to swallow your words than to be judged by them (Matthew 12:36).

And when they came to Nachon's threshing floor, Uzzah put out his hand to the ark of God and took hold of it, for the oxen stumbled. Then the anger of the LORD was aroused against Uzzah, and God struck him there for his error; and he died there by the ark of God.
2 Sam. 6:6-7 NKJV

Uzzah evokes genuine sympathy. For a thoughtless moment clothed in good intentions, God killed him. It doesn't seem fair.

He worried that the Ark of the Covenant might be damaged when the oxen stumbled. His reaction was one of instinct – and still God killed him. His sin was the sin of irreverence. He did not afford the Ark the sanctity; the Holy fear that God expected. To fault God in the matter is to call His sovereignty into question. We would be better served to take a lesson from the tragic events at Nachon's threshing floor.

Our world is increasingly casual about everything. We have moved sex from the bedroom to the front room. We have flouted moral law and devalued all things holy. Our political parties are abandoning us to worship the "fuzzy god" of public opinion. God's world is full of *rights* and *wrongs; virtues* and *sins; blessings* and *rules.*

Our world is full of *maybe* and *kind of; if you feel like it* and *if makes you feel good; please yourself* and *follow your instincts.* Take it from a dead man named Uzzah – your instincts may lead you into danger.

God's Word must be honored and His precepts obeyed, lest even our finest intentions lead to certain disaster.

So his fellow servant fell down at his feet and begged him, saying,
'Have patience with me, and I will pay you all.' And he would not,
but went and threw him into prison till he should pay the debt.
Matthew 18:29-30 NKJV

I don't remember when I started building this prison –
sometime long ago.

I cut each stone from the quarry of my resentments.
I built with vengeance to incarcerate my enemies. I set
the iron gates in place with an angry burst of adrenaline.
I issued warrants and arrested each offender. If you hurt
me, or wronged me, or disrespected me, I hunted you
down and locked you up in the prison of my graceless
heart. When my prison once reached capacity, I built
more cells. Parole was rarely granted and nobody escaped.
I've been judge, jury, and jailor – I've forgiven no one ...
until today.

Today I caught a vision of my own guilt, and of the
staggering grace that God has extended to me in Christ.
Today I realized that, having built this dark prison, I am
now cursed to guard it. Today I felt a yearning to run, to
sail away, to walk up a cold mountain stream – but as
long as I was the warden of my malefactors, I was held
prisoner in the prison I built for others. Yet, now I am
free! I've opened every prison door and set every prisoner
free. No man owes me a thing. I've nothing left to guard.
I'm leaving this prison to rot and ruin.

One look at the cross and I know – I can never hold
another captive again.

Let your speech always be with grace, seasoned with salt,
that you may know how you ought to answer each one.
Colossians 4:6 NKJV

What a waste we make of words.

They gush out of us like a torrent, void of redeeming qualities. We speak before we think. We wound people carelessly. Though we curse not, we fail to bless; and therein we lose the opportunity to demonstrate grace and instigate healing. Words are weapons against our adversary. We should use them skillfully to rebuke him. But words are also tools with which to build one another up in faith. Are our tools sharp and well-maintained, or are our toolboxes cluttered with rusty tools? Are we using words for the advantage of the Kingdom of God, or are we wasting our breath on idle chatter? Who can estimate the value of a word of encouragement? What price can be placed on a word of sympathy?

How we underestimate the simple words of recognition, spoken in passing. If you could only speak one hundred words per week, what words would you speak? If time was running out, and you were given opportunity to speak the last word into someone's life, what would you say? Time is running out. Tomorrow may be cancelled at any moment.

Choose words that save, and love, and heal. Decrease volume and increase value. A word is a terrible thing to waste.

"Blessed is the man who trusts in the Lord."
Jeremiah 17:7 NASB

Did Abraham understand what God was doing on Mount Moriah?

Did Moses understand what God was doing when He led the people to a waterless desert? Did Gideon understand what God was doing when He reduced his army to 300? Did David understand what God was doing when his son seized his throne? Did Jehoshaphat understand what God was doing when He commanded that the choir march first into battle? Did the widow at Zerapath understand what God was doing when Elijah demanded her last meal?

Did Paul understand what God was doing when He left him in jail for years on end? Did Mary and Martha understand what God was doing when Lazarus died? Did the servants understand what Jesus was doing when He commanded them to fill six water pots with water? What of the martyred legions of Hebrews 11? Did they understand what God was doing when they were flogged, imprisoned, stoned, sawn in two, and put to death by the sword?

Do you understand what God is doing right now in your circumstances? In seeking to understand, we are missing the very heart of the Christian faith. It's not about complete understanding; it's about trust!

"... for the LORD searches every heart and understands
every motive behind the thoughts. "
1 Chronicles 28:9 NIV

Carpet cleaners, electricians, landscapers, painters, sound technicians, computer consultants, copier repairmen, plumbers, carpenters, and pest control; they're like a second family when a church has multiple buildings.

If you build it, you had better be ready to maintain it, lest you lose it to fire, termites, flooding, or disrepair. Life can be just like that. We scratch and claw to obtain, only to fail to maintain. Satisfied with escaping the fires of hell, we slack off on spiritual growth. We're happy to have a spiritual experience every so often to pump us up, rather than digging in the Word, and taking in our daily bread. We're like spoiled children who leave their new toys out to rust.

Salvation is the starting line, not the finish line. Spiritual growth is a conscientious process, rather than a spiritual byproduct. When the house is falling apart, we need to fix it fast, and fix it right. Small oversights spell disaster.

The Holy Spirit is our Heavenly Building Inspector. He is the consummate professional – never missing the tiniest detail. He'll come at a moment's notice, if only we will ask. Are you past due for inspection?

Let this mind be in you, which was also in Christ Jesus.
Philippians 2:5 KJV

The mind is the battleground on which victory is secured, or defeat is insured.

Attitudes grow quickly in the fertile soil of the mind. We must weed our gardens constantly, or suffer the loss of the harvest. Attitudes require a firm hand. If we don't govern our attitudes, they will rule and ruin our lives. Good government establishes boundaries for society. Good parents establish boundaries for their children. Good employers define boundaries for employees. Governance is all about perimeters.

The mind needs clear borderlines. An unbounded thought life will soon wander the paths of destruction, far removed from safety. Thoughts and attitudes grow into words and actions. Hidden things are ultimately revealed.

We often find ourselves far removed from the highest and best. *How did I get here? Where did I go wrong? How could I stray so far?* It all starts in the thought life. We need to follow in Jesus' footsteps and feed our minds with God's Word. Jesus' example will always produce light.

The Word of God guards our hearts against corruption, our thoughts from confusion, and our feet from destruction.

The Lord is not slack concerning his promise, as some men
count slackness; but is longsuffering to us-ward, not willing that any
should perish, but that all should come to repentance.
2 Peter 3:9 KJV

TASBARRAYA, HONDURAS: Not everyone who receives a copy of the *Book of Hope* recognizes the value of the Word of God.

One child who received the book in a Honduran school tore it apart, leaving a few pages scattered on the side of the road. A fisherman named Comino walked by and picked up one or two of the torn pages. What he read touched his heart. The Holy Spirit must have been preparing him, for in that moment, with only a page or two of God's Word in his hands, Comino asked Jesus to come into his heart. He has since joined the village church. In his wallet he keeps those folded scraps as a reminder of God's goodness.

In times past, God delivered food to a prophet by way of ravens; caused flood waters to cover all of the earth; made water turn into the finest wine, and sent angels to open prison doors. Is there any question that this same God could direct the flight of paper scraps to the feet of a village fisherman that he might read the Word of God and believe?

Comino found eternal treasure in the scraps that a careless child discarded. His story reveals a God who goes to extreme measures to get His Word to lost people. How far will we go?

"Lord, if it's you," Peter replied,
"tell me to come to you on the water."
"Come," he said.
Matthew 14:28-29 NIV

Simon was probably more comfortable than the others. He was no stranger to the sudden squalls that angered the sea of Galilee.

Deepwater fishermen make an early peace with the sea, but imagine the terrors that gripped the tax collector, or the zealot, or the other landlubbers who followed Jesus' command to take the boat to the other side. Simon knew boats through and through. You can be sure that he had inspected the planking, the sails, the oarlocks, and rudder. I would guess that Simon was firmly established at the rudder, shouting instruction and encouragement as the winds rose and waves began to break over the bow. Simon was in his element – his comfort zone.

Then Jesus came like some apparition, walking on the water. Here we find one of the great lessons on faith. God's miraculous power is rarely revealed to us in our comfort zones. The one place Simon felt secure had to be abandoned so that new wonders could be experienced. Simon got out of the boat.

This morning I leave you with a Bible challenge. Search the Scripture and see if you can find God revealing some new dimension of power or grace in someone's comfort zone. Then get out of your boat!

By faith Joseph, when he died,
made mention of the departing of the children of Israel;
and gave commandment concerning his bones.
Hebrews 11:22 KJV

He was born the favored son to the favored wife in a polygamous family. From his childhood, he was looking ahead. His dreams of sheaves and stars foresaw a brilliant future.

His brothers responded with jealousy rather than joy. His naiveté put him in the wrong place at the wrong time. For a bit of cash the favored son was sold as a slave, but still, he looked ahead. Instead of bitterness, he developed readiness, and soon rose to a managerial role in a prominent Egyptian household. Once again, he found himself victimized by a lie. The house servant became a prisoner, and yet, he still looked ahead. He became a trustee; a bright spot of hope in the lowest tier of Egyptian society. Again, he chose readiness over bitterness.

One day the dreamer was asked to interpret Pharoah's dream. He was spot on, and Pharoah placed him in a tailor-made job: Forward planning for hardship. He reconciled with his brothers and looked forward to seeing his father again. At the peak of power his entire family lived in Egypt, under his provision. To the last, he looked forward, giving orders concerning the removal of his bones to Canaan.

Forward-looking people rarely make a waste of life. Joseph never looked back.

This beginning of his signs did Jesus in Cana of Galilee,
and manifested his glory;
and his disciples believed on him.
John 2:11 ASV

How did Jesus show His glory to His disciples?

It all started with an act of kindness to a young man on his wedding day. The wine failed. We know not why. Was it from inadequate preparations? Was it the result of party-crashers? Was there a breakdown in communications? All we know is that a young man was about to be publicly embarrassed – even censured – because the wine ran out. Jesus' mother, Mary, felt compassion for the couple and intervened with her Son. Against the backdrop of a common wedding feast, Jesus displayed His glory. It was more than turning water to wine. He displayed His glory by showing kindness. Kindness remains a radiant display of God's glory – even if we can't turn water to wine. Paul calls kindness a fruit of the Spirit (Galatians 5:22). Peter connects kindness to godliness (2 Peter 1:7).

Wherever it finds application, the presence of the Savior is felt. We do not need extraordinary circumstances or miraculous signs to display God's glory to the world. Every day we are afforded multiplied opportunities to be kind. Kindness without a price tag warms the coldest heart. Where His glory is displayed, men believe.

When the USSR fell, Russia – already familiar with alcoholism – opened its doors to other negative influences: drugs, cults, immorality. Pray that God will protect the children and youth from these influences and bring them into relationship with Christ.

Sasha Finds Hope in Juvenile Detention!

Sasha Smolnikov grew up in a Russian orphanage, but by age 16, the juvenile detention center was his home. The state's poor health-care and hygiene left Sasha with tuberculosis and his kidneys constantly ached after being permanently damaged by beatings in juvenile jail. He was hurting and hopeless.

But then a team of believers from Perm's New Testament Church arrived at the detention facility to tell the boys about Jesus and give them the *Book of Hope*. Sasha was one of several boys to give his heart to Jesus. During a prison service led by one of the team members, God healed Sasha's TB!

When Sasha was released at age 18, his only "family," the New Testament Church, took him in. He slept at the church and served as night watchman, and in the daytime, he sat in the classes at Bible school. During one of the church services, God healed Sasha's kidneys, too.

Recently, Sasha and other Bible school students reached out with the *Book of Hope* to a nearby village of 300 families. Teachers, parents and students have come to Jesus and the team has already planted a church there. Sasha and another Bible school student come every weekend to conduct services for the new church's 58 members.

God used His Word to reach Sasha, and now He's using Sasha to reach others. Thank you for caring enough to pray and give.

Save me, O God,
for the waters have come up to my neck.
Psalm 69:1 NIV

The office is understaffed and the boss needs you to carry a few additional responsibilities for a while.

The family is in the midst of a teenaged crisis. Your big opportunity has just materialized, but the timing is wrong. Your "forever young" parents are beginning to show their age with health related issues that frighten you. The mechanic just called – you need a new transmission. Your hard drive crashed. You sat on your new glasses. Your diet weigh-in was a blow-out. Your schedule is packed with whiners. Somebody had better rig an air tank because you're about to go under.

It's time for a simple prayer like, "Save me" or "Help!" Simple prayers are best when you're fighting to keep your head above the waters. Simon Peter uttered a simple prayer when he began to sink beneath the waves. The crucified thief prayed a simple prayer: "Remember me."

Most prayers in the Bible are simple prayers. God is not impressed with the oratory of a Churchill or the eloquence of a Shakespeare, yet He is moved by a one word prayer offered in simple faith.

I will praise thee;
for I am fearfully and wonderfully made.
Psalm 139:14 KJV

You are living inside a miracle! As you read these words, whether you dwell in a low-cost rental or an oceanside villa, you possess a masterful work of art that is priceless.

I'm talking about your body. It's awesome! An engineer wrote up a bid sheet for one human heart: fluid pump with 75-year expectancy (2.5 billion cycles); no maintenance or lubrication required; power range: .025 - 1.0 horsepower; must not exceed 10.5 ounces; must pump 2000 gallons per day; valve operation must exceed 4000 cycles per hour. The engineer could have added that the heart must work in harmony with several other systems and major organ centers, operate without interruption, and respond to every stimulus from sorrow to terror to laughter to lifting.

If God has so perfectly equipped us physically, will He not also equip us spiritually for every eventuality? Too often, we are reduced to despair when confronted with conflicts and disappointments.

Be encouraged. God has built you to take it. He won't let the temptation or trial exceed the specifications of your soul. Don't give up. Don't give in. Don't despair. The glory of the human body is but a shadow of the glory of the trusting soul.

To Him who loved us and washed us from
our sins in His own blood.
Rev. 1:5 NKJV

Blood stains are difficult to remove.

Blood-stained clothes are consigned to the rag bin. Blood-stained carpet is removed from the crime scene. Blood-stained evidence resists all efforts to stifle its testimony. Blood stains and spoils. Blood is a contaminant – just watch them rush a basketball player off the floor when the blood starts to flow. Outside of the body, blood possesses few redeeming qualities. But inside the body, blood cleanses. Two thousand years ago, John used blood as a startling word picture to describe the cleansing that comes from the sacrificial offering of Jesus Christ. John had no idea that his words were medically correct.

While you are reading, your blood is cleansing your body. Far beyond your awareness, the red cells are loading up on oxygen, dumping out carbon dioxide, transporting toxins to the kidneys, and retiring to the liver and spleen for recycling. With every breath and every beat of the heart, God's rhythmic cleansing process washes the body clean. Jesus' shed blood has a separate purpose: To cleanse the soul from sin.

Just as your body is sustained by cleansing blood, your spiritual life is dependent on His cleansing blood.

Love never fails.
1 Corinthians 13:8 NIV

"Pastor, it just seems that everything I try fails! My business is on life-support. My wife has left me. I am estranged from my dad over a money issue, and to top it all, I only feel guilt when I come to church."

Brian's self-assessment led him to an inescapable conclusion. He was a failure. In truth, there wasn't much left in Brian's life to salvage. He had a very superficial relationship with God. His priorities were shackled to his desires. His family life had been a deep disappointment. His meager accomplishments were about to be buried in bankruptcy. His attitude was lousy. Self-pity ruled the day, and I wondered how I could tell Brian that he needed to try love.

It all seemed too simple, but the evidence he offered made it clear that Brian had never really put biblical love (1 Corinthians 13:1-13) to the test. His life had centered on getting rather than giving. His self-portrait showed a man marked by impatience, abrasiveness, selfishness, arrogance, anger, malice, greed, and dishonesty; in short, the antithesis of love.

At the bottom, Brian was looking for a new game plan. Maybe you're looking for a life that works. Have you tried love? Real love? Biblical love? It never fails.

We are therefore Christ's ambassadors,
as though God were making his appeal through us.
2 Corinthians 5:20 NIV

Instant and ready communications have given modern day ambassadors a reasonable assurance that they can speak for their principal any time, any place.

Not so long ago, news and inquiries traveled across the ocean waves in wooden sailing ships. The ambassador might be out of touch with his homeland for months on end. It was essential that the ambassador have a thorough knowledge of the whims and wishes of his king or minister. Paul chooses to describe everyday, ordinary Christians as ambassadors for Christ. It would follow then, that we should know Him well if we have any hope of properly representing Him to a desperate world.

Could it be that much of the confusion that clouds the Christian witness can be traced to an inadequate knowledge of God? Could it be that we have settled for just enough religion to get our hides into heaven, but not enough relationship to gain Jesus a serious hearing in the public arena?

If we were hired to represent a golf ball manufacturer, we had better know and love golf. If we were hired to represent the dairy industry, we had better enjoy milk and cheese. What if we were called to represent Jesus?

Good morning, ambassador.

Now then we are ambassadors for Christ,
as though God did beseech you by us: we pray you in Christ's stead,
be ye reconciled to God.
2 Corinthians 5:20 KJV

Ambassadors must never forget where their allegiance lies. If an ambassador becomes too rooted in his assigned country, he may neglect his core responsibility: To represent his king.

He is far from home, subject to temptation, pressured to compromise, and plied with comforts. One day the ambassador wakes up to realize that he doesn't feel like an alien, or think like an alien, or act like an alien – he considers himself quite at home. On that day, the ambassador is prone to fail amidst great comforts, forgetting his allegiance – his homeland – his master – his purpose. Ambassadors for Christ must be constantly reminded that Jesus' Kingdom is not of this world (John 18:36). We are aliens (1 Peter 2:11). We have become new creatures in Christ (2 Cor. 5:17). The only reason we have for being here is to speak for Christ, to love like Christ, to live in Christ, and to be canvas on which God paints redemption's story!

Ambassadors must not sell out. They could be recalled for an accounting any day – at any hour. The distinction between the Kingdom of God and the kingdom of darkness must weigh constantly on the ambassador's heart. His calling is an honor – and a trust!

Have you pledged your allegiance today?

Now then we are ambassadors for Christ,
as though God did beseech you by us: we pray you in
Christ's stead, be ye reconciled to God.
2 Corinthians 5:20 KJV

The king's ambassador carries the king's authority so long as he speaks the King's will.

As an ambassador, I cannot tell the rulers of the country where I am stationed what to do. I don't have that authority. As an ambassador, I cannot make demands or manipulate political advantages lest I bring shame to my King. I must confine myself to proactive, purpose-driven activities that reflect the will and heart of my King.

When we speak outside of the authority of God's Word, our words are no more than dust in the wind. When we speak the Word of Jesus, we speak with authority. When we give ourselves to the fulfilling of the great commission, we move with authority. When we shape our lives only after His will, we have all authority to complete His agenda and return home with honors.

Let's move away from opinions, philosophies, and experiences as a basis for action in spiritual matters. Rather, let us seize upon the King's will, understand the King's Word, and make our presentation a mirror image of Jesus' life. If we will do so, we will never lack divine authority nor power.

We are Christ's ambassadors. We have His authority. We must make His Word our perimeter.

Ask of me, and I will make the nations your inheritance,
the ends of the earth your possession.
Psalm 2:8 NIV

E.M. Bounds made a statement to the effect that when God's house on earth is filled with prayer, God's house in heaven gets busy.

Have you ever thought of what your prayers cause in heaven? Are angels dispatched as we pray? Is provision set in motion when we intercede? Are circumstances manipulated when we pray for a lost son or daughter? Does Satan cringe under the blows of our prayers? Do our prayers live forever before God? When we have forgotten, does God still remember? What happened in heaven when D.L. Moody prayed? Were demonic forces not put to flight? Did not whole cities experience the power of God? A sincere prayer is more powerful than the whole of the United Nations.

Nothing significant has ever been affected for the Kingdom of God unless prayer was in the vanguard. No time will be better spent today than the time you spend in prayer. Is heaven busy on your account this morning? Are angels rising to put the adversary to flight? Is the curtain of gloom parting as you call on the incomparable name of Jesus?

We must never forget that what we see on earth can be, and will be, marked by our prayers – or their absence.

Train a child in the way he should go,
and when he is old he will not turn from it.
Proverbs 22:6 NIV

I am the proud daddy of three teenaged girls.

I am a future wedding pauper. I am the lord of three grand fountains of emotion. I am the final word on licensing, dating, curfew, friends, and grounding. I bleed money, trip over shoes, buy hair brushes by the gross, and weep whenever I hear somebody sing "Butterfly Kisses." I "love" every new haircut, hair color, hair crimp, hi-light, and gel job – and you should love it, too. If you don't, please don't say so – it complicates my life. I am a mood reader, a private investigator, and the only hug they really need.

I regard all males thirty or younger as sworn enemies. I expect any suitor to be twice as mature as I was at their age. I am the pit bull that guards the door. Break their hearts, and I'll break your thumbs. I will not lose my girls to the culture, peer pressure, the devil, bright lights, or pretty boys. I will pray like Daniel, fight like David, preach like Peter, work like Paul, and love like Jesus so that I may see them safely through to a Christ-centered adulthood. I long to see my grandchildren and beyond, serving Christ.

Have you a spiritual goal for your family? Are you parenting by design or by default?

But the king said,
"What have I to do with you, you sons of Zeruiah?"
2 Samuel 16:10 NKJV

The sons of Zeruiah were among the mightiest of David's mighty men.

These distant cousins distinguished themselves on the battlefield and demonstrated a filial loyalty to David. While they projected the power and authority of David's kingdom, they did not share the king's heart. The sons of Zeruiah had one fail-safe plan for every kind of opposition: Kill it. Have you ever run into David's distant cousins? They are a capable and dynamic tribe, but sympathy, compassion, humility, and brokenness are not to be found among them. When David's kingdom was usurped by his renegade son, the sons of Zeruiah wanted blood, without regard for David's feelings. When David was insulted on his skulking exodus from Jerusalem, the sons of Zeruiah wanted blood.

They could not conceive that God might have a hand in their shameful procession. When the crisis had passed and David regained his kingdom, they lobbied for the blood of his enemies. David wisely chose to mark his return with mercy rather than murder. Though Zeruiah's sons were mighty, they would never be used beyond the military.

Power is not the only evidence of God's presence and approval.

For the word of God is living and powerful.
Hebrews 4:12 NKJV

OREKHOVO-ZUYEVO, RUSSIA: Andrey's mother manages a meeting hall on the outskirts of Moscow. She has opened the doors for all kinds of groups and meetings, often listening but not hearing the business being conducted or the officer being elected.

You see, Andrey's mother was often thinking about what to do with Andrey. At 28 he had been through several programs to cure his drug addiction – without success.

Andrey's mother unlocked the doors for a visiting group of Americans. She watched and listened with increasing interest as young people shared their testimonies of deliverance from drug addiction. At the close of the crusade Andrey's mother asked for prayer for her son and for a copy of the *Book of Hope* to take to him. Team members and local pastors surrounded her with prayer and sent her home with a book for Andrey. Andrey's mother insisted that he come to the crusade. He came to the Lord on the closing night and was delivered from a five-year drug habit.

Andrey's mother heard the story, asked for help, delivered the *Book of Hope*, and witnessed the miracle of a changed life. Is it any wonder that in a matter of days, Andrey's mother was saved?

If ye shall ask any thing in my name, I will do it.
John 14:14 KJV

Hen we have prayed, God opens the doors of opportunity, sends divine help, casts mountains into the sea, and floods our hearts with delight.

Until we have prayed, we are left to shadowbox ourselves to exhaustion. A prayerful life is a directed life. A prayerless Christian is crippled, deaf, and blind. Prayer is the main event. Miracles and victories are the fruit of prayer.

The great men and women of the Bible lacked much of what is required today for success. Most of them gained little by way of education. None of them ever attended a leadership seminar or strategic planning summit. Few of them possessed any political influence. Widespread popularity came only to a few Old Testament kings. Unfettered by degrees and methodologies, they turned their world upside down. They called upon the Lord. They prayed day and night. They asked God for the impossible. God answered with the incredible.

Every one of us can make the world a better place today. We can do it by praying. Prayer is more effective than any human endeavor.

Have you prayed today? Have you humbled yourself before God? Have you asked Him to do something great?

We are fools for Christ's sake.
1 Corinthians 4:10 KJV

"Don't look at me, look to Jesus," said the worship leader with purple hair. "We're just here to glorify Jesus," he said, as the band broke into a funky-town-boogie-sidestep-shuffle.

"Let's rock, let's give it up, let's worship," he shouted as he pranced around, a sad caricature of an aging rock star. "It's not about me, it's all about Him," he cried, as he ripped off a tortured guitar solo. I felt like I was witnessing a poor brand of Christian karaoke. When Paul said, "We are fools," he was not endorsing foolish and infantile behavior. He was chiding the sinful Corinthians who supposed themselves to be super-wise. Paul's use of biting sarcasm has oft been used to defend outrageous flamboyance on the part of charlatans and pretenders. If a man teases a rabid Doberman, he is a fool, and no Christian virtue can be found in his dangerous acts.

Christians cannot defend stupidity by claiming that we are "fools for Christ." Neither should we accept carnal, self-serving behavior as somehow "spiritual" because Jesus' name is invoked, or Paul's statement is quoted out of context.

God is not honored by carnival hysterics, but by sincerity, integrity, meekness and humility.

Where there is no counsel, the people fall;
But in the multitude of counselors there is safety.
Proverbs 11:14 NKJV

I bought a little four-wheel drive wagon – the one pitched by the Australian guy with a crocodile smile.

I liked its sturdy look. Few men can resist four-wheel drive. Add the masculine image of our Australian friend and the sale was complete. I found a used one at a good price and blazed down the road feeling rugged and manly. All I needed was a tan and a sweat-stained hat.

I took notice of every similar model I met. To my dismay, the overwhelming majority of my sister vehicles were driven by . . . sisters. It seems that women really like the leather-skinned Australian bloke with the sweat-stained crocodile hat. I searched in vain for men behind the wheel.

I suddenly felt like I was driving one of those pink Mary Kay cars. I thought that the car appealed to manly men, but it was really targeted at soccer moms.

It's not the first time I've acted without considering all the angles. Sometimes the cost of a hasty decision runs a lot higher than a car payment. God has given us the ability to reason, the availability of mature counsel, and an ever-open audience at heaven's throne.

Employ all three when making long-term decisions, or build a bigger garage for your regrets.

When I was a child, I talked like a child, I thought like a child,
I reasoned like a child. When I became a man,
I put childish ways behind me.
1 Corinthians 13:11 NIV

Forget all this talk about teenage independence and individuality. Teenagers are a schooling species – I know – my house is like the Great Barrier Reef.

Since I have three daughters, we seem to attract our fair share of sharks, flounders, barracudas, puffers and groupers (or is that groupies)? Decisions are made by a pilot fish within the school who zigs and zags according to whim. Everybody follows. Purpose and achievement are secondary to "hanging out" and the school doesn't seem to mind if they swim over the same reef a thousand times.

This meandering school rarely sleeps, with the exception of Sunday morning worship service. They eat anything and everything, being a scavenger species. They love the comforts of the school, often more than the comforts of home. Their greatest fear is to be alone.

When abandoned, they fall prey to a shark or hide among the rocks in fear. Ideally, they move beyond the schooling stage and learn to swim against the current and out of harm's way. Some never seem to break free, and spend their lives in a weary adolescence.

God help us to help them make the break, lest their God-given beauty be lost in the silvery flash of the school.

. . . put a knife to your throat if you are given to gluttony.
Proverbs 23:2 NIV

We've reached an all-time high. We are bloated beyond precedent. Look for wider doorways and fifty-gallon bucket seats.

We are eating ourselves into oblivion. 61% of American adults are too fat. 35% are overweight while 26% are obese. Only 47% of the adult population was overweight between 1976 and 1980. 25% of American children between ages 2 and 20 are, or are at risk of becoming overweight or obese. This represents a twofold increase over a decade ago. 61 million Americans, 1 in 5, have some sort of cardiovascular disease. In 1998 alone, nearly one million died because of it.

Today, someone will die every 33 seconds from diseases that are often preventable with good nutrition and a little bit of exercise. Nearly one-third of cancers of the colon, breast, kidney, and digestive tract can be tied to low exercise and excessive weight gain. Church people are often very judgmental on issues of smoking, drinking, and drugs, while gluttony is given a chuckle and a pass.

I wonder where we draw the lines between the man who poisoned his liver with alcohol and the woman who stopped her heart with a Big Mac and fries? We're killing ourselves for a lack of self control.

For even when we were with you, we gave you this rule:
"If a man will not work, he shall not eat."
2 Thessalonians 3:10 NIV

I have this advice for the lazy: Get used to poverty!

Lazy and waste go hand-in-hand to produce nothing less than a steady drain on relationships, families, cultures, and churches. I once had a man make a serious attempt at convincing me that God had told him not to work. He was freeloading on a couple of well-meaning friends and expecting the church to give him a couple hundred dollars to help him make ends meet. I took him to Paul's admonition to the Thessalonian church concerning working and eating. He was unmoved. "God won't let me work," he said. I replied that the Apostle Paul wouldn't let me give him any money.

He was deeply offended by my insensitivity. I was deeply disgusted by his contempt. I fought the urge to give him a boot as he shuffled out of my office to go con some other church. He was smart, well educated, talented, even handsome, but dreadfully lazy and arrogant. He probably found a preacher somewhere to pay his bills until God lifted his ban on earthly labor.

The Christian community could have a powerful impact on the world next week if every believer would work as though they were working for the Master. In truth – we are!

Warn a divisive person once, and then warn him a second time.
After that, have nothing to do with him.
Titus 3:10 NIV

There are some people you need to write out of your life! Paul identifies them as "divisive." These folks have a keen ability to drive wedges, stir-up strife, twist words, and change colors like a chameleon.

You're kidding yourself if you think you can fix what is wrong with a truly "divisive" person. You will exhaust yourself in the process. You might as well spend a year trying to convince your dog that he's really a cat! Paul offers grace in the form of two warnings. Beyond the second warning he recommends a complete severance.

Some may think that your withdrawal from a divisive person is "un-Christian." Paul indicates that withdrawal is the "Christian" thing to do. When you're confronted with a divisive person, remember Paul's qualified words: *"If it is possible, as far as it depends on you, live at peace with everyone"* (Romans 12:18 NIV).

Living at peace does not indicate a close intimate relationship. Sometimes peace is the best we can do. Realize that you can only hold up your end of a relationship. A divisive person will never hold up their end. Don't waste your time trying to tame a crocodile. When you're dealing with a divisive personality, it's only a matter of time until you get bit.

When I heard these things, I sat down and wept.
For some days I mourned and fasted and prayed
before the God of heaven.
Nehemiah 1:4 NIV

The city of David is a mere shadow of its former greatness. The walls lay in rubble. A cadre of exiles have been repatriated; a dispirited people without hope or heroes. Strong armies dominate the region, insuring that Jerusalem shall never again rise to prominence.

For the Jew, Jerusalem is an unending nightmare – a testament to God's severe judgment. She is a bankrupt city, a hopeless shell, listless and reproached. But as another gray morning is dawning over Jerusalem, God is working for her redemption through a king's servant named Nehemiah, some seven hundred miles to the east.

As Jerusalem shakes herself from slumber, Nehemiah is praying. He has been praying for four months. His plan is audacious, as are all great plans born in the sweat and tears of prayer. He has no experience in urban renewal. He is unqualified as an engineer. Nehemiah has risen to a place of honor among his captors, yet he remains a slave. He has nothing to work with, and yet he will succeed in restoring the ancient city. His success is insured before the first stone is moved – insured by four months of prayer.

No great work for God is ever birthed except for the labor and travail of prayer.

So we built the wall, and the entire wall was joined together
up to half its height, for the people had a mind to work.
Nehemiah 4:6 NKJV

It is amazing what can be accomplished when people have "a mind to work."

The people living amidst the ruins of Jerusalem believed that God had raised up Nehemiah for the task of rebuilding the wall. Rather than resist, or refrain, they put their hearts and hands to the task. The third chapter of Nehemiah gives testimony of the unanimous nature of their cooperation. Each household took a portion of the wall, each doing their part. God's work is always advanced when people do their part. When everyone exercises their spiritual gifts, the church thrives. When everyone tithes on the increase, the church thrives. When everyone embraces a ministry, the church thrives. When all stand behind the cause of Christ, the church thrives. Jesus prayed fervently for us before He ascended to the Father, that we may be one (John 17:11).

Unity creates synergy. A symphony is a travesty unless everybody stays on the same page. So the church is either madness or movement depending on our unity. Miracles await us when unity binds us together for a great cause.

Days spent in quarrels are days lost for eternity. If you're going to build your part of the wall, you have to give attention to connecting with your neighbor.

So I sent messengers to them, saying,
"I am doing a great work, so that I cannot come down.
Why should the work cease while I leave it and go down to you?"
Nehemiah 6:3 NKJV

Great purposes are often thwarted by petty issues.

Our adversary works first to distract, and then to destroy. Just about the time Nehemiah's project reached critical mass, his enemies launched their final offensive. It started with a desire for Nehemiah's attention. "Come, let us meet together," said Sanballat, Tobiah, and Geshem. The walls of Jerusalem had been raised from the rubble. Only the gates remained unset. In this "almost, but not quite" setting, the enemies of Israel made a last desperate move to stop the work. Whenever we are growing spiritually and accomplishing the work of God's Kingdom, the enemy of our souls will go to extreme measures to get our eyes off Jesus. Some minor irritation will suddenly become a troublesome boil. A thousand "urgencies" will rush in on the four winds. A long settled conflict will suddenly find new life.

If we are not on guard we will delay obedience, depart God's pathway, and involve ourselves in lesser things while great things are abandoned. Learn a lesson from Nehemiah. He would not "come down" from a great work to deal with a devilish distraction.

Stay focused on Christ's great cause, lest your labors be wasted and the victory lost.

Yea doubtless, and I count all things but loss for the excellency of the knowledge of Christ Jesus my Lord: for whom I have suffered the loss of all things, and do count them but dung, that I may win Christ.
Philippians 3:8 KJV

No man can produce a resume that qualifies him for the great work of the Kingdom of God.

Paul could site the privilege of birth, a lawful life, a stellar education, recognition in the highest levels of government, and the reputation as a rising star in Jerusalem. Yet Paul says such lofty credentials are to be considered as "dung" when compared to the greatness of the knowledge of Christ.

The late Malcolm Muggeridge achieved fame, respect, notoriety, and wealth as he captured his readers with wit and intelligence. He came to Christ in the late years of his life and stated that his lofty achievements were a "positive impediment when compared to one drop of living water which only Christ can give." We often say of some talented musician or popular star, "If only they were saved – they could do such great things for God."

While we should be zealous for all men to be saved, we're wrong to think that greatness is dependent on anyone's talents. God can raise up rocks and stones to praise Him. He uses the weak and lowly, ignoring the strong and confident.

Greatness begins for us when we confess that we are hopeless sinners. It is only at this point that God has something He can work with.

"Call to Me, and I will answer you,
and show you great and mighty things, which you do not know."
Jeremiah 33:3 NKJV

D.L. Moody said, "When God has an impossible task to do, he finds an impossible man and He breaks him."

His statement brings the Apostle Paul to mind. The devil's chief prosecutor became the Gospel's chief promoter. Paul's legacy is a legacy of greatness. When a nation in decline needed a mighty warrior, God chose an unlikely farmer named Gideon found hiding his meager crops from the big bad Philistines. Gideon is not remembered as a farmer, but as a cunning commander of men. Gideon's legacy is a legacy of greatness. To march a nation out of bondage, God chose a fugitive shepherd named Moses. Moses' path was marked by the great acts of God. He shared a shepherd's vocation with a boy named David who would leave a legacy of unparalleled greatness, and a lineage that would deliver God's own Son into the world.

No man comes to God to offer a resume of greatness. God always begins with an empty page, a broken heart, an obedience bought by tears, even failure of spectacular dimension.

This is the glory of the matter: That God can use anyone to accomplish His incredible purposes. Do you dare ask God to do great things through you?

"Nazareth! Can anything good come from there?"
Nathanael asked.
John 1:46 NIV

Read the Old Testament and study the location of the great works of God. More often than not, they were performed in small towns, not great cities.

Trace the steps of Jesus and chart the locations of His great miracles. More often than not, they occurred in the country barrens or fishing villages surrounding Galilee. Messiah bypassed the splendor of Rome, the beauty of Athens, the glories of Alexandria, even the golden city of Jerusalem to be born in a Bethlehem stable. Jesus was not raised a couple of blocks removed from the temple, but removed by several days' journey in the disreputable town of Nazareth. Even when the miracles started, Jesus did not rush to the great population centers. He moved among common people in out-of-the-way places.

God can do great things in your small town. He does not need massive population to accomplish His divine purposes. Where two or three gather in His name, He is there.

In a world impressed by big numbers and slick production, God is found to be out of fashion. Yet, He will show His glory in a tiny church at a country crossroads where people seek Him with a whole heart.

It's not about numbers – it's all about Him.

If in this life only we have hope in Christ,
we are of all men most miserable.
1 Corinthians 15:19 KJV

Four hours had passed since the stricken submarine ground to a halt on the bottom of the Barents Sea. Twenty-three sailors held slim hopes of rescue in the cold silence of the after compartment. Ninety-five shipmates were already dead. Who can imagine the horror of those last dark moments in the Oscar-class Russian submarine Kursk?

Waiting in the dark, Lt. Dmitry Kolesnikov wrote by touch. "It seems there is no chance, 10-20 percent. We hope that at least someone will read this." And then later, "Hello to everyone, mustn't despair."

Dmitry's last thoughts were for those left behind. His brave message, found in his pocket, was beamed all over Russia and around the world. When I first heard it on a newscast, the scene it suggested tugged at my heart-strings. The more I thought of it, I found myself wishing that Dmitry could have said "I'll see you again one day soon." Had he ever heard of Jesus? Had he any understanding of eternal life? Could anyone in the after compartment have offered a prayer?

Book of Hope Affect Destiny Teams are doing their best to insure that the sailors in tomorrow's Russian Navy have, at least, heard the story of Jesus. It's the one story everybody ought to know.

But God hath chosen the foolish things of the world to confound the wise;
and God hath chosen the weak things of the world
to confound the things which are mighty.
1 Corinthians 1:27 KJV

God has never needed golden boys, A-Teams, blue ribbon panels, marketing firms, or Ivy League educations.

This is not to say that God does not use our talents or education. God uses our strengths and weaknesses according to His sovereign will, but He doesn't need them. God has always done more with less than men thought adequate. Remember how He downsized Gideon's great army until only three hundred remained? What about feeding thousands with a little boy's lunch? Who can forget His strategy for reducing the fortress of Jericho? When the wine ran out at Cana, Jesus only required six pots of water. Everybody knows you need more than water to make wine, right? Wrong! Jesus didn't choose His disciples from the top of the class.

At best, he chose 'C' students. I am not commending mediocrity, by any means. I am only pointing out that what He can do is always the prime consideration, not what we can do. Every sunrise opens all doors and windows to the unlimited potential of Christ in us.

Live with the preoccupation of His ability rather than your inadequacy. God always does more with less than man thinks adequate.

Therefore say to them,
'This is the nation that has not obeyed the
LORD its God or responded to correction.
Truth has perished; it has vanished from their lips.'
Jeremiah 7:28 NIV

America has never been richer in possessions and more bankrupt in morals.

This nation was founded on godly principles and she is falling due to their erosion. You can argue and debate the spiritual acuity of the founding fathers. You can assume that they were theists and deists. You can even assume that they were far from spiritual giants, but this must be granted: our founding fathers believed that the seeds to the greatness of a nation could be found in the Bible. We were once a nation under God. Now we are a nation under a cloud. We were established with a God consciousness.

But that establishment has been overturned with a self-centeredness that threatens to shred the fabric of the American ideal. With the rapid globalization that followed the war years, moral landmarks were shifted or removed all together. We became a particularly secular nation. The cost is measured in a lost generation and a people increasingly sophisticated in evil. Prayer is abandoned – Abortion is a right – Morality is no longer a prerequisite for leadership – Christianity has been increasingly marginalized in our culture.

Jeremiah seems strangely current when viewed in a contemporary setting.

While he was sitting on the judgment seat, his wife sent to him, saying,
"Have nothing to do with that just Man,
for I have suffered many things today in a dream because of Him. "
Matthew 27:19 NKJV

Pilate should have listened to his wife. I wonder what she dreamed? Did she foresee her proud husband disgraced in Rome? Did she foresee his last tragic act of suicide?

Something shook her up to cause an interruption at the judgment seat. The situation was weighty and multi-faceted. Pilate found himself on the horns of a political and religious dilemma. For a moment he thought he had devised a foolproof plan to diffuse the situation. He would give them the choice of Barabbas or Jesus. Surely they would not suffer the release of the wicked Barabbas for this quiet prophet Jesus? Pilate's plan is like looking at divine redemption through a mirror . . . it's all back-wards. Pilate sought to redeem the life of a sinless man with the life of a scandalous sinner. God sought to redeem the lives of scandalous sinners with the life of a sinless man. Pilate's quickstep was without effect. The Jewish leaders demanded the freedom of Barabbas and the crucifixion of Jesus.

For our sakes, it's a good thing that Pilate didn't lis-ten to his wife that day. It's a good thing that his political maneuvering came up short. Jesus died so that Barabbas, and every other scandalous sinner might live – forever.

When Pilate saw that he could not prevail at all,
but rather that a tumult was rising, he took water and washed
his hands before the multitude, saying,
"I am innocent of the blood of this just Person. You see to it."
Matthew 27:24 NKJV

He knew! Pilate knew that Jesus was an innocent man. He did not fail Jesus for a lack of judgment. Pilate was a very wise ruler; a skilled politician.

There we find the roots of his failure. Pilate, knowing what was right, chose to do what was expedient. He weighed the value of a troublesome prophet against the prospect of political unrest. He maneuvered with the skill of a dancer to place responsibility on the heads of the Jewish leadership, symbolically washing his hands of all guilt. But time has not exonerated the governor. He left an innocent in the hands of violent men. He fed the wolves so that they would not devour him. His clever dodge numbered him forever with cowards. Will we be found numbered there?

Pilate stepped back in the face of mob violence. We shrink back at the prospect of embarrassment. Pilate could claim that he had prevented a great catastrophe that dark Friday. We have no claim to hide behind. Pilate could site public safety, ethnic relations, political sensitivity, the will of the people – but we can only site ignorance or cowardice when one is left in darkness who could have known the Light.

In our silence, Pilate looks almost . . . noble.

This is the confidence we have in approaching God:
that if we ask anything according to his will, he hears us.
1 John 5:14 NIV

I started to notice a change in Ted about two months ago.

At first, I thought he was just having a good run of circumstances. He had always been a melancholy sort of guy, not morose by any stretch, but much given to worry and weariness. He wouldn't have made my top ten happy people list . . . he wouldn't have made my top fifty! When circumstances got a little rocky, I would expect to see the old Ted again. But something was changing here. This morning he walked past my table at Starbucks and I couldn't help myself – I had to ask. He was "breezing" through the place with his head held high and his Bible tucked under his arm. "What has happened to you?" I asked. His eyes were dancing, and he answered, "Remember when we met about eight months ago and you encouraged me to get my prayer life in order? That's what I've done. I never miss my morning devotions and prayer."

That was it! That was all! Ted didn't look like the same guy I had come to know over the years. He was wearing his prayers. He was clothed in the confidence that comes from a great relationship with the Lord.

What are you clothing yourself in today? Wear your prayer!

For if you forgive men when they sin against you,
your heavenly Father will also forgive you.
But if you do not forgive men their sins,
your Father will not forgive your sins.
Matthew 6:14-15 NIV

There once was a man who sinned against me, and I struggled to drag him before the throne of God for judgment.

Every time I got a real good grip on his collar, I lost my bearings to the King's throne-room. For years I exhausted myself trying to drag my oppressor to justice – until I met a wise old sage. "What are you doing with that man?" he asked. "I'm taking Him to God's judgment seat," I cried. "So it is God you seek?" he asked. "Only He can judge between this man and me," I replied. His eyes flashed bright and he offered his help. "Just turn to the right, and over this rise you will find God," said he. I thanked him and hurried my prisoner over the rise, but when I topped the hill, I found no judgment court. I found my King – but He was hanging on a cross.

That cross revealed my sin in such fullness, I immediately scanned the horizon to see if anyone else could see my shame. In that moment, I knew that I had no hope of escaping the penalty of my sins. But then, with the King's dying breath, He took my sins away. Suddenly, the scene was changed.

I stood alone in perfect peace … and what of my prisoner, you ask? I lost my grip when I caught a glimpse of the cross – I lost my case to grace!

Please Pray for Muslim Children

Islamic extremism killed thousands on September 11, 2001 because the devil deceived some Muslims and led them into murderous madness. We must pray that God intervenes in the lives of Muslim children and families around the world to prevent further tragedies by bringing all the children and youth into a relationship with Jesus!

In a Muslim Nation, God's Word Still Triumphs!

Although we cannot give you complete details of how the *Book of Hope* is reaching children in predominantly Muslim areas of the world, we can share a story from one large Muslim nation. We have withheld names to protect confidentiality.

A teenaged girl in a large mostly Muslim nation had become addicted to drugs and alcohol, but she had two friends who were believers, and they were praying for her salvation. They had shared the Gospel with her, but they couldn't seem to get through.

Then they were able to get the *Book of Hope* to her. She ignored it for an entire month, but one evening as she was feeling hopeless and afraid, she began to look through it.

She rang up her friends and told them, "All the words put so much peace in my heart." Her two friends hurried to her home, read through the book with her, and led her in prayer to give her life to Christ.

Today, she has kicked her addictions and is a vibrant young believer.

*"Stand at the crossroads and look; ask for the ancient paths,
ask where the good way is, and walk in it,
and you will find rest for your souls."*
Jeremiah 6:16 NIV

The weakness of a man-made government is that it is man-made. Like a state-of-the-art jetliner brought down by human error, even the very best system of government is ultimately subject to the moral code of the people who make its laws and interpret its constitution.

The Virginia Declaration of Rights voiced the assumption that drives a democracy: *"That all power is vested in, and consequently derived from, the people."*

What if the people are immoral, or profit-driven, or blood-thirsty? Power has no inherent goodness, so those of us who see our democracy in a state of moral meltdown are left to wonder what kind of nation shall be shaped by generations to come should God be driven from the public arena and good be gutted by relativism.

James Madison, second President of the United States, wrote, *"We have no government armed with power capable of contending with human passions unbridled by morality and religion ... Our Constitution was made only for a moral and religious people. It is wholly inadequate to govern any other."*

If ever we needed good and godly leaders, it is now. We are fearful of international terrorists. We should be equally concerned about domestic termites.

Speak and act as those who are going to be judged by the law
that gives freedom, because judgment without mercy will be shown
to anyone who has not been merciful.
Mercy triumphs over judgment!
James 2:12-13 NIV

It doesn't take a lot of people to change the world.

Fueled by hatred, suicidal bombers in jet cockpits left an indelible scar on the American landscape. Willingness to die for a cause invests that cause with incredible potential – for good or for evil. The destructive power of an evil cause boggles the mind. What horrors are set in motion by hatred! How helpless we become when self-preservation is subjugated. If slaves to hatred and fear could so change the world with violence, how much more could the world be transformed by slaves to love? Our cause is the highest cause. The power of love has no equal, but who will live and die for THE CAUSE? Until we act, we only possess potential. When we love, we demonstrate God's redeeming power.

It is time for "sleepers" to be activated to extreme acts of love and mercy. When love is awakened, the gates of hell are assaulted. When love hides its face, this world becomes a very dangerous place. Our world cries out in an extreme anguish that can only be assuaged by extreme love.

We must never forget that evil's greatest enemy is good, and that justice must be tempered by mercy.

See, I am doing a new thing! Now it springs up; do you not perceive it?
I am making a way in the desert and streams in the wasteland.
Isaiah 43:19 NIV

Larry works as a research chemist for a manufacturer of non-woven fabrics. His college degree is in Forestry.

Tim's master's degree in English Literature doesn't seem to fit his role as a heavy equipment mechanic. Bill earned two business degrees, and then chose the Christian ministry. Harry Truman left retail for politics. Radio commentator Dr. Laura Schlessinger counsels the masses, but her Ph.D. is in physiology, not psychology. Starting points and milestones are not faithful indicators of where a life might end.

We live in the age and land of great opportunity. We serve a God who made a Shepherd into a King; a Persecutor into a Missionary; a Fisherman into an Apostle. Have you looked lately at where your life is leading? Are you stuck in a rut that leads down the wrong road? Does your future look dull, mediocre, or pointless? God's way leads us to purpose and fulfillment. Maybe it's time for a jailbreak?

Take the class, start that exercise program, withdraw from toxic friends, invigorate your prayer life, re-evaluate your goals, re-focus your energies, renew your marriage, resign from "deadwood" activities, do something self-less. Refuse to let a boring life run its course.

From whom the whole body fitly joined together and compacted
by that which every joint supplieth, according to the effectual working
in the measure of every part, maketh increase of the body unto
the edifying of itself in love.
Ephesians 4:16 KJV

It's an odd collection, I'll grant you that – and I really can't tell you why I haven't tossed it out. I've kept a bag full of extra parts from all of my "some assembly required" projects through the years.

I've got screws and dowels, cinches and anchors, tabs and plugs, bolts and hinges for desks and chairs and shelves and stands. I stare at this odd collection, poured out on my desk, and smile at the knowledge that almost everything I have ever assembled is missing a critical part or two. I struggle with patience. I've done a fair amount of backtracking in my time.

In the body of Christ, there are no "extra" parts. Every person has a place, a calling, a perfect fit. The secret of abundant living is to find that place and integrate one-self with a Kingdom motivation and shared purpose.

Don't waste your time trying to hammer a square peg into a round hole. You might finally achieve your goal, but the splintering pain and ultimate disfigurement of forcing the issue will leave you with a lonely question: Why?

Find God's place and purpose. The process isn't always simple and trouble-free, but the peace He gives when we have found His will is well worth the journey.

You were running a good race.
Who cut in on you and kept you from obeying the truth?
Galatians 5:7 NIV

Is your faith growing? Are your prayers being answered?

If not, maybe you had better take stock in the people you're surrounding yourself with. Proverbs 27:17 says "As iron sharpens iron, so a man sharpens the countenance of his friend." To the incorrigible Corinthians, Paul writes, *"Do not be misled: "Bad company corrupts good character" (1 Corinthians 15:33).*

Faith is either stirred up, or beat down by our closest friends. Are you living in the company of fire-lighters, or fire-fighters? Do your nearest and dearest challenge you to a higher plane or are they dragging you back to mediocrity or worse? Billy is in prison today because he was behind the wheel when a friend's friend pulled a trigger. Billy had never met the shooter before, but his poor choice of friends landed him in Central Prison for a seven-year stretch for accessory to murder. Have you been hanging out with shooters . . . people who assassinate the character of others? Have you been running with people who are constantly running their mouths?

Make a friend of somebody who is living at a higher spiritual level. Run from people who drag you down. Faith does not grow amidst fools and whiners!

He did what was right in the eyes of the LORD,
but not wholeheartedly.
2 Chronicles 25:2 NIV

I magine a wedding where the celebrants made a mutual commitment to love and to cherish for . . . five years.

Imagine the groom turning to his radiant bride and pledging to be faithful "90% of the time." The marriage covenant is a forever covenant, and so is the covenant we make with God. A half-hearted commitment invariably results in broken dreams, broken homes, broken lives, and broken hearts. Amaziah's tragic reign ended in exile and shame. He started well but could not finish. He did some good, but the dark influence of his father bore bad fruit. Doing the right thing with half a heart only deepens the sense of tragedy when sin has conceived and brought forth death.

The Christian life requires fidelity, a singular affection. The Lord requires of us that we love Him with all our heart, soul, mind and strength. We cannot make life work with a divided heart. Like an adulterous affair, a divided heart leaves all parties wounded and demeaned. Does God have your whole heart today? What other loves draw you away? Is it a job, an addiction, greed, a lust for power, or is it laziness?

Whatever keeps you from a wholehearted devotion robs you of life itself.

Do your best to present yourself to God as one approved,
a workman who does not need to be ashamed and
who correctly handles the word of truth.
2 Timothy 2:15 NIV

No matter the noble cause of science, it seems that we have always found ways to weaponize our discoveries and destroy ourselves.

The quiet and unassuming study of physics gave rise to bombs that level cities and microwave initial survivors. Long ago, nature yielded her natural poisons to unnaturally advance the procession of the Caesars or rid us of other troublesome characters. Biology stored and studied the most virulent living strains of virus and bacteria, only to unleash the horrors of Anthrax, the threat of Smallpox, and the terror of Ebola in the hands of madmen. Psychological warfare uses thought itself to defeat an adversary. There are few implements or machines that we have not used as human erasers.

The Bible is a sword to be wielded against the devil, and a light to be shined into a sin-darkened world. It is the most efficient weapon we possess for spiritual warfare. How true we are to our fallen nature when we use the Bible as a weapon to hammer one another.

Truth must be handled with love, lest the ultimate good be used for evil. We need only read of inquisitions and crusades to recognize the danger. We need only use the Scripture to a selfish end to repeat the pattern.

For the things which are seen are temporary,
but the things which are not seen are eternal.
2 Corinthians 4:18 NKJV

TAMBOV, RUSSIA: The biology teacher offered a cynical smile as I finished my presentation of the *Book of Hope.*

"This is, of course, very interesting to us," she said in a voice dripping with sarcasm. She reached for a plastic model of the human brain and held it up for the class to see. "Perhaps you can understand our problem," she said, pointing to the model. "Can you tell us how you can find any room for God here? We can examine the brain, and God is not there." Her utter contempt was breathtaking.

Before I could respond, my interpreter was chattering away. I didn't know what she was saying, but the response of the class and the sudden indignation on the face of the teacher told me that the tide had turned. In the hallway I asked what she had said. "I asked the wise teacher if she could tell the students where to find love in that brain, though we were all certain that love is real," she said. I couldn't have answered better than that.

Though we may be far removed from that cynical teacher, we too tend to trust only in things that we can see. Although God is at work in His creation and revealed to our five senses, His greatest revelations come only by faith to the spirit of man.

As soon as all the people saw Jesus,
they were overwhelmed with wonder and ran to greet him.
Mark 9:15 NIV

1975 and 1969 are years that are forever connected in my fond memories. In 1975, I got my driver's license and bought a 1969 Camaro.

Dad co-signed and followed me home. Mom was waiting at the side door when I pulled into the driveway like a conquering warlord. For a sixteen-year-old boy, this was triumph; this was the ultimate.

My love for that car was extravagant. I bought her the best wax. I spent all of my money and most of my time upgrading and detailing. Rust was surgically removed. Dirt never saw the sunrise. A new paint job, a new exhaust system (Hush Thrush), new mag wheels, high-perform-ance parts, and a "nuclear" stereo system were lovingly applied. I spent entire Saturdays working in and on my car – it was all that mattered.

I sold her in 1977 with a lump in my throat. The buyer totaled her six months later. For all my love, she rusts away in an Iowa junkyard. In the process of grow-ing up, I've learned to love people and use things. But I've also noted that growing old often destroys our sense of wonder.

We all should know that feeling of sixteen-year-old wonder, not because of what we possess, but because of what possesses us.

"I hate divorce," says the LORD God of Israel,
"and I hate a man's covering himself with violence as well as with
his garment," says the LORD Almighty.
So guard yourself in your spirit, and do not break faith.
Malachi 2:16 NIV

He climbed to the top, only to find the pinnacle to be a cold and heartless place.

A 1.1 million dollar home overlooking Lake Washington could not shelter this troubled man. Success could not light a single room in his darkened heart. And so, with life's most displaced courage, he pulled the trigger and took his own life with the severe violence of a shotgun blast. He was just 27-years-old. His records sold copies in the millions. He defined his own genre of disaffected music to a generation we called X. He wrote songs like, "I Hate Myself and I Want to Die;" a chilling self-prophesy.

Curt Cobain added his name to the long list of suicidal superstars who had everything but a reason to live. An interviewer, probing the dark nature of Cobain's lyrics, asked what Curt considered to be the greatest tragedy of his life. His response was chilling. He answered, "The divorce of my parents when I was eight-years-old." The horrors of heroin addiction took a back seat to childhood trauma; a trauma lived out day-by-day in America.

Terrorism has indeed come to America. Its victim is the family. Its assault is relentless. Its arch weapon is divorce.

But at midnight . . .
Acts 16:25 NKJV

The little conjunction "but" is one of the more dramatic words in language. It signals a change in course.

For example, if I say, "I went to the store," you might imagine that I had purchased something. However, when I say, "I went to the store, but...," all assumptions are off. Paul and Silas were brutalized in the city of Philippi. Their backs were laid open with rods carried by the magistrate's assistants. It was common practice for a foreigner (a non-Roman) to be beaten, even before trial, as a means of gathering evidence or coercing confession. No effort was made to discern the citizenship of Paul or Silas. The beaten men were then placed in stocks for an overnight stay in the local jail.

At this point, we would normally assume that they suffered through the night and got out of town at the first opportunity. *"But" at midnight, Paul and Silas were praying and singing hymns to God.* The outcome is completely unexpected. It is no wonder that the early Christians were accused of turning the world upside down – they were living upside down!

We could learn something from the Philippian prison choir. They turned a prison into a prayer room; suffering into salvation; and a jailor into a saint.

"Sirs, what must I do to be saved?" So they said,
"Believe on the Lord Jesus Christ, and you will be saved."
Acts 16:30-31 NKJV

Believing in God and believing on the Lord Jesus for salvation are not synonymous.

Asking if a person believes in God only answers the question of atheism. The pantheist finds god in everything. The animist endows the mountain with a soul. The syncretist assembles a "designer god" according to whim. The Buddhist depersonalizes God, convinced that He is unknowable. The Hindu has too many gods to know. The Universalist believes that all roads lead to God (he has no basis, but he believes it because it satisfies his sense of logic). Islam claims to show a path to God without need of Jesus.

When someone says that they believe in God, they could mean just about anything. James points out that even demons believe in God (James 2:19). Jesus said, *"I am the way, the truth, and the life. No one comes to the Father except through Me" (John 14:6 NKJV).* He claimed absolute exclusivity.

The Philippian jailor could not be saved by simply acknowledging the existence of God; he had to believe in the efficacy of the saving work of Jesus, God's son.

The one true God will not be joined to a pantheon. He stands above, and alone, and we can only know Him through Christ.

But these two things shall come to you in a moment, in one day:
The loss of children, and widowhood. They shall come upon you in
their fullness because of the multitude of your sorceries,
for the great abundance of your enchantments.
Isaiah 47:9 NKJV

Dave teaches middle school.

That fact alone would certify him for sainthood or lunacy by the application of most measures. Day in and day out, Dave slogs through the valleys and climbs the lofty peaks of the adolescent emotion, looking for teaching points and pointing kids in the right direction. I always enjoy talking school with Dave for the up-to-the-minute perspective he brings on family life in America.

"The top two struggles I see in the kids are the divorce of their parents, and the absence imposed by dual-career households." In both cases, at issue is the loss of family security and connectivity. What kind of "family" will today's middle-schooler create? What will result from hours that should have been spent with Mom and Dad having been spent with MTV? It's a frightening proposition. How much sadder, the kids who grow up in a "nuclear" family and still miss the intimacy; the connection; the mentoring that should flow through a loving and involved family life.

In an age of isolation, parents must lovingly intrude in the lives of their children. Refuse to be marginalized. Parenting cannot succeed from a distance.

The rich ruleth over the poor,
and the borrower is servant to the lender.
Proverbs 22:7 KJV

"Mr. ... Uh ... Graftree?" A reflex action rolled my eyes to the back of my head. I had another telemarketer on the line, and I knew that it would take three rejections to clear the deck.

I wanted to say, "No, no, no!" but I was too slow. The telemarketer was already reading off her 3x5 card, extolling the virtues of the latest credit card offering from First National Bank of Pequoima, so I waited and answered, "I have no interest in any new credit offerings."

She read on – "But Mr. Crabtree, FNBP offers zero percent interest." I thought I had her now – "I could never really value a credit account that didn't charge interest." She finally threw in an air miles deal, which I had to reject (it didn't include military helicopter miles). Three offers – three rejections – I was now expecting her to rattle off an 800 number I could call if I changed my mind. To my surprise, she burst out laughing ... "Military helicopter miles ... that's funny," she said. "Glad I brightened your day," said I. She clicked off to dial up another mark. I'll bet she's used to rejection.

In a culture that screams, "I want and I need," nobody needs more debt!

I saw among the simple, I noticed among the young men,
a youth who lacked judgment.
Proverbs 7:7 NIV

Life goes in circles. It's funny how a change in seating alters one's perspective. When I was seventeen, a girl's father had the audacity to "discourage" me from pursuing his daughter. He talked in poorly constructed parables and uttered thinly veiled threats. I heeded his warnings, and labeled him a jerk!

From my present seating at life's table, he now seems to be a very reasonable man. As a matter of fact, I've strengthened one of his parables (the parable of the lost limb) and made it my own. His "threats" now seem to me as firm promises. I'm making promises to all prospective suitors. My daughters have reached the dating years, and I'm just getting over the shock that they would actually want to go to dinner with any other male besides me. People say, "Don't you remember how it was when you were seventeen?"

Of course I do – which explains my Rottweiler and gun collection. I don't think I'm too unreasonable. A three-generation background check can give a young man a deep appreciation for his family heritage.

Promises can really motivate a young mind. I'm thinking about continuing my education by learning how to administer a test with a lie detector. Watch what you sow – harvest is coming!

So teach us to number our days,
that we may apply our hearts unto wisdom.
Psalm 90:12 KJV

Terry would give anything for one more day to spend with her stockbroker husband. He perished in One Trade Center one sunny New York morning. With a wistful smile, she dreams of what she might do with just one more day, and then the sadness comes again.

Frank would give anything for another hour with his dad. Minor issues fueled male ego until reason was crushed under the weight of bitterness. When his father was taken to the hospital with chest pains, Frank decided to stay at work. When he finally arrived at the hospital, he was ten minutes too late. Just one more hour – Frank wants just one more hour – he could make it right if he only had one more hour. Tania wishes she could have ten words back. Ten words destroyed one friendship and damaged several others. It would only take a minute to set things right if she could replay a single moment, and take back ten words.

Today, we have that moment, that hour, that day. Today, we can love, lead, reach, embrace, forgive, restore, enjoy, rejoice, and build. We can only do this day once. We mustn't miss its power nor squander its potential.

Wake up and smell the roses. You are living somebody else's dream.

"The heart is deceitful above all things, And desperately wicked; Who can know it?"
Jeremiah 17:9 NKJV

The movie actress was afforded every courtesy by the talk show host. She was pushing her new book on relationships, and he was doing his best to coax an intelligent statement from her collagen-enhanced lips. She had become an *expert* on relationships by tanking three of her own marriages and wrecking one or two more.

She spouted a mix of cliché and psycho-babble, admonishing us to love ourselves and accept the reality that few relationships last forever. She had learned to "follow her heart." A few more husbands and a couple more books will probably earn her an honorary doctorate and guest appearances with Oprah, Nikki, Sally, Jerry, Jenny, Maury, and Montel.

Following our hearts almost always leads to disaster. Jeremiah warns us not to follow our hearts. We need guidance that transcends our emotions, finding roots in principle and truth. We need to choose our paths according to right and wrong, not desire and circumstances.

The actress prattled on about her road to enlightenment, spinning pop psychology and hedonism into one great and confused web. How sad that today's experts rise not out of lives well-lived, but rather from a catalog of self-induced horrors survived.

"My grace is sufficient for you."
2 Corinthians 12:9 NKJV

God said to Paul, "My grace is sufficient for you." I'm glad God put His great promise in the present. If God had said, "My grace was sufficient for Moses," we would simply bear witness to historical truth. If God had said, "My grace will be sufficient in the end," we would grit our teeth and hold on for "some golden daybreak." God said, "My grace is sufficient for you."

I am so glad to know that no matter what day, what trial, what season, God's grace is all I need ... NOW! When I'm under attack, His Word says that I am *"more than a conquerer" (Romans 8:37).* When darkness falls, He is *"my light and my salvation" (Psalm 27:1).* When I'm picking up the broken pieces, He is *"the restorer of life" (Ruth 4:15).*

When I feel alone, He is *"the friend who sticks closer than a brother" (Proverbs 18:24).* When my mother and father forsake me, *"the Lord will lift me up" (Psalm 27:10).* When my resources are exhausted, He is a *"very present help in time of danger" (Psalm 46:1).* When I want to quit, He *"renews my strength" (Isaiah 40:31).*

Grace is a present blessing. Learning to trust God in the present is the key that unlocks His bright tomorrow.

But Jesus said, Suffer little children, and forbid them not,
to come unto me: for of such is the kingdom of heaven.
Matthew 19:14 KJV

She can't be more than seven-years-old. What is she doing alone on the sidewalks of St. Petersburg? That cute little boy looks as though he doesn't have a care in the world. What is he doing in an orphanage in Arkangelsk? Her eyes are as green as emeralds, and her smile could light up any room. Why does she sit apart from the other children at school #62 in Tambov? He giggles and laughs like a normal eight-year-old boy. How did he end up in a seven-by-seven prison cell in Chita?

A hundred other Russian children come alive in my memories. Thousands more blend into an overwhelming sea of need. I wake sometimes in the wee hours of the morning having been to Russia in my dreams. The sights, the sounds, the pastel-colored buildings, the over-crowded trains, the rocking of the subways, the school director's greeting, the roar in the hallways between classes - it's as if I've stepped across a continent in a moment - surprised to wake in America.

For some, its the children of the Philippines. For others, its the dark-eyed children of Peru. But for all of us who have given a *Book of Hope* to a child, it's a shared dream, an uncommon passion, to move beyond our borders and reach the children of the world.

I can do all things through Christ which strengtheneth me.
Philippians 4:13 KJV

For the most part, the church lives with false self-imposed limitations that have nothing to do with God's Word or will. Look carefully through your Bible and see how God works.

Age is not a limiter. Abraham was 100 and Sarah was 90 when the promise was fulfilled. Failure is not a limiter. Moses blew forty years trying to do God's will his way. Singleness is not a limiter. One with God is a majority – and more than enough. Location is not a limiter. He is the same whether in a dungeon, or on a mountaintop. Ethnicity is not a limiter. The Gospel crosses every color, tongue, tribe, and strata. Education is not a limiter. He uses the scholarly Pharisee (Paul) and the lowly fisherman (Peter). Background is not a limiter. He uses former demoniacs, prostitutes, swindlers, soldiers, and kings. Opportunity is not a limiter. He is the Way-Maker; the Gift Giver; the Window of Heaven, and the Door no man can shut.

He doesn't need a passport or visa. He doesn't need an investment banker or a project cost analysis. He is our Healer, Sustainer, sufficient grace, and ever-present help in times of trouble.

It's high time we cast aside our limitations that we might rise to our potential.

And his servants came near and spoke to him, and said,
"My father, if the prophet had told you to do something great,
would you not have done it?"
2 Kings 5:13 NKJV

Namaan fell into a common trap. He failed to realize that God rarely asks us to do spectacular things. He asks us to consistently perform simple tasks; to walk in a simple obedience; to live our lives quietly (1 Thessalonians 4:11).

Namaan was put off by the simplicity of the prophet's instruction. Elisha told him to go dip seven times in the Jordan River. The prospect of dipping in a muddy river lacked the dignity that Namaan had anticipated. If he were asked to sacrifice fifty oxen, lead a prayer processional through the Syrian capital, donate fifty talents of silver to the poor, and fast for a week, he would have done it. Dipping in the Jordan was just too simple; too earthy; too private for Namaan.

God grows greatness out of small obedience. We need a new awareness of the power of everyday faithfulness. What flows out of us is far greater than what can be seen in us if we take care of the little things.

God's probably not asking you to take your city, but He is asking you to love your neighbor. He's not asking you to give all you have to the poor, but He is asking you to give when you see your brother in need. Greatness cannot grow except from simple obedience.

And put a knife to your throat if you are a man given to appetite.
Proverbs 23:2 NKJV

My wife put me on her diet. Tonight I was introduced to "butter" in a bottle, no-fat salad dressing,
and dry brown rice. I'm allowed eight vanilla wafers a little later if I avoid snacking before bedtime.

Right now I'd shove my grandma aside for two hot
Pop Tarts and a cold glass of whole milk. Necessity and
pleasure don't always make a connection. I need to drop
a few pounds, but I'm not really looking forward to the
journey.

Tell me that the reward will be sweet. I can't hear you
now for the giant dinner bell that's clanging in my head.
Give me a Snickers bar and my hearing might return.
What's that? I need to improve my attitude? Meet me at
Wendy's and we'll discuss my attitude over a double-
cheeseburger.

Norman Vincent Peale couldn't paint a happy face
on a diet. Battling appetites and starting an exercise program are difficult undertakings. To refuse the challenge
only hastens the undertaker.

Only five-percent of people who successfully complete
a diet keep the weight off, but I'm going for it anyway.
Inertia has a crippling effect on body, soul, and spirit.

They shoot from ambush at the innocent man;
they shoot at him suddenly, without fear.
Psalm 64:4 NIV

The assassin chose his position with great care. He needed maximum cover, a crowd to lend the element of confusion, decoys to throw off all pursuit, and a clear line of fire.

The target had been living for weeks with a heightened sense of danger. Rumors had been traced to dead ends, indistinct warnings had sounded on his perimeters. He was being stalked – he knew it, he could feel it, but the assassin covered his tracks, leaving ghostly evidence. The target would not live in fear or go into hiding, so the ghastly shadow dance continued day into day, week into week.

The assassin was a patient man, moving beneath the radar. Killing was easy. Getting away clean presented the greater challenge. He chose his weapon with great care. Lying in a shooter's prone position, he slowed his breathing as his target came into view. It really came down to a question of timing. The target stepped into the crosshairs. The shooter let out a long controlled breath, squeezed the trigger, and quietly walked away.

Another perfect hit; another clean escape; another day in the life of a highly-skilled gossip. The target never knew what hit him; shot through the heart; another hapless victim of the character assassin.

But Samuel said to him, "I will not go back with you.
You have rejected the word of the LORD,
and the LORD has rejected you as king over Israel!"
1 Samuel 15:26 NIV

I am fascinated by people who choose to live in the shadow of a volcano; build on barrier islands; rebuild in a flood plain; marry thrice-divorced playboys, or smoke after lung surgery. They are gamblers at heart, or unaware of the odds. Sooner or later, volcanoes blow, hurricanes reshape the beach, rivers flood, character is unmasked, and cigarettes kill. When wisdom takes a backseat to desire; when emotional attachments bind us to bad ground; when the thrill of a chase exceeds the capture, we are destined for disappointment and disaster.

King Saul chose to build on a fault line. He ignored God's specific instruction and rewrote God's plan after his own desire. This was no small slip; no minor oversight. Saul showed contempt for God's will and his life began to sink down in the quicksand of rebellion. Obedience is always a simple thing. Cover-up and deceit become increasingly complex. God's judgment on Saul was concise and terrible: rejected . . . rejected by God!

We make a grave error when we picture God as an over-indulgent parent. We're only fooling ourselves when we think our indiscretions carry no consequence. Impulse closes our prison door, and rebellion turns the key.

> *Then Samuel left for Ramah, but Saul went up to his home in*
> *Gibeah of Saul. Until the day Samuel died, he did not go*
> *to see Saul again, though Samuel mourned for him. And the LORD*
> *was grieved that he had made Saul king over Israel.*
> *1 Samuel 15:34-35 NIV*

At this point, the madness begins. The bright promise of the king who stood head and shoulders above his countrymen will never be realized. From this point, we trace the meanderings of a madman in kingly robes. Samuel has abandoned him. Insanity races within to consume his mind and cloud his judgments.

Never again will Saul know the comfort of God's presence, nor the power of His prophetic word. His administration will flounder in incoherence. The glory days are past. Once-bright hope smolders in the wreckage of a life that could have been. His house will never throw off this mantle of tragedy. He is the subject of God's regret.

He is a lesson for the ages. Because he did not consider the commandment of the Lord above his own desire for personal glory, he is abandoned. A dread disease would have been better. Sudden death on a field of battle may have softened his remembrance. Rather, Saul was left to rule, and to live, devoid of God's presence. It is no wonder that David, who watched from afar, would plead with God after his own moral failure, *"Do not take Your Holy Spirit from me"* (Psalm 51:11).

Beware that you never lose the wonder; the power; the pleasure of God's presence.

. . . God, who gives us richly all things to enjoy.
1 Timothy 6:17 NKJV

I learned a lesson in the Starbucks line; a lesson I've learned to apply. When you're filling life's cup for the daily routine, always leave room for the cream. It's the "cream" of life that takes off the bitter edge. It's the "cream" that softens the blow. It's the "cream" that adds richness to an ordinary blend.

"Cream" re-colors the blackest daily grind. When your cup is too full and your schedule too busy, the meaning of life is easily lost. When there's no room for laughter, there's no room for living. When daily joys are pushed out by pressure, you're heading for a spill.

Leave room every day for the simplest of pleasures; a quiet thanksgiving; a memory that brings a smile; a crimson sunrise; a morning cup of your favorite brew; a child's hug; a tender embrace; a hopeful thought; a thoughtful word; time in the Scriptures; a whispered prayer; genuine laughter; genuine love; misty-eyed gratitude; remembered priorities. Schedules, deadlines, quotas, and career devour our time without remorse. Success leaves us empty and rewards demand more. There's always more trouble waiting at tomorrow's door.

Learn a good lesson as you follow your dream. Life is always better when you leave room for the cream.

. . .God was in Christ reconciling the world to Himself, not imputing their trespasses to them, and has committed to us the word of reconciliation.
2 Corinthians 5:19 NIV

The corridor of the old music building was dark, narrow, and long. Well-worn indoor/outdoor carpet of an indistinguishable blue/green masked the popping of the old floor joints as I stepped lightly down the hallway. I was very nervous – and that surprised me – I was rarely nervous about anything.

I paused in front of the last door on the right, took a deep breath, and knocked. The instructor greeted me with mild surprise and invited me in. We exchanged a few "how are you's" and then – an awkward silence. I cleared my throat and stammered, "I – I've come ... I – I just wanted to ... I finally framed my request and sighed in relief. Sweat was running down the small of my back – sweating in February!

I have no memory of the words that followed. We shook hands, and he opened the door. I moved quickly down the hallway. With a misty eye, the instructor had given his daughter to me. My knees felt weak. On the sidewalk, it occurred to me that he had "committed to me" his most valued possession.

I still strive to prove myself worthy of such a sacred trust. Yet, there is a greater trust that God has placed in us. To us, He has entrusted His message to the world; the only hope of eternal life.

Rejoice in the Lord always. Again I will say, rejoice!
Philippians 4:4 NKJV

How dull and dead the church becomes when we reduce God to church-going and ritual. I wonder, should we have ears to hear on Sunday morning, if God does not shout from heaven, "Oh please, you're not going to do that again, are you?" The Bible reveals a God who is incredibly creative. Just three verses into the Book we find Him at work: "Let there be." Just a few verses before the curtain drops with a final amen in Revelation, we find Him declaring, *"Behold, I make all things new."*

We serve the God who revels in the work of transformation, reformation, recreation, and reconciliation. We serve the God who rescues, renews, and revives. We serve the God who made everything from nothing; brings to nothing the plans of my enemies; plans our days and sets our paths in right places.

We serve the God of the new day, the new year, the new life, the new creation, the new birth, and the new covenant. The heart of God grieves over his faithless and stubborn children. I wonder if God finds His children incredibly boring?

Christ is come to the earth. It's time to sing, and dance, and build, and reach. We have the most exciting mission on planet earth. Get out of the box. It might be a coffin.

But he disdained to lay hands on Mordecai alone, for they had told him of the people of Mordecai. Instead, Haman sought to destroy all the Jews who were throughout the whole kingdom of Ahasuerus – the people of Mordecai.
Esther 3:6 NKJV

Hitler was not the first despot to seek the destruction of the Jews. From antiquity, they have fought to survive in a hostile world. God has miraculously delivered His people again and again.

On the day of her rebirth in 1948, Israel was attacked on three borders. She prevailed. Throughout modern times, all attacking armies have ultimately given up ground to Israel. To this day, there is a virulent strain of enmity living in the Middle-East, working for the complete annihilation of the Jewish nation.

How contemporary the book of Esther seems against this modern backdrop. The villain of the book of Esther was an evil man named Haman. For vanity alone he plotted genocide. This fact alone must place him in a rogue's gallery of despicable humanity. Surely in Haman we see the worst of men. He hated a race. He hated the innocent. He hated the unknown. Offended by Mordecai, he revealed a grotesque arrogance.

This same arrogance lives today in the bigot's heart. He judges himself superior. He hates without reason. He strikes the weak, revealing a cowardly heart.

Don't allow even a dusting of bigotry to pollute your soul. Remember Haman. Bigots often hang on their own gallows (see Esther 7:10).

And she said, No man, Lord. And Jesus said, Neither do I condemn thee: go thy way; from henceforth sin no more.
John 8:11 ASV

SIERRA MAESTRA, NICARAGUA: Brenda lived a double life. She worked at the school by day and worked the streets at night. Abandoned by her husband, she sold her body to provide for her children.

The hopelessness in such circumstances numbs the soul even as it wastes the body. Brenda needed a real friend; someone to break her out of her prison of darkness. On June 22 of last year, an Affect Destiny Team from California visited Brenda's school. They delivered the *Book of Hope* and invited Brenda to the Crusade that night. Brenda was waiting outside before the doors were opened. She heard a simple Gospel message, and when the altar call was given, she came weeping. "I want to change my life," she said. "I can't continue living the way I'm living."

What can a group of American volunteers offer someone like Brenda, struggling in the grips of poverty and prostitution? They can offer her truth that sets a captive free. They can offer her a local church to minister to her family and disciple her in the Scriptures. In a word, they can offer her HOPE!

Brenda left the crusade with a glow on her face and peace in her heart. For the first time in a long time ... Brenda held hope for the future.

Please Pray for South Africa
Population under age 18: 16,550,000

South Africa struggles with poverty, race relations, apartheid's brutal history, dissolution of the tribal system, and perhaps most difficult to overcome: an AIDS epidemic. Recently, it was reported that one in five people in South Africa was already HIV-positive. Please pray that the *Book of Hope* wins souls and that God's power transforms lives to defeat this deadly disease!

Enine Learns to Resist the Devil!

Enine was a beautiful 15-year-old South African girl, whose family struggled with abject poverty. Usually there was enough to eat, but just barely.

Like other teenagers, Enine wanted desperately to be grown-up, especially if it meant she could have some nice clothes and jewelry of her own.

That's why she was overwhelmed when people from the Church of Satan offered her exactly what she wanted: clothes and jewelry. Enine started sneaking out at night to attend midnight black masses.

Then Enine received the *Book of Hope* at school. She knew that, as a Satanist, she should get rid of the book. But she was intrigued.

Enine saw herself in the story of Satan's attempt to tempt Jesus in the wilderness. And when she read of the little girl whom Jesus raised from the dead, Enine found hope. Enine had been desperately afraid that she, too, might die, as so many have from AIDS. But in the pages of the *Book of Hope*, she found One who could defeat death!

Enine joyfully gave her heart to Jesus. Then she returned the clothes and jewelry to the church of Satan. Today, Enine, her mother and her little brother and sister have all come to Christ and attend church together.

Fight the good fight of the faith; take hold of the eternal life,
to which you were called and for which you made the
good confession in the presence of many witnesses.
1 Timothy 6:12 RSV

It seems that Paul finds his protégé to be a bit timid. "Fight!" Paul says. "Fight the good fight of faith." The church needs a few more fighters these days. I'm not talking about infighters, but rather those who can wield the Sword of the Spirit to do battle against our real adversary.

We are adequately supplied with weaponry (Ephesians 6:14-18) and allies (1 Corinthians 12:14). We fail to appreciate what God has given to us. Instead of embracing one another and consolidating our power, we fight like children over trinkets and toys. Instead of walking by faith, we shuffle in fear. Instead of taking hold of our weapons on a battlefield, we're found finger-painting in the nursery!

Instead of triumphant confidence, we overestimate the strength of our adversary. Instead of boldness, we idle in uncertainties. Instead of pulling down strongholds, we pick apart one another. Instead of manifesting the power of God, we languish in meanness and mediocrity.

The church is at her best when united for Christ, and against evil. Shoulder to shoulder we are intimidating. Separated we are easily intimidated. Victory is sure for those who unite, and fight!

. . . I will build my church.
Matthew 16:18 KJV

These five words have saved my life! To know that God is wholly committed to the building of His church rescues and revives me. I've witnessed levels of commitment in churches that runs so low that it is amazing the doors are kept open. I've struggled with my level of passion and commitment to the church. At times I've felt so weary I thought about turning in my hard hat and finding another line of work.

But no matter what level of commitment I see or feel, God is committed to the building of His church. Building is always costly. Church visions are a dime a dozen. Fifty good books point out fifty good ways to get the job done, but no plan comes cheap. Building is costly! It eats up commitment. It devours human capital. It wearies our spiritual muscles. It challenges our limitations. If it weren't for the renewal God promises (Isaiah 40:31) we would give out in no time!

God is totally committed to seeing this project to completion. Have you ever envisioned God in a hardhat studying a thick set of blueprints? It's not far off the mark! The prints are perfect. The Builder is *"out of this world!"* The possibilities are mind-boggling. Put your faith in the Master-builder.

*Wise people store up knowledge, But the mouth of the
foolish is near destruction.*
Proverbs 10:14 NKJV

Idle talkers take no thought for the damage they do.
Twisted values feed destructive behaviors that destroy
families, churches, businesses and friendships. Tearing
down is cheap. "A monkey with a match can destroy
more in an hour than a thousand wise men can build in
a year," said Clovis Chappell. The Chicago fire was started in a shed by a cow.

I've seen bigger fires started in churches by fools. I
helped put out a fire like that last week, but there wasn't
much to salvage. A year invested in rebuilt trust was
smoked with a bit of slander followed by a lie. The arson-
ist was caught, but I doubt if she will ever stop playing
with matches. Some people just can't resist a tasty bit of
gossip.

Every Christian should think before they speak. Our
words should build (Ephesians 4:29). They should reflect
value and beauty. Proverbs speaks of the wise "storing up"
knowledge. We would be a healthier people if our store-
houses were full and carefully guarded by discretion.

You don't have to say everything you know. A little
bit of self-editing will keep you from disaster. A foolish
word invites a firestorm.

...and the gates of hell shall not prevail against it.
Matthew 16:18 KJV

Gibraltar will crumble before the church is conquered. She is inevitable, invincible, inescapable, incredible, enduring, overcoming, and unbeatable. She is endued with power, entrusted with redemption, encouraged by the Spirit, engaged in a winning warfare, and equipped for every good work.

We fail to appreciate the gift that God has given to us in one another. Instead of embracing one another and consolidating our power, we fight like children over trinkets and toys. Instead of walking by faith, we shuffle in fear. Instead of taking hold of our weapons, we're found finger-painting in the nursery! Instead of triumphant confidence, we overestimate the strength of our adversary. Instead of boldness, we idle in uncertainties. Instead of pulling down strongholds, we pick apart one another. Instead of manifesting the power of God – we languish in mediocrity.

God's overcoming power is ours for the taking. Together, we can change the world as we unite our hearts. God has guaranteed our complete triumph against our hellish foe. Though the signs of the time are dark and foreboding, the greatest hour for the church is at hand.

Let the church BE the church!

Humble yourselves in the sight of the Lord, and He will lift you up.
James 4:10 NKJV

Want to test a friendship? Tell your friend that he needs to humble himself. Chances are, he won't perceive it as a positive development in the relationship (this gives light to the shallow nature of most relationships). Humility is a character trait that we honor, respect and revere . . . in other people!

Humbling oneself is generally cast in negative light, as though humility were punitive in nature. Humility finds its antithesis in pride. Pride is the natural, boastful prerogative of our fallen nature. Humility is the healthy offspring of repentance and discipline. Pride carries a false sense of grasping and achieving. Humility carries the sense of releasing, even losing. Pride is all about ascending. Humility is all about descending. Pride is about rights and status. Humility is about surrender and servanthood. Pride is widely regarded as necessary for success. Humility is the spiritual basis of greatness. Pride precedes every great fall. Humility precedes every great deed.

Proud men stop praying. Humble men stop sinning. Proud men admit no wrong. Humble men receive great grace.

The good news is that we can humble ourselves. The bad news is that most men won't.

For where your treasure is, there your heart will be also.
Luke 12:34 NIV

My eldest daughter was just issued a driver's license. I just paid the insurance premium. An insurance executive just bought a new Learjet. I need a money machine. Correction – I am a money machine!

Birthdays, graduation, anniversary, insurance, and college have made me into a 24-hour ATM. I can't turn around without someone pushing a button for fast cash. I'd like to hang a sign on my window that says, "Out of Order." It's only going to get worse. I'll soon have three girls in college at the same time (What were we thinking?). I'll soon have two additional insurance premiums. This spend-fest will reach its apex when I preside over three weddings. I'll smile in all the pictures – or will that be a grimace? I hope they marry insurance executives with Learjets – just kidding! A crumbling stock market got me thinking about true value investments.

The work of advancing God's Kingdom is, without question, the greatest investment a man can make. Investment in family takes up the second position. I recently interviewed a man who has mounds of money and a bankrupt family life. Though he didn't know it, he helped me re-align my values.

Where goes your treasure – there goes your heart.

For we are God's fellow workers; you are God's field,
God's building.
1 Corinthians 3:9 NIV

Many people imagine God as a white-robed, white-headed, backlit, distant Monarch enthroned in an ethereal chamber amidst the clouds. Have you ever pictured God as a Master Builder surveying a site with blueprints and a plumb line? Have you ever caught a glimpse of the Creator brooding over a desolate wasteland?

I have seen Him, this Master Builder, blueprints in hand, gazing out over the barren Russian steppe. I have seen Him, this Creative Genius, surveying the great cities of the world. I have seen Him set massive foundations in the blood-spattered ruins of Bosnia. I have seen Him, this Brilliant Innovator, building a mighty church on martyr's blood in China. I have seen Him, marking off dimensions, gathering in His laborers, assembling His equipment, inspecting every footing, strengthening every column, assigning every task, and empowering every willing worker. I see, in Him, divine ability, perfect planning, uninterrupted supply, power to dig, power to lift, power to demolish, power to fabricate, power to annex, and power to finish!

We are His ultimate project. We are His passionate vision. We are His work in progress, and He is determined to bring us to completion.

For you died, and your life is hidden with Christ in God.
Colossians 3:3 NKJV

HIV is classed as a retrovirus. Unlike viruses that invade the body to be killed off by our immune systems, HIV copies its DNA blueprint into the host cell's chromosomes. Even if HIV is overcome by the body's immune system, the copied blueprint begins to churn out new HIV. To kill the invader, you have to kill the host.

Sin is not a floating virus picked up by mankind at some stage in our lifecycle. Through Adam's fall, sin was written into our spiritual DNA, like a retrovirus. To kill the invader, you have to kill the host.

Paul understood this principle nineteen centuries before we knew of viruses and retroviruses. The eradication of sin comes only through death. Victory over sin comes only through the resurrection life imparted to us by God through the death of His Son Jesus. The glory of the cross is that sin can be "killed off" in the host through the death of another. Jesus took on himself the sins of the whole world that we might be clean to the very core of our being; to the DNA of the soul (1 John 2:2).

We are modern-day miracles. We are creatures of eternal significance. Through Christ, we have triumphed over the ultimate death. In Christ we have gained eternal life.

Of whom we have many things to say, and hard to be uttered,
seeing ye are dull of hearing.
Hebrews 5:11 KJV

You are sitting at the sonar table in an Ohio class nuclear submarine. The operator places the hydrophones over your ears and asks you to identify anything you can hear. To help you out, the boat has been brought to all-stop. You are suspended in the inky blackness of the ocean in the most silent of submarines, straining to hear something – anything. There is a gentle swishing, that just might be the sound of blood rushing through your ears. A few gurgles and clicks almost cover a slight groaning in the distance.

"What can you hear?" asks the chief of the boat, with a silly grin on his face. You close your eyes tightly and concentrate on vague whispers that tell no secrets. "Nothing," you say. "Stone-cold silence."

"Let Bobby give a listen," he says. Bobby dons the phones and listens for about ten seconds. "Russian Akula class submarine 1500 yards off the port bow; surface contact – probably a fishing trawler – beyond the sub; three, possibly four whales off the starboard bow . . . and it's raining on the surface." "Don't feel bad," says the chief. "Bobby knows what to listen for. He's spent *hours* listening and training."

Have you ever wondered why some people seem to hear God's voice so clearly?

For all the gods of the nations are idols.
Psalm 96:5 NIV

The synthetic god of American pluralism watches over a decaying culture with unseeing eyes. Fashioned from the grief and shock of crashing towers, he now lists to the left, irrelevant and forgotten.

He never stood a chance, this synthetic god assembled for the sake of unity. He is as dead as Baal and Dagon of old. He is a meaningless sentiment shared by the godless clerics of godless religions. He is a silent god created in committee. He does not offend, he does not demand, he does not judge, he does not speak, he does not love, he does not intervene, and he does not redeem. His umbrella is large enough to make room for Buddha, Mohammed, and forty million Hindu gods. Because he embraces all things, he stands for nothing.

He is a cosmic contradiction; a compendium of confusion. He is popular among philosophers, convenient for politicians, the darling of new-agers, and the slave of human wisdom. He is one man's higher power, another's guiding principle, another's spiritual inner journey, and yet another's quick remedy for a throbbing conscience.

What shall become of the people who follow this synthetic god, but an ever-creeping darkness followed by eternal night?

*For I have told him that I will judge his house forever for
the iniquity which he knows, because his sons made themselves vile,
and he did not restrain them.*
1 Samuel 3:13 NKJV

The most popular 21-year-old in the world takes the stage clad in skin-tight leather and a no-secrets halter. Her energy level could light a small city. The band is world-class. The dancers move as one to create a provocative backdrop for the platinum blonde superstar. She belts out a lyric that really doesn't matter.

If you don't know what this show is about, you're dead or crazy. The kids have no trouble getting the message. The sexually charged performance doesn't seem to bother Dad or Mom who shell out twenty-five bucks for twelve-year-old Sally to attend the concert. Nobody seems worried about role modeling, appropriateness, influence, or (dare I say it) holiness.

Dad sure doesn't like it when Sally starts to dress like the rock star, and dance like a pagan, but what can he say? He bought the ticket! Mom doesn't like the rising rebellion she sees in her daughter and friends, but what can she say? She buys the CD's and videos!

Dad is asleep at the switch. Sally's attitudes are out of control. Mom notices that Sally seems to be losing interest in the church – "Hmmm – must be something wrong with the youth pastor."

... you shall be witnesses to Me in Jerusalem.
Acts 1:8 NKJV

This morning I listened to a great missionary. Far removed from friends and family, he labors in a dangerous and deprived location. He knows few creature comforts. His life is consumed with one compelling purpose: to get people to Jesus.

The missionary's message awakened awareness in me to the compartmentalized nature of my life. When the day's work is done, I go home to predictable comforts. I am surrounded by plush. I am enveloped in plenty. Though I am always accessible through telephone, it is not difficult to leave the office at the office. Though I respond to occasional emergencies, I enjoy a life of ease when measured against the life of my missionary colleague. I know that God called me to this home field, but I must never make the fatal error of divorcing myself from the missionary endeavor.

We are all missionaries. The passion that drives a missionary into the frontier should drive us into the heart of our fallen culture. Spiritual fulfillment can only be found as the great commission infuses everything we say and do with life-giving power.

If I cannot relate to the life of my missionary friend, I must go first to my knees – then, to my world.

That they may set their hope in God.
Psalm 78:7 NKJV

SOUTH AFRICA: One in five are affected with the AIDS virus in South Africa. Health officials expect that half of the children under sixteen will die before they reach sixteen.

Amidst the bright hopes of a prosperous and pampered nation, we forget so many live in a culture of death. What hope can the philosopher offer to the millions living on a razor's edge? Medical breakthroughs come at a snails pace. When a magic potion is discovered, Africa will receive it last; economics rule the world. What hope can we offer, living on the other side of CNN, well insulated from the epidemic? What message can comfort a nine year-old girl, moving through the early stages of decline? She has watched the disease ravage her family and friends. She knows what awaits her. Shall we preach acceptance and help her resign herself to the hard ways of the world? Will she die without hope? This culture of death cries out to us for the only message adequate to meet the needs of the crisis: the message of eternal life in Christ. Even now, the *Book of Hope* is being distributed in South Africa.

Pause a moment and pray for the children and the workers. Help us change the world, one child at a time - before it's too late.

Sow your seed in the morning, and at evening let not your hands be idle,
for you do not know which will succeed, whether this or that,
or whether both will do equally well.
Ecclesiastes 11:6 NIV

I'm scrambling again! I put off my shopping until the last minute. I can't find a card that sends the right message. I've had to settle for a late reservation. My magical night is turning into a nightmare. Procrastination got me again – so I'm limping along, hoping to salvage and save face.

Procrastination always leads to a lousy destination. Tom is scrambling again! He has neglected his marriage for years. He says he loves her. She says she's leaving. He's playing catch up. He's not catching up fast enough. Shelly is scrambling again! She chased the big career and lost touch with her son. Now she's spending her profits on his rehab bills. Guilt is eating her alive. She would give her Lexus to turn the clock back ten years. Ted is scrambling again! He has played games with the things of God and quite suddenly his life fell apart. *"Where do I even begin, Lord? I can't save face with You. How can You ever make something good out of this mess?"*

Truth is, we all waited a little too late to come to Jesus. We all would have been better off if we had sought Him earlier. The wonder of the cross is that Jesus' grace is extended to procrastinators too.

Don't wait another minute. Some things are too good to miss.

*Then Moses gave an order and they sent this word throughout the camp:
"No man or woman is to make anything
else as an offering for the sanctuary."
Exodus 36:6 NIV*

Can you imagine a church service where the preacher stands up halfway through the offering and says, "Stop giving, we have more than enough? John, put that hundred dollar bill back in your pocket now ... we have all that we need." Can you imagine such a thing? I can't either!

It happened during a church construction project in the Sinai. The people gave beyond the need. They willingly gave daily until Moses ordered them to stop (Ex. 36:3). I marvel at the wilderness spectacle. I search for the keys to such spontaneous generosity and commitment. Exodus doesn't give us much in the way of personal thoughts and motives, but we can identify a few keys. These people had witnessed the power of God in miraculous provision. They lived in the years of manna in the morning and quail fillet at night. They were *certain* of God's provision.

Could it be that we are guarded in our giving because we doubt the surety of God's provision for us? Must he provide manna in the morning and quail at night before we grant him complete access to our hoarded resources? Through the generosity of nomads He built His tabernacle. Now He builds His Kingdom. Can the same generosity be found among us?

*"A farmer went out to sow his seed. As he was scattering the seed,
some fell along the path, and the birds came and ate it up."*
Matthew 13:3-4 NIV

He was a "sloppy sower," this farmer who went out to sow his seed. It seems that he took no care to target his seed on the best soil. Seed fell on the path, seed fell on the rocky places, seed fell on shallow soil, and seed fell among thorns. The farmer didn't care much for detail work. He knew what he could, and what he couldn't do. He could not command the rains, therefore, he could not make the seed germinate. He could not command the sun, therefore, he could not command the crop to grow. He could not guarantee the measure of the yield, therefore, he adopts a wise strategy of maximum coverage.

A "detail guy" might avoid the more obvious dead zones, but the farmer didn't want to lose the grain that grew tall on the edges of the path. The targeted planner might avoid the rocky places, but the farmer knew that there was a small harvest to be gleaned in the clefts of the rocks – and the farmer survived on that margin.

The parable speaks loud and clear to the sowers of God's life-giving seed: SOW IT EVERYWHERE! God's great plan for a spiritual harvest demands that every man be given the opportunity to receive the seed. He will give the increase, if we will scatter the seed – EVERYWHERE.

*Keep your lives free from the love of money and be
content with what you have.*
Hebrews 13:5 NIV

In the year of my birth, even the homely Rambler had tail fins. 1959 was the peak year for useless and gaudy auto design. Cadillac, Chevrolet, Ford and American Motors stretched the average car by an average foot and a half in length, and a half-ton in weight.

Harley Earl is recognized as the father of the tail fin. He was an eccentric designer, but you already knew that if you have laid eyes on a '59 Cadillac. Earl was employed for one purpose: To make Americans believe that last year's design was out of date.

Tail fins did the trick, and Detroit produced metal monsters that caused a Methodist bishop to bellow, "Who are the madmen who built cars so long they cannot be parked and are hard to turn in corners, vehicles with hideous tail fins, full of gadgets and covered with chrome, so low that an average human being has to crawl in the doors and so powerful that no man dare use the horsepower available?" The madmen knew the marketing power of discontent.

Take a minute and catalog your desires. Do you really need the biggest and best, or are you off chasing tail fins and gadgets? When desire trumps design, we're apt to end up in the land of the bizarre!

I will never leave thee, nor forsake thee.
Hebrews 13:5 KJV

Abandoned. Is there a greater terror than to be rejected and isolated? I've seen it in the red-rimmed eyes of a husband who came home to an empty house. I've seen it in the angelic face of a Russian orphan. I've seen it in a downcast worker, laid off after twenty-two years. I've heard it in the mournful cry of a woman who found the evidence of her husband's intimacy with another. I've felt it in my heart as a couple left my office, and the church. Abandoned.

People walk away for a great number of reasons. Sometimes it's for self-preservation. Sometimes it's for selfishness. Sometimes it's for the better. Most times, it's for the worse.

Jesus' prayer for the church was that the Father "make us one." We are made for relationship, not rejection. Running is always easier than wrestling through hardship. The grass is always greener on the other side of the fence – but it's not your grass. We would do well to emulate the Father who demonstrates fidelity though we wander. It is the message that Jesus held until His last minute here on earth (Matthew 28:20).

When you want to run from trouble, run to the Word instead. Faith and flight have little in common. Short-term relief comes at a very high price.

But each one is tempted when he is drawn away by his
own desires and enticed.
James 1:14 NKJV

The devil is expert at closing the deal! Our own desires sell us empty promises. When we are "drawn away," then we are enticed.

The best understanding of the Greek word for enticed is "entrapped." At the root, it is the language of the con, a bait and switch proposition. I am convinced that our adversary is more skilled than the most seasoned sales manager at closing the sale. He springs the trap when our desires have taken control of our senses. When we fail to battle temptation, we are selling our own souls.

Against such a powerful adversary, how can we stand? We must recognize that God has placed a limit on the Devil's power to tempt us. Paul advises us that God will not allow us to be tempted beyond our ability to resist (1 Corinthians 10:13). He will make a way of escape. The imagery is powerful. Our desires draw us closer and closer to danger – Satan positions himself to spring the trap – desire takes us to the edge of sanity – God provides a sudden open door.

Victory is won or lost at this critical point. One step more and we're tumbling into the abyss. This is no place to linger. We must flee (1 Corinthians 6:18, 10:14). Run like the wind. You are not pre-destined to fall (Jude 1:24).

Wait for the LORD; be strong and take
heart and wait for the LORD.
Psalm 27:14 NIV

Sometimes you just have to hold on. Don't try to fix it. Don't launch a new plan. Don't give in. Don't lose hope – just hold on. Sometimes we exhaust ourselves in the midst of a storm, which, by its very nature, will pass over.

Richard Exley said it this way: "Only a fool would try to dig a storm cellar in the middle of a tornado." I've witnessed that level of foolishness. I've seen families destroyed through impatience and over-reaction. I've watched ministries sink because a leader panicked and pulled the plug. I've presided over the tragic funeral of a desperate man who couldn't find a door, so he pulled a trigger. Hold on! Paul had a hundred chances to quit. Shipwrecked, disappointed, run out of town, stoned and left for dead – and that's just the beginning. Paul spent years imprisoned, often without knowing when his case might be heard.

What could he do? Sometimes, he just held on. He wasn't writing every day. He didn't have visitors every day. At times, the most important missionary in the Bible sat still – alone – in a cell. Paul held fast in the darkness, and the Lord opened up bright new opportunities. This storm will pass. A new day is dawning. You'll see His plan in time, if you just hold on.

By pride comes nothing but strife.
Proverbs 13:10 NKJV

The valet of the late Kaiser Wilhelm II said, "I cannot deny that my master was vain. He had to be the central figure in everything. If he went to a christening, he wanted to be the baby. If he went to a wedding, he wanted to be the bride. If we went to a funeral, he wanted to be the corpse."

I've met a few little Kaisers in my time. They belong to the "hurt class" of people in a church. The "hurt class" are constantly offended, continually whining, forever needy, never happy, and always finding fault. They would portray themselves as perpetual victims, but their discontent is rooted in their longing for attention.

Since they cannot have "center stage," they draw whatever spotlight they can manipulate. Foolishly, we rush in to try to give them a sense of security that can only be found in relationship with the Lord. We wonder why we can never give enough to these folks.

We wonder why they drain us so. We wonder why, for all our efforts, no progress is made. The answer is simple: only Jesus can anchor a drifting soul, and our labored efforts are a sorry substitute.

Insecurity that is not remedied by divine encounter will never be successfully treated through the greatest of human intention.

Then He will answer them, saying, "Assuredly, I say to you, inasmuch as you did not do it to one of the least of these, you did not do it to Me."
Matthew 25:45 NKJV

The girl caught my attention as she weaved her way along the sidewalk. She paused for a moment, hollow-eyed, twenty-something, emaciated. I held her gaze for a second, and then her eyes shifted as she took two faltering steps. Her lips moved soundlessly. The light turned and I shot across the intersection toward the safety of the middle classes. Conversation swirled around me, but I couldn't hear a word.

All senses were arrested by a voice that whispered somewhere in the back of my mind . . . *"She's somebody's little girl! She's the hope child turned hopeless! She's a shattered mother's dream – a walking corpse on a Florida sidewalk."*

She is one in millions – uniquely created by God and lost in a zombie world that rarely collides with mine. I've heard it said that America is "over-evangelized," but I don't believe it. They surround us – the lost, the lonely, the losers, the least, the last. They confound us – addicts, drifters, abandoned, molested. They repulse us – yes they do – and that truth should break our hearts and blind our eyes with tears.

It's no wonder Jesus is absent from our fine cathedrals and plush sanctuaries. We've forgotten the "least of these," and we've left Him in the streets.

Jesus said to her, ". . . My hour has not yet come."
John 2:4 NKJV

Jesus lived an intentional life. His movements were measured, yet He never seemed to be in a hurry. His purpose and His practice formed a perfect union. No life since has been lived so efficiently.

If you will study His life, you must consider how you conduct your own. Are you living life, or is life living you? Are you purposed or pointless? Are you proactive or reactive? Is your hand on the rudder, or are you lashed to the mast?

Satan gets great mileage out of discouragements and distractions. We're often surprised that trouble seems to come in bunches, but that is just how the devil works. Multiple attacks at unprotected moments leave us reeling like a punch-drunk fighter. We expected sunshine, but we got a blizzard. We expected happiness, not a hassle. We expected an easy walk in the park, but the park turned into a jungle, and the walk turned into a chase.

It's true that trouble comes in twins and triplets. Multiple distractions rob us of a singular focus. A singular focus for Christ is the devil's worst nightmare.

Live an intentional life. Pursue a Godly purpose. Don't let anything come between you and the great commandment (Mat. 22:37) or the great commission (Mat. 28:19).

Now Cain talked with Abel his brother; and it came to pass,
when they were in the field, that Cain rose up
against Abel his brother and killed him.
Genesis 4:8 NKJV

Evolution is a hopeless theory. Darwin grappled with its dark side when he recognized that the evolutionary track of mankind would necessitate the elimination of the weak. Upon the death of a friend, Alfred Lord Tennyson captured the violent and godless nature of Darwin's theory in the poem, "In Memorium": *"Are God and Nature then at strife, that Nature lends such evil dreams, So careful of the type she seems, so careless of the single life. Who trusted God was love indeed, and love Creation's final law – Tho Nature, red in tooth and claw, with ravine shrieked against his creed."*

In the absence of God, nature plays His role with a cold and brutal violence. The last century seems to be the confirmation of Darwin's darkest fears. The greatest atrocities and slaughter of innocents in the history of the world have occurred under the watch of our most educated generation.

From the killing fields of Cambodia, to the mass graves of Rwanda, to the burning churches in East Timor, to the violent inner cities of America, godlessness holds the door for violence. The answer to our violent propensities cannot be found within us. We need outside help, lest Darwin's darkest fears become our present nightmare.

*Beloved, do not avenge yourselves, but rather give
place to wrath; for it is written,
"Vengeance is Mine, I will repay," says the Lord.
Romans 12:19 NKJV*

Getting even is a costly waste of time. The sweet taste of vengeance conceals a venom that numbs the soul. Revenge is a powerful and deceptive emotion. It fills up our prisons. It destroys our relationships. Revenge is obsessive, consuming, and insatiable. The pride that feeds it disables a man's security system. Anger dulls his judgment. Clear thinking goes out the window when vengeance walks through your door.

Though "revenge is sweet," it usually invites extended spiritual illness. I've watched it make fools out of smart people. I've seen grown men reduced to pouting adolescents.

When revenge is finished devouring its prey, it begins to devour you. You probably know somebody who is "eaten up" with vengeance. Taking vengeance takes out the best in us as it brings out the worst in us. You can be sure that God isn't in it. Taking vengeance is a gross violation of God's authority.

Paul admonishes the Romans to leave vengeance to God. It's His business. He "will repay" in just the right measure. Nobody really gets away with anything. God keeps a perfect set of books. That truth does not comfort my heart. It causes me to fear for my oppressor.

Follow me, and I will make you fishers of men.
Matthew 4:19 KJV

Standing on a stone quay I witness the dawning of a glorious morning. Gulls wheel overhead in a never-ending quest for food. The waves beat a steady cadence on the rocks sending the occasional curtain of spray to wash the quay. I have no reason to be here – except for some primal urge to greet the dawn and taste the ocean breeze.

The inlet is churning with life as the fishing fleet makes for the freedom of the open sea. The deep-throated growl of marine diesel power rises and falls with the wind as the fishermen busy themselves with bait and gear. A solitary gull feathers a perfect landing and struts alongside like a dog at heel. I've nothing to offer, but the gull seems to enjoy my company. The fishing boats are soon past, melting into a silvery horizon as the wind erases their sound. The tiny harbor is clogged with luxury yachts and sailboats that gleam in the sunlight. They wait in silence for their weekend visitation; a short sail in calm waters; a picnic lunch at the dock; a few hours of restful leisure.

It's not unlike a church on Sunday morning. Too few will go out fishing. Too many will remain firmly tethered to the dock. The season soon will come to an end. Jesus needs a working fleet.

*And he went to him, and bound up his wounds, pouring in oil and
wine, and set him on his own beast, and brought him
to an inn, and took care of him.*
Luke 10:34 KJV

The popular Christian song says it best: "People Need the Lord." We are surrounded by people who are spiritually dead. We can give them life, if we only will. We need to meet them where they are. A sixty-minute church service isn't going to make their list of choices. The good Samaritan didn't stand on the far side of the road shouting instructions through a bull horn – he had to go to the beaten man and carry him to the inn.

We need to show them the "real thing!" They won't sign up for Bible lessons – they're looking for an example to follow. We need to walk them through the process of discipleship. One cannot assume that a seeker has any religious foundation these days. We must become mentors lest we be found guilty of dumping the wounded Samaritan on the doorstep of the inn. Post-Christian America is a demanding mission field. The pagan culture we used to evangelize abroad lives right next door.

If we don't instruct, if we don't equip, if we don't set anchor points, the seeker will keep seeking and drown within sight of the shore.

The "always and forever" message of the Gospel can change the world when it's demonstrated in a life, spoken in love, and felt in the touch of a church turned inside out.

The fool has said in his heart, "There is no God."
Psalm 14:1 NKJV

In searching for information on DNA, I was struck by the language used by scientists concerning design. How anyone can study DNA and not believe in a Designer is beyond me.

Consider the following: "Building a person involves following a set of instructions. Your body stores those instructions in a long, twisted molecule, DNA. It controls everything about the way you look, from the color of your eyes to how tall you are to the width of your feet."

It has been estimated that if the information carried by DNA in one cell were printed out, it would require 400,000 pages at 500 words per page to give full expression to that one cell. Scientists estimate that your body contains between 60 and 100 trillion copies of your genetic code, yet all of your DNA combined composes only .0007% of your body weight.

Forget about microchips and hard drives. God's means of storing information is so compact that the combined genetic code of every person that is living, or has ever lived, could be contained in a thimble.

Purposed design demands a Purposed Designer. Standing on the horizon of the genetic frontier, I see the Lord.

As soon as you hear the sound of the horn, flute, zither, lyre, harp,
pipes and all kinds of music, you must fall down and
worship the image of gold that King Nebuchadnezzar has set up.
Daniel 3:5 NIV

Music is one of the most powerful influences to any generation. It speaks to the mind and soul. King Nebuchadnezzar wanted the nations of the world to bow to his idol, so he commanded the people: "When you hear the music, bow down and worship."

In the last decade, MTV turned on the music and a global youth culture bowed down and worshiped. The Christian message through such a powerful medium as music and video should be fully utilized. Generational preferences should be set aside. We might not think it's good music, but it is their music and through that medium the message of the Gospel shines. Though technology and music are dominant forces in our culture, there is yet a stronger medium for the Gospel.

The risen Christ, lived out in a loving Christian, is the most powerful witness to a fallen culture. With all of our advances, we are drowning in a sea of information. Words don't carry much weight with the next generation. They are watchers. They spend an average of seven hours per day in front of a television. What this generation needs is *"human video"*. . . real life examples of Christ in action in us. They'll sit up and pay attention when they see real love offering real life.

And the LORD God caused a deep sleep to fall on Adam, and he slept;
and He took one of his ribs, and closed up the flesh in its place.
Then the rib which the LORD God had taken from man
He made into a woman, and He brought her to the man.
Genesis 2:21-22 NKJV

There are five things every man should know about his wife; five things that keep you from trouble. There were five steps in God's creative process, and they speak volumes: 1) God caused Adam to sleep. Adam had no say in the design. Adam was not asked His opinion. He was not consulted on final specifications. A wise man does not belittle God's creative genius. 2) God took a rib. This indicates partnership and intimacy. Although the man is set in place as the head of the wife (Ephesians 5:23), He is to treat her as his ultimate life partner. 3) God closed the flesh. God's creative Word did not harm Adam in any way. The marriage relationship should leave no scars. 4) God made the woman. She is God's craftsmanship of the highest order. Some women jokingly say that when God created woman He got it right. In truth, when man and woman were placed together in the garden – everything was right. 5) God brought the woman to Adam. She is God's gift; an undeserved blessing; an answer to man's incompletion; an intimate to whom none can compare.

Rejoice in your wife. She is God's good gift. I know a man who spent five years trying to change his wife. He now lives alone.

They shall besiege you at all your gates until your high and fortified walls, in which you trust, come down throughout all your land.
Deuteronomy 28:52 NKJV

In ancient China, the people wanted security from the barbaric tribes to the north; so they built the great Chinese wall. They took great pride in their massive fortress. It was so high they knew that no one could climb over it. They built it so thick that nothing could break it down.

Content with their handiwork, they settled in to enjoy their hard won security and raise their children in peace. During the next one hundred years China was invaded three times. The wall was never successfully climbed or breached. The barbarians simply bribed the gatekeepers and marched through opened gates. The Chinese were so secure behind their walls of stone that they forgot to teach integrity to their children. I see a tragic parallel in America.

We have built a nation great and strong. We remain the world's only super-power. It is unlikely that American soil will ever be forfeited through war, but the American soul has been lost to succeeding generations of negligent gatekeepers. We can no longer sing "Faith of our fathers living still" with a straight face. The Great Wall of China speaks a message across the centuries: Beware of misplaced confidence. He who guards the gate is greater than he who builds the wall.

In Ukraine, Lilia and Her Daughters Find Hope For Eternity!

A single mom in Dnepropetrovsk, Ukraine, Lilia was struggling to provide for herself and her two little girls on something less that $3 per month. She almost went to jail for stealing just to make ends meet!

Broken and hopeless, she turned to drinking and men to ease her pain.

Then, one day, Lilia's children received the *Book of Hope*. After they went to sleep, Lilia began to read it. She says:

"My goodness! I do not have the words to express what happened to me. Some unknown feeling filled my heart and brought a strong desire to change my life completely."

Lilia, her little girls, and her mother all committed their lives to Christ, and today they are faithful members of their local church. Says Lilia, "I am no longer afraid or ashamed to look into the eyes of other people, but more

important, into the eyes of my children! Our new life has just begun, and I believe for the very best."

Now Moses was tending the flock of Jethro his father-in-law.
Exodus 3:1 NIV

Moses thought he was banned for life. He had traded regal robes for the common garb of a shepherd. He had mortgaged his future by murder and flight. He had blown his opportunity, missed the key connection, and lost his calling in the shifting sands of Egypt.

Can you relate to the fugitive shepherd? Are you certain that life has passed you by? Did you marry the wrong person? Did you turn down a "once-in-a-lifetime" opportunity? Did you lose your membership in the winners club? Moses' story is one you have to hear. When it came to delivering God's people, Moses was about as far out of the picture as a man could be. He was a runaway shepherd. His life now revolved around livestock. His royal years were forty years behind him. It seemed that he was quite content to take care of Jethro's sheep and live out his years in the Midian wilderness – and then God called.

A late-life mission wrote Moses' name into the hero's hall of faith in heaven (Hebrews 11:23). Life's story doesn't end until our hearts beat the final cadence. Fatalism is a deceptive mindset that blinds us to God's redemptive purposes. You may be down, hurt, weary, and bruised, but you're not out yet. Expect to hear His call – again.

In every thing give thanks: for this is the will of
God in Christ Jesus concerning you.
1 Thessalonians 5:18 KJV

I 've put on a few extra pounds. My hairline is in a full panicked retreat. The hair that has chosen to stay is turning gray. I've developed tennis elbow. I don't play tennis. My knee aches from my running years. My new glasses are giving me fits. The dentist says I need a root canal. I'm thirty days behind on a deadline. I've been working on a mild form of insomnia. I think I have a mild hearing loss. I've been through a thorough back-stabbing. I've got more commitments than time to fulfill them. I'm stressed about the board meeting tonight. My wife's car needs a front-end job. My girls need a car. I need a money tree.

The schedule is killing me. Humidity is drowning me. Coffee is poisoning me. My computer froze. My back is aching. My sinuses are clogging. My eye is twitching. I caught a virus. My computer caught a virus. I'm getting forgetful – I think. There's no end in sight. There's no help on the horizon … but I'm walking on air!

I don't have any real problems. I just left the bed-side of a friend in intensive care. I'm fighting the blues – he's fighting for breath. I'm living – he's dying. It's amazing how storm clouds flee with a little change in one's perspective.

He said to them, "Go into all the world and
preach the good news to all creation."
Mark 16:15 NIV

This morning, as you read, I am on my way back to Russia. This will be my fourteenth year in partnership with the Book of Hope. For the next two weeks I will be giving the Word of God in every venue God opens.

Though my primary means of service is carried out in the role of a pastor, I have a second calling. I am a short-term missionary. I am not a replacement for the full-time variety. Indeed, my brief encounters with the mission field have left me with a deep respect and resolve to send them and keep them on the cutting edge of the harvest. I am not the new wave in foreign missions. I am not a reckless cowboy looking for a new frontier. I am just one responding to the Great Commission with more than money and prayer.

The great commission is my personal challenge. It is imperative that I go. I hold an eternal hope for a short-term encounter. For that hope I am willing to go anywhere. I want to make the Master's last command my greatest concern. I want to use western affluence to make a difference. So I'm going back to Russia with a few friends who share the same vision. I'm going because He called, and because I can.

Is God calling you across an ocean . . . across the street?

"The LORD has kept me from having children. Go,
sleep with my maidservant; perhaps I can
build a family through her."
Genesis 16:2 NIV

Solomon, a man of some experience with women, wrote: *Better to dwell in a corner of a housetop, than in a house shared with a contentious woman* (Prov. 21:9). Sarai was desperately unhappy, impatient, and self-pressured. Her biological clock was ticking so loudly she could not hear the voice of faith and reason whispering in her heart. God had promised a son, but with the passing of each month, her sense of hopelessness deepened.

Finally, and fatally, she took matters into her own hands. Hagar, the maidservant, was a slave, and thus, Sarai's property. Sarai was simply applying a cultural remedy to the problem of barrenness. The choosing of a surrogate wrote the first chapter in a tale of suffering and hatred that continues to this day.

Whenever we try to improve on God's plan, or rush to shortcut God's design, we end up with a solution that fails to satisfy, and consequences we could have never imagined. Sarai found no comfort in the birth of Ishmael – quite the opposite, her discontent spread like a cancer. No doubt, Abraham was open to any remedy. His house was not a happy place.

Think twice before you tinker with God's plans and promises. Your short-term solution may birth a long-term tragedy.

But in fact God has arranged the parts in the body,
every one of them, just as he wanted them to be.
1 Corinthians 12:18 NIV

The old warehouse claimed to be a trailer supply store, but it was a lot more than that. Over the years, the owners had dabbled in everything from go-karts to chainsaws to garden supplies to sailcloth.

It was a real "guy place." I doubt if the gritty concrete floors had ever known the clicking sound of high heels. The girl at the register chewed gum and knew where to find a reverse-threaded brass fitting for a twenty- year-old barbeque grill. As a matter of fact, the girl at the register could probably have welded a barbeque grill from scrap iron. The aisles were cluttered. The place smelled like worn leather and hydraulic fluid. Every aisle held a mystery to be uncovered.

When the store moved to a brand new, girl-friendly place across the highway, it grieved me, like seeing the town diner replaced by a McDonald's. Everything is shrink-wrapped at the new place, and I'll bet you can find nail polish on aisle three. It might as well be a Mega-Mart Supercenter.

God created an infinite variety in mountains, rivers, forests, and people. We are gravitating towards strip-mall uniformity in the name of political correctness. Learn to enjoy and appreciate our differences. Blind conformity veils the creativity of God.

*Fathers, do not exasperate your children; instead,
bring them up in the training and instruction of the Lord.
Ephesians 6:4 NIV*

In ancient Greece, the ideal man was the thinker the philosopher. In China, the ultimate man was the sage the scholar. In the middle ages, the great men were architects and builders. In the sixteenth century, the pre-eminent man was the artist. In nineteenth century England, he was the man of letters. In the twentieth century, he was the warrior, giving way to the statesman. At the same time, we witnessed the rise of the industrialist who gave way to the entrepreneur.

In historical perspective I have not been able to accurately define an age where the ideal man was embodied in fatherhood. Perhaps we can catch a glimpse of exalted fatherhood in a small pocket of history in America. Perhaps in the fifties, when post-war America determined to build a better world for her children. Right or wrong, our best intentions were lost in countless hours of overtime, absence from the crib-side, and negligence in spiritual training.

We've produced a better light bulb, bigger business, greater opportunity, global communications, pills and cures and a better education. Yet, something is lacking. Oh, for a generation of fathers who give themselves to produce better sons and daughters.

For we do not have a High Priest who cannot sympathize
with our weaknesses, but was in all points
tempted as we are, yet without sin.
Hebrews 4:15 NKJV

"You don't know what it's like to be poor!" said the protester. "You don't know what it's like to be black!" said the marcher. "You don't know what it's like to be a woman!" said the crusader for fair wages. All points conceded. Trying to feel what others are feeling outside of experience is like trying to understand a new foreign language. We can all claim to sympathize – to feel pity and sorrow for a sufferer. But to claim "empathy" we must "feel the pain."

In a job fair classroom, a Vietnam veteran listened as his instructor used multiple military illustrations to make his point. He implied that his students were soft, untested, and weak. He was going to "put some steel" in their resolve. The vet raised his hand. "Have you ever been under fire?" The silence was deafening. The trainer stared into the dark eyes of the vet. In that moment, he saw the tracings of a hundred battles – blood, terror, and valor. "No," he whispered dryly, "I never saw combat." Nothing more was said. The message was clear: *"You have nothing to say to me."*

God knows what it is to be human; to suffer pain and rejection; to feel elation and dejection. He is uniquely qualified, in every case, to speak with authority.

And Nathanael said to him,
"Can anything good come out of Nazareth?"
Philip said to him, "Come and see."
John 1:46 NKJV

Stereotyping and profiling can rob us of enriching relationships. What if Nathanael had turned down Philip's invitation? What if he had said, "I wouldn't cross the road to hear someone from Nazareth?" Although Nathanael had some kind of negative history with Nazarenes, he didn't allow his presupposition to completely close his mind.

I grew up with a stilted view of Russian people. I was raised in the cold war, and thus, was certain that all Russians were cold, inhospitable people. I couldn't have been more off base. The finest hospitality I have ever enjoyed has been at Russian tables spread by generous and loving Russian hosts (Thank-you Yuri). In a world so deeply divided in ethnic strife, we would do well to demonstrate the triumphant power of Christ's love.

It is the demonstration of love that convinces the world of our authenticity (John 13:35). It is our pointless bickering and strife that convinces the world that we are no different than the rest. Think what Nathanael would have missed if he had given into his irrational prejudice. He would have missed God in flesh reconciling a shattered world through perfect love.

What are you missing for a foolish presupposition?

Then we who are alive and remain shall be caught up together with them in the clouds to meet the Lord in the air. And thus we shall always be with the Lord. 1 Thessalonians 4:17 NKJV

The media blankets the world. My cable service boasts four twenty-four hour news outlets. The Internet offers another means by which instant information can be delivered. A plane crashes. We know it in minutes. The World Cup is played out on another continent. We watch it live. The infrastructure for world-wide reporting is poised and ready for a story that will rock the world. I expect it in my lifetime: "MILLIONS OF PEOPLE – DISAPPEAR!"

Experts will be called in to talk about everything from UFO's to Bible prophecy. The story will find no geographical center. People will be missing from every continent, every nation, every race, and every tongue. Reports of missing bodies will trickle in, mingling with a flood of "live" disappearances. The "vanished" will number in the millions. It could be today, or tomorrow, or next week, or year.

The only certainty is that it will happen. Christ came to the earth to save us, and He will come again to embrace us forever (John 14:3). God has never failed to keep a promise, and this promise is given to us with crystal clarity.

We should live our lives to be the big story – we sure don't want to be here watching as it's reported.

*"Do you want to be made well?" The sick man answered Him,
"Sir, I have no man to put me into the pool
when the water is stirred up."
John 5:6-7 NKJV*

The lame man could not see beyond his experience. Because others had been healed when the waters were stirred, he believed he could only be healed in the troubled waters. The One who sculpted the mountains and created light was standing within a few meters, but he wasn't aware of His identity.

Though we know who Jesus is, and how He works, we often follow the pattern of the lame man at the pool. We fix in our minds a rigid framework of what needs to be done, and how it needs to be done. For example, a man needs a job – prays for a job – seeks a job – but will not consider anything outside of his field of past experience. A woman cries out for deliverance from depression. Because she is convinced that her husband or wayward daughter is the cause of her depression, she prays that God would change them.

God doesn't always approach our problems on a familiar path. He is creative beyond our imagination. He sees the whole picture while we see only shadows. Sometimes grace is sufficient. Sometimes His answer has never entered our minds.

It's not about troubled waters – it's about the presence and power of the Lord. Don't presume that God will be limited to a single course of action.

But the LORD said to Gideon, "There are still too many men.
Take them down to the water, and I will sift them for you there.
If I say, 'This one shall go with you,' he shall go; but if I say,
'This one shall not go with you,' he shall not go."
Judges 7:4 NIV

The great violinist Itzhak Perlman took the stage at Avery Fisher Hall in New York City. Crippled by polio, Perlman walks with the aid of two crutches and leg braces. Audiences sit in silence as he labors to take his place. When ready, he nods to the conductor and the audience is treated to a rare virtuosity. As Perlman began, a string broke.

What would he do? How long would the concert be delayed? Reporter Jack Reimer writes, "He closed his eyes and then signaled the conductor to begin again. The orchestra began and he played from where he had left off. And he played with such passion and such power and such purity as they had never heard before." Perlman completed the concert on three strings to a standing ovation. Afterward, when he had quieted the crowd, he said, "You know, sometimes it is the artist's task to find out how much music you can still make with what you have left."

Have you experienced loss, a setback, abandonment? What kind of music will you make with what you have left? How long will you grieve over a broken string? How will you respond to unexpected circumstances, undeserved calamity, or inconvenient timing? God has a well-established history of doing more – with less!

"Suppose one of you wants to build a tower.
Will he not first sit down and estimate the cost to see if
he has enough money to complete it?"
Luke 14:28 NIV

For a number of years my wife had expressed a longing for a golden retriever. Last Christmas, I gave in and placed a card under the tree bearing the promise of a puppy as soon as one could be found. It took several months to locate the perfect pup, but I kept her placated with books about "Goldens."

After three months of searching, puppy day arrived, and our house suffered the invasion of an eight-week dynamo. "Cute" and "cuddly" were soon matched up with "messy, smelly, hungry, nippy, and whiney." Within a fortnight, the puppy did what puppies do and my wife and three daughters were ready, I mean *READY*, to sell the puppy. I resisted on the basis that this was my Christmas gift to my wife, and that the "critter" had somehow wormed its way into my heart.

I'm writing this in April, and I think I've saved the puppy from auction on eBay! She's growing like the beast in Revelation, and if she messes in the dining room again, I don't think I'll be able to save her. Her vet bills make my dentist look like a real bargain.

Here's a simple lesson on counting the cost: Sometimes your best intentions come with pricey consequences. Next year I'm thinking "gift certificate."

And the Word was made flesh, and dwelt among us,
(and we beheld his glory, the glory as of the only
begotten of the Father,) full of grace and truth.
John 1:14 KJV

Let me give you a thumbnail sketch for a new screen-play. I'm sure the idea has been tried a few times, but here goes. Our movie would center on a man who suffers a sudden and comprehensive amnesia. He wakes up one morning to a life he does not recognize.

While all treat him with affection and familiarity, he does not recognize the woman who claims to be his wife, nor the children who call him Daddy. He is a blank page. For our movie to have any chance of being made, we must somehow resolve his dilemma. We could introduce a love interest to grant the man a new identity (sigh). We could have the man fall in love all over again with his wife (how sweet). We could have his memory restored through some dramatic mechanism (eureka!). We might even grant him some extra-sensory powers in the post-traumatic phase of the story (sci-fi).

While we have many options open on the writer's table, there is one storyline that will sink our picture: We could leave the man in a state of confused ignorance. But without identity, we have no story! So it is with Christ in the Scriptures. He must be God's only begotten Son; God in flesh. If we cannot fully establish His identity, we have no story.

Now when Ahithophel saw that his advice was not followed,
he saddled a donkey, and arose and went home to his house, to his city.
Then he put his household in order, and hanged himself,
and died; and he was buried in his father's tomb.
2 Samuel 17:23 NKJV

A broken relationship often exacts a terrible price. Ahithophel was David's friend and advisor. Somehow, their relationship soured. Some commentators have suggested that Ahithophel was the grandfather of Bathsheba, the object of David's illicit affections. If so, it would offer a plausible explanation for a fractured relationship. It cannot be proved, but something devoured their friendship (Psalm 55:14).

When David's renegade son, Absalom, overthrew his father in a bloodless coup, Ahithophel joined the insurrection. Disaster followed. Absalom's cunning was offset by an undiscerning heart. His own deceit left him blind to deceit in others. He chose to ignore the advice of Ahithophel and follow the counsel of David's spy. The aged advisor, estranged from his king, could not handle the rejection of a pretender. He died at the bitter end of a rope in the shadows of his own conceit. He is not the first, nor the last man to be hung by pride.

Unforgiveness bears the bitterest fruit. Reconciliation seems a high price to pay until the cost of our pride is fully calculated.

Is your life a collection of fractured relationships and secret resentments? Surely nothing good can come of it.

*When they saw the courage of Peter and John and realized that they were
unschooled, ordinary men, they were astonished and
they took note that these men had been with Jesus.*
Acts 4:13 NIV

With no more than 3-½ years of training, Jesus is
going to leave the scene, commissioning His disciples with the daunting task of taking the Gospel to the
uttermost parts of the earth.

Does He choose deep-water sailors, explorers or frontiersmen? Does He choose diplomats and politicians who
can stand tall in the halls of power? How does He shape
His team? Surely He will search the great cities, looking
among the schools of learning for the best and the brightest.

You might think that He would draft twelve men
with the pedigree of Paul; men of breeding, men of letters, men of action. What strategy should one employ in
trying to build a team that will change the world?
Wisdom calls for a broad search ... but no! Jesus goes
home to a backward region, far removed from the halls of
power of Jerusalem. He reaches down into Capernaum,
Bethsaida, and Cana.

All of the disciples were plucked from this rough collection of Galilean hamlets and fishing villages, with the
exception of Judas Iscariot. The choosing of the twelve
disciples sends a message across time that common people
need to hear. It's not about us – it's all about Christ in us.

Be still before the LORD, and wait patiently for him.
Psalm 37:7 RSV

6:00 A.M. Starbucks. Post-holiday Friday morning. Triple-venti-One-Sweet-n-Low-No-foam latte. Low volume coffee traffic. No background noise. That's the best part. The music system is broken and I can hear the clicking of the keys on my laptop.

I usually pick my table with consideration for speaker locations. I'm in luck when they're playing old jazz. I'm in pain when its reggae. This morning I'm enjoying the sound of the expresso grinders and the hiss of steam. I hope the music system is fried for at least a week. I could really get used to this.

Much of life is cluttered with background noise. Everywhere we go there is something playing in the background. Last week I was trying to buy a pair of jeans. I had to shout my size to the attendant. He shouted and pointed to a general area near the back of the store. We didn't connect. A symphony was sawing away in the grocery store. The restaurant was playing songs in Italian. The music store had rock and roll.

We have developed an aversion to silence. It's as if we're afraid to be alone in ourselves, for even a single moment, without a lyric or riff to fill in the dead space. Give silence a slot in your daily schedule. You might be surprised to hear the whisper of God.

*Then He said to His disciples, "The harvest truly is plentiful,
but the laborers are few. Therefore pray the Lord of the harvest
to send out laborers into His harvest."*
Matthew 9:37-38 NKJV

Book of Hope Distribution: An Aeroflot jetliner is taking me back – back to the land that has defined missions for me over the past eleven years. I'm going back to Siberia.

Every September since 1991, my wife and daughters have seen me off on Book of Hope distributions. This one is special. This year, my three daughters are team members and they seem to feel the same passion I feel for short-term missions. This year, we are working with a young pastor who was won to the Lord through a church we planted in 1992 in Kraznoyarsk. This year, we are going to a people group that was classed as "un-reached" just five years ago. This year, I'll see the mission field in a different light; a mission field and mission work conveyed to a rising generation. This year, my children will be telling Russian children about Jesus.

While my heart is bursting with pride, I cannot escape the disquieting truth: We are not doing enough. More than three billion people have not heard the Gospel. Suddenly, twenty laymen and thirty-thousand books seems a paltry investment. Jesus pleaded with His disciples, "Pray the Lord of the harvest" – more laborers! God is calling. Is He calling you to go?

Blessed is the nation whose God is the LORD,
The people He has chosen as His own inheritance.
Psalm 33:12 NKJV

November 17, 1800: It was moving day in Washington. A homeless government moved into a new Capitol Building. Whether it has been a "habitat for humanity" depends on your level of political cynicism.

I was born outside these United States, and my first visit to the Capitol was fascinating, awe inspiring, and emotionally moving. For all the wrangling and demagoguery, the world is a better place for the good that has flowed out of her domed chambers. The Capitol Building that I visited was quite different from the one occupied by Congress, the Supreme Court, the Library of Congress and the D.C. Courts in 1800. My Capitol was wrapped in security precautions.

If you had been around on moving day in 1800, you could have walked right in and had a look around. There is an inscription in the dome of the Capitol that few people know about. It says: "One far-off divine event toward which the whole creation moves." It's a line by Tennyson captured in the Westminster Confession.

It is also a sign that we once gave reverence to Christian doctrines and Divine Providence. I hesitate to mention it. Someone may challenge it under the establishment clause and sue for its removal.

Jesus saith unto her, Woman, what have I to do with thee?
mine hour is not yet come. His mother saith unto the servants,
Whatsoever he saith unto you, do it.
John 2:4-5 KJV

When Mary steps in to rescue a failing party, Jesus is reluctant to act owing to the fact that His "hour is not yet come." Mary ignores this and instructs the servants to follow the Lord's instructions.

Why did Jesus yield to Mary's request? Was it because she was Mom, and the commandments require honor (Exodus 20:12)? Was it a moment of compassion for the groom? I don't think so. Read the life of Christ with an eye for His response to faith. Jesus could not resist when people demonstrated faith.

Matthew holds four clear examples. A Centurion came to Jesus seeking healing for a paralyzed servant. Jesus was amazed at his faith (Matthew 8:10). Four friends brought another paralyzed man to Jesus. They tore up a roof and lowered his stretcher. Jesus was amazed at their faith (Matthew 9:2). The woman with the "issue of blood" pressed through the crowd to touch Him. Jesus responded to her desperate faith (Matthew 9:22). A Canaanite woman shows a stubborn persistence that moves Jesus deeply. Her daughter was healed (Matthew 15:28).

So it seems that Jesus, rushed into action before His preferred moment, responds to the absolute faith of His mother. How persistent is your faith?

And he will be called Wonderful.
Isaiah 9:6 NIV

Slowly, our sense of wonder is dying. If you listen, you can hear its death-rattle as we find natural explanations for all that surrounds us. Science, apart from God, stands on the assumption that everything can be ultimately explained. Miracles are left to the movies.

The supernatural is filed under "fantasy." Our culture strives to leave nothing in the realm of mystery, wonder, or faith. If archaeologists were to uncover the Ark of the Covenant, we would soon be treated to a Discovery Channel special explaining its power. No doubt, a psychologist or two would discount its biblical history to the power of superstition and fear. The end result of our theories is a world of marvel without mystery; amazement without reverent awe.

God is not absent from our scientific discovery. All that we uncover is but the fingerprint of the Almighty. DNA points to a Master Designer. And what will we find when we develop the ability to look beyond DNA?

What is the sum of our knowledge captured in libraries and organized into textbooks? It is but a single drop to the oceans when compared to the One whose very name means "full of wonder." Don't be deceived. We are living in a supernatural world.

> *O God, You know my foolishness;*
> *And my sins are not hidden from You.*
> *Psalm 69:5 NKJV*

It's amazing how much of ourselves we leave laying around. The latest wave of forensic science has revealed a wealth of physical evidence we constantly trail behind. The good guys have taken some big steps forward over the past few years. Fingerprints, hair, fiber, and DNA are common courtroom themes.

You don't need Colombo, Holmes or Miss Marple anymore. Just bring on Sally with her swab kit and UV light wand. I'm counseling a growing number of men caught up in Internet pornography. How did they get caught? They didn't understand that walking around on the Internet is like wearing new boots in damp clay. Your own "personal" computer is tracking your every move on "the net." It's enough to make you paranoid. Internet journeys are recorded with markers called "cookies." Someone is out there reading your "cookies" to get a better handle on how to sell you something – or worse (am I paranoid?).

God is the ultimate "tracker." The Bible tells me that He never takes His eyes off of me. Internet retailers track me to sell me something. The adversary tracks me to accuse me, but God tracks me because He loves me. Outsiders consider this invasive. I find it very comforting.

*"And you shall know the truth, and the truth
shall make you free."*
John 8:32 NKJV

Pete chose to ignore his drinking problem. His boss offered a rehabilitation center, but Pete felt he had it all under control. His best friend brought it up on a weekend fishing trip, but Pete told him he was over-reacting. His wife tried to understand him; to defend him; to cover for him. Finally, she reached a breaking point and left him.

Winston Churchill possessed a keen insight into a man's prideful heart when he wrote, "Men occasionally stumble over the truth, but most of them pick themselves up and hurry off as if nothing has happened." After he lost his wife, Pete lost his job. After he lost his job, he lost his house and car. He followed a predictable downward spiral that led him to a shelter, and finally, to the streets.

Today, Pete is making a comeback. He lives at a Teen Challenge center, and has committed his life to Christ; but Pete's wife has married another man and his kids call somebody else "Daddy."

Self-deception is an incredibly destructive indulgence. The truth could have saved Pete's family and career. The truth could have saved him from unspeakable sorrow. Truth ignored is a date with disaster. "The truth shall make you free." A lie will make you foolish.

Be sober, be vigilant; because your adversary the
devil walks about like a roaring lion, seeking whom he may devour.
1 Peter 5:8 NKJV

Momentum gained is hard to stop. Momentum lost is hard to gain. When Christians lose their forward motion, lethargy comes like a leech to drain away our energy. When churches lose their forward motion, it takes renewal to get the train moving down the track again.

We need to be moving. We're in the business of life and death. We have a very real adversary who seeks to destroy our souls. Columnist Herb Caen wrote in the San Francisco Chronicle: "Every morning in Africa, a gazelle wakes up. It knows it must run faster than the fastest lion or it will be killed. Every morning a lion wakes up. It knows it must outrun the slowest gazelle or it will starve to death. It doesn't matter whether you are a lion or a gazelle; when the sun comes up, you'd better be running."

We need to be running. Paul says we're running a spiritual race and we are to run in such a way as to win the prize. To win, one must train, push, stretch, strain, breathe, eat, and rest – every day! To win, one must hit the ground running every day. To win, one must consecrate, sacrifice, strategize, prioritize, and visualize. Good morning! Get up! Better pray – better move – better watch – there's a lion out there somewhere.

For the leaders of this people cause them to err;
and they that are led of them are destroyed.
Isaiah 9:16 KJV

Christian leaders need the "right stuff." I've watched enough burn up, burn out, blow up, wipe out, break up, walk out, crack up, and wash out. Stay out of leadership until you are certain of God's call and prepared for God's people.

Here's a bit of help as you analyze your calling. Do other's failures annoy you? Are you a user of people? Do you have to get your own way? Are you critical of your leaders? Do you have a hard time keeping secrets? Have you any hidden sins? Do you pout when things go wrong? Do you quit when things get tough? Do you strike back when smitten? Are you confused in crisis? Are you a gossip? Is anybody following you now? When you get a position, do you have to constantly remind people that you're the leader? Can you handle a delicate situation? Has anyone ever called you bull-headed? Do you take everything personally? Do you need, need, need approval? Do you make people nervous? Are you a strong finisher? Do you hold grudges? Are you a pessimist?

If you can't see yourself at all in these questions, you may hold promise. If you see your own shadow here, go slow. If these questions read like your biography, please stand down. We'll all be better for it.

... that I may finish my race with joy.
Acts 20:24 NKJV

The Indianapolis 500 is the most celebrated motor race in the world. The flag drops and forty incredible machines rip around the track at more than 200 miles per hour – a spectacle.

Before the race starts, sports commentators rush from pit to pit, hoping to catch an interview with driver or crew chief. Before the race, attention is divided between forty racing stories. Every driver climbs into a shining bullet. Every crew chief wonders if this will be his big day. Every owner sees himself in victory lane. Every driver's wife envisions her husband safely home. The pace car leads the field through warm-up laps. The tension mounts as all await a green flag-with a thundering crescendo the cars cross the start/finish line. The crowd stands as one. The race is begun.

At this point everything shifts from start to finish. It doesn't really matter how, or where a driver started. What matters is how he finishes. If a driver gets reckless, he courts disaster. If a driver gets sleepy, he's in the wall. The race is a race for the finish!

Life is that way. It's not how you start, it's how you finish. It's not where you've been, it's where you're going. It's not about a good beginning, it's about the checkered flag.

"Awake, you who sleep, Arise from the dead,
And Christ will give you light."
Ephesians 5:14 NKJV

I wonder what would happen all over the world if Christians were to suddenly get very busy in the Lord's work? I wonder what breakthroughs would be achieved, what barriers would fall, what blessing might be poured out if we were to experience a sudden stirring to action?

George Sweeting offers the following bit of history: "During the reign of Oliver Cromwell, there was a shortage of currency in the British Empire. Representatives carefully searched the nation in hopes of finding silver to meet the emergency. After one month, the committee returned with its report. 'We have searched the Empire in vain seeking to find silver. To our dismay, we found none anywhere except in the cathedrals where the statues of the saints are made of choice silver.' To this, Oliver Cromwell eloquently answered, 'Let's melt down the saints and put them into circulation.'"

Maybe we should be praying for some kind of "meltdown." Some churches are absolutely frozen in time, frigid in fellowship, rigid in worship, and suspended in outreach. If only we could experience a meltdown that put saints into circulation, love into action, life into liturgy, and momentum into our disabled movements. We might just change the world!

*So then, just as you received Christ Jesus as Lord, continue to
live in him, rooted and built up in him.*
Colossians 2:6-7 NIV

A boy grows up with interchangeable video friends.
He flips through twenty channels in forty seconds.
His compressed attention span demands information
packaged in fifteen second sound bites.

Why watch a movie when a music video tells it all in
three minutes? Why read a book when a video supplies
imagination? Why grapple with reality when "virtual reality" offers a broad selection? He's growing up in a world
high on choice and low on commitment. He speeds
through adolescence bouncing in and out of short-term
relationships. By the time he reaches mid-life he is stung
by the realization that his life has no direction. He is a
masterpiece without a master plan . . . an abstract.
Constant change has left him physically, emotionally and
spiritually overdrawn.

In the absence of commitment his choices become
increasingly tiresome. Nobody ever told him that you
could take a multiple-choice test and choose all the
wrong answers. By fifty he agrees with Donald Trump:
"Nothing in life is what it's cracked up to be." Life, with
unlimited options, does not work without commitments,
foundations, and vows.

Commit! Stick to it! Follow through! No man can
truly live without roots.

As a dog returns to his own vomit, So a fool repeats his folly.
Proverbs 26:11 NKJV

WASHINGTON, D.C. July 14, 1865: Exhausted by the close of the Civil War, President Lincoln affixed his signature to government documents before taking in an evening of entertainment at Ford's Theater.

Unknown to all, he had just performed his last official act. Within hours, Lincoln was fatally wounded by gunshot. At the cessation of North/South hostilities, just five days before, the army was relieved of its guardianship of the presidency. Lincoln sat in Ford's theater without protection. Sixteen years later James Garfield was assassinated by gunshot. Two presidents had fallen, and still no steps were taken to offer protection. Twenty years later (1901), President McKinley became the third president to die at the hands of an assassin.

If only we could learn our lessons with one fall. Unfortunately, we often have to hit the bottom repeatedly before we reach up. Neglected lessons have a recurrent tendency. Get off that merry-go-round and run to higher ground. Repentance marks a new beginning.

History is sprinkled with irony, and few so sobering as this: That last document that Lincoln signed before leaving for the theater was a document creating a new federal agency . . . the Secret Service.

He who believes and is baptized . . .
Mark 16:16 NKJV

Have you accepted Christ as your personal Savior? Yes? Wonderful! Have you been baptized? What's that you say ... "You're praying about it?" You don't have to pray about water baptism. It is not an option. Baptism is a commandment.

You wouldn't pray about whether you should commit adultery or not, would you? Of course not . . . adultery is clearly covered in the Ten Commandments (Exodus 20:14). Baptism is covered in Jesus' final instruction to the church (Mark 16:16). It is a commandment; a first step. Everybody knows how important first steps are to a process or relationship. If we neglect God's prescribed course for life, should it be any wonder that life doesn't seem to work? If I leave a few footings out of the foundation, should I be surprised when the house caves in?

When you came to Christ and accepted His offer of salvation, the man you used to be died, and a new man was born. The corpse of the old man is to be buried in the waters of baptism (Romans 6:4). It is no wonder that many among us are spiritually weary and constantly struggling. Who wouldn't be exhausted after a few days or years of dragging around a corpse? If you've missed the first step, see your pastor. Be baptized.

But when he heard this, he became very sorrowful,
for he was very rich.
Luke 18:23 NKJV

Tom has a beautiful sixteen-year-old daughter named Abbie. Tom has a 2002 BMW 745Li with a license tag that reads "EXES!". Abbie just left on her first date with a guy named Stevie. Tom wouldn't even think about letting Stevie borrow the BMW for the evening, but he didn't think twice about letting Abbie go on a date. The question here is value. If the young man couldn't be trusted with a car, should he be trusted with a daughter?

Frank just installed a five thousand dollar fence and a two thousand dollar security alarm system at home. He's made more home improvements than anyone in the neighborhood. His wife, Terri, is begging Frank to take her away for an overnight marriage retreat in the mountains. Frank says they can't afford it. The question here is value. If a man invests thousands in his house, and won't invest two hundred in his marriage, can he have a happy home?

A rich young ruler came to Jesus. He wanted *eternal* life, but he assigned greater value to temporary comforts. Faulty values led to a downward cycle of sorrows. In the quest for God our values are questioned. In accepting Him, our values must be changed.

Pastors in Ukraine say the youth there face many challenges: crime, alcohol, drugs and witchcraft, to name a few. Please pray that the local believers will be able to give God's Word to every child and youth in Ukraine and see the next generation protected from Satan's attack and brought into God's kingdom!

In Zambia, HOPE Changes Christabelle Forever!

Christabelle came to school that morning with a heavy heart ... her family was in turmoil, and she had no hope for the future. In fact, the only thing she could focus on was how desperately she needed help – and how she had nowhere to turn for it!

This 15-year-old girl from Lusaka, Zambia was surprised when she got to school, and a young American woman took the stage to address a schoolwide assembly. She seemed to be speaking directly to Christabelle's heart!

The young lady was Amy Minnich, a missionary associate with Book of Hope Response Teams. The associates devote a year or more of their lives to Book of Hope ministry, traveling the globe to distribute the book and tell kids about Jesus.

Amy bravely told the students of Lusaka Girls School of her own past: how her parents divorced, and she was left feeling hopeless and alone. It was exactly what Christabelle had been feeling. But then she explained how she came to Christ and found that Jesus loved her unconditionally! She invited all the girls to find hope for eternity in Jesus, and the team gave each student the *Book of Hope*.

Afterward, Christabelle had to find Amy in the crowd and tell her: she had accepted Jesus as her Savior, and now she knew that there was Someone who loved her, and that there was hope for her and for her family!

After these things the Lord appointed seventy others also,
and sent them two by two before His face into every city
and place where He Himself was about to go.
Luke 10:1 NKJV

Biysk, Siberia: Book of Hope Distribution. The travel schedule is grueling. To journey half way around the world to an obscure location in a foreign culture means delay, change of plans, hurry up and wait, sleeping when you can, and struggling to adjust to jet lag.

When it's team travel, it's complicated by a variable multiplier. Four flights and a three hour bus ride have brought us to this place; another Siberian city set up for Book of Hope distribution. Tomorrow, seven teams will leave the hotel in taxis loaded with books. Tomorrow, a few stay-at-home moms, a building inspector, a computer specialist, a nurse, an engineer, a jack-of-all-trades, a school teacher, four teenagers, two kids, and a preacher will tell the story once again. Tomorrow, a life will be changed forever as God's Word causes faith to rise in the heart of an elementary school boy, or a high school senior, or an English teacher, or an administrator.

Our interpreters are ready. Our rookies are anxious. Our host pastor and his staff are putting the finishing touches to the schedule. Some on our team have prepared for two years to do this distribution.

'Tis the night before another Book of Hope distribution – a night for hopes and dreams; faith and vision; obedience and destiny.

"For I am the LORD, I do not change."
Malachi 3:6 NKJV

It is estimated that within three years, 62 million Americans will be under the age of fourteen.

The world that housed my generation is virtually unknown to them. They have never seen a black and white TV, a record player, or an eight track. They cannot conceive of a world without computers, microwaves, and compact discs. They view the family as a flexible and changing set of relationships rather than a fixed and tight-knit community.

In most cases, they can solve the computer problems their parents create. They have been raised in a culture that denies the absolute, so they have no allegiance to fixed principles. More than any other generation, they are the children of change. Every generation must adapt to reach the next, but with the increasing pace of change, the gap is widening so fast that we struggle to keep ourselves educated, let alone integrated. My grandfather saw two generational shifts in his lifetime. My father has witnessed at least four generational shifts. In my lifetime I can expect to witness eight or ten major shifts.

Changing times grant us an incredible opportunity to introduce the "Changeless One." We need to be careful that we don't lose our bearings in our attempts to stay on the cutting edge. Don't wear yourself out trying to keep the pace. Keep the faith! "Real" is always relevant.

*I plead with Euodia and I plead with Syntyche
to agree with each other in the Lord.*
Philippians 4:2 NIV

In May, 1976, Jim McCoy and Willis Hatfield shook hands in a public ceremony dedicating a monument to six victims of the infamous feud that marked their families in American history. The Hatfield/McCoy feud was front-page news in the 1880's.

It ran for ten years in the hills of Kentucky, costing the lives of a hundred men, women, and children. No one is quite sure what started the feud. Some cite Civil War tensions: the McCoys sympathized with the Union; the Hatfields with the Confederacy. Others say it began when the McCoys blamed the Hatfields for stealing hogs.

A fight often outlives its cause. Feuds often take root in churches. The results are spectacular, tragic, and predictable. No winner can truly be declared and casualties litter the landscape. Church feuds are rarely settled with a single battle. They tend towards guerilla warfare that drags on as testimony is lost and opportunities evaporate.

I think Paul was trying to head off a church feud in (Philippians 4:2). It's almost as if Paul is saying, "Now stop it, you two!" Church folks could learn something from the Hatfields and McCoys. We can be truly reconciled to one another. Jim McCoy died Feb. 11, 1984 at age 99. He bore no grudges and had his burial handled by the Hatfield Funeral Home in Toler, Kentucky.

Whatever you have learned or received or heard from me,
or seen in me – put it into practice.
Philippians 4:9 NIV

In the last half-hour I have experienced three near misses and a couple minor miracles. I have come within a hair's breadth of mailboxes, mail trucks, and Monte Carlos. My heart rate is ninety percent of maximum. My senses are razor sharp.

I sit in the passenger seat of my own vehicle, wishing for additional seatbelts and a crash helmet. I am firmly buckled, my jaw is set, and my knuckles are white. My daughter has just received her driving permit, and I am stunned at the inadequacy of her training (that light was red!). My other daughter has also received her permit – she wants to go for a drive after supper. My third daughter gets hers in a couple of months. I need some form of sedation. "Relax Dad," she says, "my teacher said I was a good driver" (pedestrian!). That driving instructor must have nerves of steel and/or blindness (brake, Brake, BRAKE!).

Most things in life can only be learned through experience. Books, videos, and classes provide a framework, but life requires practice. We're approaching my driveway (Parked car! Parked car on the right!). We've made it home, and I'm awfully glad to be back in my own driveway – even if we are parked sideways.

In the beginning was the Word.
John 1:1 KJV

John gives us keen insight into the mystery of God with six words. At the core of all things is/was the Word! Six words jumpstart the Gospel with two seminal truths: God is, and God spoke.

Communication is rudimentary to relationship. Speech is miraculous. Consider: a Christian is stirred by a thought concerning Jesus. That thought is shaped by an experience and by faith. The mind grasps the thought and launches it across the great gray landscape of the brain. In a microsecond the diaphragm contracts and air is pushed through the voice box. Sound produced by vocal cords is distinctly shaped by the tongue, teeth, and lips. This shaped charge disturbs airwaves as it drifts across space until it collides with an ear. The ear pulls the sound waves into a tiny canal where they cause tiny bones to vibrate. Vibrations are translated to chemical/electrical signals that race across the brain where they are met by faith, confirmed by God's Spirit, and galvanized into a confession of faith.

Through the miracle of the spoken word, somebody is translated from darkness to light! The message communicated by the living Word changes everything. Tell the story. Speak the Word; it is the beginning of all things.

"Your fathers, where are they?
And the prophets, do they live forever?"
Zechariah 1:5 NKJV

I'm in the middle of the birthday season. Within a fifty-five day span, my three daughters celebrate birthdays. These celebrations are happy/sad occasions for me. My girls are pictured, just above my computer screen, at ages five, three, and two.

When I look at the picture, I am always visited by a familiar wish: the wish to hold all three of them at once, laughing and giggling; the wish to wrestle once more in the family room; the wish for pillow fights, crayon artwork, and neck-wrenching hugs.

I don't live there anymore. I'm dealing with driver's education, emotional roller-coasters, boys, bucks, cat fights, and clothing wars. I can't get them all in my lap anymore (I tried last week and threw my back out). I'm not infallible anymore. I'm not omnipotent anymore. I'm not the only male that matters on the planet anymore, and I'm not taking it well.

By summer's end they'll be eighteen, sixteen, and fifteen. It seems like only yesterday they were five, three, and two. Slow me down Lord. Teach me to cherish the moment. Loosen my tongue to say the right things. I'm so busy building with mortar and stone that I soon forget that life . . . is but a vapor.

Praise the LORD from the earth,
You great sea creatures and all the depths;
Fire and hail, snow and clouds; Stormy wind, fulfilling His word.
Psalm 148:7-8 NKJV

The snow fell early and stayed late in New Brunswick, my childhood home. Most Christmases were white. We celebrated with snowballs, sleds, toboggans, and snow skis. If we got ten inches it was no big deal.

I now live in a city where snow is a nuisance. We rarely have more than two snowfalls per year. People don't know how to drive in the stuff. Four inches shuts down half of our city. Schools close. People go crazy in grocery stores, clearing the shelves of bread and milk. Eight inches shuts down the other half of the city. Reporters cover the story like Watergate. A festive "holiday" spirit infects people who cannot drive to work, but seem to find a way to get together for a snow party. Twelve inches shuts down everything except monster trucks and the fire department. The storm gets its own name like "Blizzard of '85" or "The Big Whiteout."

The difference between New Brunswick and North Carolina is preparation. In Canada, we knew we had to live with lots of snow, so we were prepared for it. In North Carolina, it's a novelty. If you know a life storm is coming – be prepared for it. If one catches you off guard, don't panic – ride it out. No storm lasts forever.

Dear friends, let us love one another, for love comes from God. Everyone who loves has been born of God and knows God. 1 John 4:7 NIV

(O)ur entire lives revolve around the giving and receiving of care. Unless you go live alone in a cave somewhere, that which matters in life can be measured in caring relationships with others. The richness of a marriage can be measured in the quality and quantity of demonstrated care. Raising children is an exercise in care. Friendships are all about caring, helping, reaching, lifting, and loving.

Among the coldest words a person can hear are the words, "I don't care!" A new baby requires a high level of care. Each stage that follows requires care of differing texture and color. The "care train" never stops rolling for Moms and Dads. When the kids are gone, our parents require a greater level of care. When our parents are gone, we are not far from needing additional care ourselves.

God created us for the warmth of the human touch; the comfort of human love; the communion of human language; the security of human acceptance; the joy of the human family. He made us for His good pleasure (Revelation 4:11), but He also made us for one another. The latter is a reflection of the former.

We are never so like God than when we truly care for one another.

And he brought him to Jesus. Now when Jesus looked at him, He said,
"You are Simon the son of Jonah. You shall be called Cephas."
John 1:42 NKJV

Every year, twenty-nine professional gamblers roll the dice in Madison Square Garden at the annual National Basketball Association Draft. The gamblers carry titles of "General Manager" or "Vice-President In Charge of Player Personnel," but they're gamblers none-the-less.

They're laying millions on the line, hoping to uncover the next Michael Jordan, or Magic Johnson, or Larry Bird. They will gamble on unknown players like Miaden Sekularac of Yugoslavia, because they know, "It's not what you are, it's what you *could* be." These executive gamblers have studied all the statistics, attended workouts, assembled personality profiles, and conducted family interviews. They have caucused to debate strengths and weaknesses. They approach the draft with ten different scenarios. The best a gambler can do is assess possibilities and probabilities.

On the shore of Galilee, Jesus drafted players for a team for the ages: world-changers. A basketball GM sees a player and says, "You could be." Jesus looked at a fisherman named Simon and said, "You shall be." Christ imparts the power to become all that God planned before we drew our first breath. You're not a gamble to God. You're a *sure thing.*

Before a word is on my tongue you know it completely, O LORD.
Psalm 139:4 NIV

Myers-Briggs says I am an ESFJ. By temperament I am a sanguine/choleric. By culture I am mid-America. My politics are conservative. My theology is Pentecostal, and my hobby is writing. Do you think you know me now?

Here's more. I hate golf, love pasta, despise Duke Basketball, admire musicians, read a book a week, drive, eat, and talk too fast. If I were Gen-X, I'm certain I would be diagnosed with some hyper-disorder and drugged into a manageable state.

Have you got a read on me yet? A few more bits and pieces: I'm running low on faith in politicians, chiropractors, weathermen, tax cuts, stock markets, and "sold-on-TV" products. I rejoice in fatherhood, weep at the thought of an empty nest, laugh at least twice a day, sing with a voice only God could love, dream big dreams, believe in miracles, hold out with optimism, and always take three where a dosage of two is recommended.

If you were to add to this list my complete self-knowledge, my wife's insight, and my daughters' input, you would have but a shadow of a fingerprint compared to God's complete knowledge of me. And when *all* is said, and *all* is known, He loves me still. Amazing grace!

"For who has known the mind of the LORD?
Or who has become His counselor?"
Romans 11:34 NKJV

What a mystery, the human mind. What incredible compressed capacity the brain affords. Where do ideas come from? Where are great inspirations birthed? How can an undisciplined mind offer up the creative genius displayed in soaring spires, where disciplined intelligence creates a warehouse?

One is blessed with a lofty IQ, but robbed of social graces. Another is dull, but irresistibly lovable. Go figure! One can lock out everyone in a crowded room. Another is distracted by the ticking of a clock in a monastery.

What stamina the brain exhibits. Studies exhaust us, but the mind never really shuts down. Even at rest, it works. Concentrating on a dry equation evokes boredom. Concentrating on a love interest provokes action. A short change of pace renews the power to concentrate again.

Amazing! What is a thought, a feeling, an impulse, except an electrical charge that races through a million crossroads to make connections that form a basis for action, a call to nobility, an unspoken preference?

If we cannot grasp the greatness of the human mind, how can we begin to comprehend the unsearchable depths of the wisdom of God.

To every thing there is a season, and a time to
every purpose under the heaven.
Ecclesiastes 3:1 KJV

For all of our technological wonders, a simple drought can bring us to our knees. What good is a gazillion-gigahertz computer chip when your backyard paradise becomes a desert?

Yards burn, crops die, temperatures rise, restrictions are imposed, and everybody looks to the skies with hope when clouds roll in. Politicians take fire for a lack of vision and drought planning. Newscasters count down the days to the next round of water restriction. I'm watching the clouds roll by right now, but there's no forecast of rain. Yet I know that it will rain. It's just a matter of time. Drought and flood, fire and rain, wind and heat – it may be delayed a while longer, but it's coming, and we'll probably complain about the rain and grumble over canceled picnics.

Spiritual droughts are seasonal, too. They often come and go without warning. Are you in a dry season? Does it seem that the heavens are silent and your spirit is drying up? Don't panic. Keep the weeds out of your heart and trust the Lord. Create a logjam of prayer at heaven's gate.

God answers persistent prayer. As long as you continue to seek Him, the rains will come again – it's a sure thing! It's amazing how fast God can turn our troubled worlds around.

...but Paul did not think it wise to take him,
because he had deserted them in Pamphylia
and had not continued with them in the work.
Acts 15:38 NIV

"Just quit!" Have you thought about it? Have you, in the rehearsal hall of your mind, stomped into your supervisor's office and dropped your keys, your I.D., your last assignment in his lap? Have you thought about tanking your marriage, leaving your church, quitting school, running away, or dropping off the map?

Be careful what you quit. Quitting is habit forming. Most closed doors lock behind you. I've never read a book that honors quitters. I've never seen a statue raised to remember deserters. For the most part, quitting is a dishonorable disengagement. Quitting comes at a high cost. Most of the time the quitter moves down, not up.

I can't count the number of times someone has come to our doors seeking financial help after quitting a good paying job. Unable to delay the gratification of being free of an oppressive workplace, unable to stay the course in the pursuit of a better option, they opted for the door — and now they're standing at mine, about to go under.

John Mark had called it quits in Pamphylia. It was not the proudest day in his life. He made it back (2 Timothy 4:11). John Mark is a rare exception. Most quitters have left their best days behind.

But his delight is in the law of the LORD,
and on his law he meditates day and night.
Psalm 1:2 NIV

People who allow their minds to wander soon find themselves lost in hostile territory. The thought life is not a private retreat without boundaries. It must be disciplined, guarded, and directed (Philippians 4:8). Thinking flows to action like a river to the sea.

Our best and our worst began with a thought. God knows our thoughts afar off. *He knows* that what is formed in the mind is birthed in our deeds. We should be concerned and consumed with right thinking. Too often we concern ourselves only with action.

God desires to take pleasure in our thoughts. David's first Psalm points out that the blessed man is one who meditates and delights in the Law of the Lord.

Such a man's thought life holds prophetic implications for blessing or cursing (Psalm 1:3-4). Is it any wonder that David was called "A man after God's own heart" (1 Samuel 13:14)? He invited God into the center of his thought life. He welcomed God with the dawning of each new day. He worshipped God with the setting of the sun.

We would do well to bookend our days with thoughts that flow out of God's Word.

Then the seventy returned with joy.
Luke 10:17 NKJV

Biysk, Siberia: Book of Hope Distribution: I watched the teams returning; their taxis drifting through the haze like ships making for harbor. Three car doors opened as one and their smiles told the story. It had been a good day for distribution.

One team had been pressed hard by a psychology professor, but the testing of their faith gave increase to their joy. Another team had been offered just one classroom presentation, but the administrator's heart thawed as they interacted with the children. A third team returned in a state of amazement; the teacher had virtually asked for a testimony of how Jesus could change a life. Ray didn't hesitate. A private man gave a very public testimony.

My three daughters returned with their teams. Today, they shared the Gospel in hostile and friendly settings – a fifth-generation witness in a place their forefathers could not have imagined ministry. Tomorrow, we will go to orphanages, schools, a prison, and a tiny village school about forty minutes from here.

My heart is full. Yet, as I look into the blackness of the night, I am reminded of millions in this part of the world who have not heard. It is enough to break your heart – it has certainly broken mine.

Honor one another above yourselves.
Romans 12:10 NIV

From the thirty-third floor we enjoyed a magnificent meal overlooking Boston Harbor. Dusk gave way to the jeweled beauty of a sprawling city radiant in the darkness. We gathered to celebrate a birthday; to savor the matchless connection of family; to laugh at stories we all know so well; to mark a key point in time; to cast a memory for posterity.

Being there was a blessing in and of itself. The food, the view, and the company made it a night to remember. I realized, at that table, how incredibly rich I am. My discovery had nothing to do with the price of the meal, nor the quality of the restaurant. True wealth is measured in terms of relationship, not accumulated stuff, nor aggregated luxuries. My worldly wealth is measured in a loving family, immediate and extended. It is a wealth that I must protect through investment in the next generation. I want my grandchildren to gather, as we have, to celebrate the greater moments in life.

There is a "moment" approaching on your family calendar. Birthday, anniversary, graduation . . . the occasion presents a celebrative opportunity in an all too sober world.

Don't miss the "moment." Celebration is a tested and proven vaccine against regret.

Therefore, since we are receiving a kingdom that cannot
be shaken, let us be thankful, and so worship
God acceptably with reverence and awe.
Hebrews 12:28 NIV

The mid-fifties computer guy sitting in 27F proved to be an easy conversationalist. We talked of common roots in the Northeast and summer vacations on the lakes of Maine. We eventually got around to careers.

When I tell people I'm a pastor, they get chatty, quiet, or intense. He got chatty. "Let me tell you, this is a low day for me," he said. "I've been down here for a new system training course. I didn't get my certification. I don't know what I'm going to tell my boss." He was amazed that young people seemed to have an immediate grasp of the new technology. He struggled with his inability to adapt from his "main frame" roots to a whole new computer culture. I tried to encourage him: "You'll pick it up. It's just new to you now." He readily agreed, but I could see the doubt behind his eyes. A two-week training course had pushed him firmly into the mid-life maze.

Rules change. Career tracks spin. Pace increases. New today is obsolete tomorrow. We need something fixed and solid. We need an anchor point so that changing winds don't blow us away. We need the "unshakable" in a world that quakes in uncertainty. He is the fixed point of all creation. Bind your soul to the Changeless One.

O LORD, you have searched me and you know me.
You know when I sit and when I rise; you
perceive my thoughts from afar.
Psalm 139:1-2 NIV

What peace I find in the fact that God knows. Nothing about me surprises Him. Nothing is hidden from His sight. He hears the faintest whisper of my heart. He moves in the shadows of my thoughts. He is witness to the birthing of my desires. He counts my tears. He hears my prayer. He sees what I see, and what I cannot. He hears every beat of my heart. Since conception, He has never taken His eyes off of me … not for a single moment. Born to sin, by blood He bought me. Born to die, in Him I live.

In my darkness, He did not lose sight of me – not for a second. God knows! Except for grace, it is a terrifying thought. He witnessed my most shameful moment. He heard my cursing, saw my greed, felt my indifference, endured my ignorance, suffered my rebellion, outlasted my resistance, exceeded my hopes, and fulfilled my dreams. He knows my tomorrow, helps in trouble, leads by example, loves beyond measure, lifts me in sorrow, fills me with power, and hides me in the hollow of His hand.

I have known His rebuke, conviction, correction, affirmation, pleasure, provision, guidance, and peace. He knows me, and somehow, He loves me.

Such love demands my heart and inspires my soul.

"And on earth peace, goodwill toward men!"
Luke 2:14 NKJV

The checkout lines go on forever. Shredded by the rush and crush, I clutch the doll that walks, talks, wets, and cooks stir-fry. The line closes just as I reach the register, causing me to wring the neck of the dumb doll. The lady next to me looks like she might file charges. The Scripture that claims the last shall be first does not apply to the checkout line at Toys-R-Us.

The parking lot is packed, and several cars prowl like wolves, waiting for any sudden opening. There is no charity in the parking lot – this is serious business – this is Christmas. A BMW with a sorry-looking tree strapped to the top is parked sideways, taking up two spots. Sap drips onto the hood, ruining the paint the driver protected by taking two spots – poetic justice.

At 3:00 this afternoon, I found the wimpiest Santa in Greensboro. Thin and anemic, he sat in his sleigh with his boots up, his beard pulled down under his chin, staring off into space. Santa's little helper finished her cigarette, hacked out a dry cough, and swore under her breath. The shoppers around me look exhausted.

Cheap decorations and throwaway toys make me long for the real spirit of Christmas – one that features peace, goodwill, and a silent, holy night.

*"Behold, the virgin shall be with child, and bear a Son,
and they shall call His name Immanuel,"
which is translated, "God with us."*
Matthew 1:23 NKJV

The detail and retail of the Christmas rush overpower the most compelling Christmas truth: God in the Bethlehem manger!

Shepherds knew they had seen the deliverer, but did not realize that they had seen the face of God. Fishermen knew He was a great teacher, but they failed to recognize that God was using their boat for a platform. The moneychangers must be counted among the most fortunate of men. They ticked-off God and got away with a whipping. Roman soldiers didn't realize they were piercing the hands of God when they nailed Jesus to the cross. Israel's wisest teachers, experts in the Scriptures, students of God, didn't recognize Immanuel: *God with us.*

Though we have the benefit of hindsight, we, too, can miss the glory of His presence. We find what we seek with a singular purpose. Too often we are seeking everything but God. We are a driven generation, looking for big scores and cold cash security. God is oft reduced to a Sunday addendum as we grasp for the brass ring. Are we as blind as the Pharisees?

Every day is a quest for God – more and more of Him. Don't let trivial pursuits take center stage. We are not just living out a creed; we are walking with the one and only God.

I bowed down heavily, as one who mourns for his mother.
Psalm 35:14 NKJV

Childhood Christmas memories revolve around my grandmother. The Christmas fires burned bright in the Crabtree home, and she was the keeper of the flame. She was to Christmas what Carson was to late night, or Cosell to Monday Night Football. She loved Christmas with the enthusiasm of a child.

A snow-covered house on Court Street in Bangor was alive with lights and ribbons, the smell of turkey, and the laughter of Helen Crabtree and her adoring grandchildren. We gathered around a large mahogany table for a Christmas feast. Grandpa was responsible for the prayer. Grandma was responsible for the party. When she got sick, she saved her strength for Christmas.

In my memories, Christmas marked her decline. One year she greeted us from a walker, then a wheelchair, then – a hospital bed. When Grandma died, she left a void no one could fill. We felt it most at Christmas. Grandpa became the guest, rather than the host. My parents made it a grand occasion – but Christmas changed when she died. No one could supply the "magic" she held in her heart. Her life enriched others.

The great English preacher, G. Campbell Morgan said it best: "Live so as to be missed." She did, and she is.

*"A man's life does not consist in the abundance
of his possessions."*
Luke 12:15 NIV

Christmas shouldn't be hampered by a sluggish economy. If the quantity of gifts measures our Christmas, we're in sorry shape indeed. Sure, it's great to choke the tree with gifts and clothe the season in generosity, but things often become a substitute for love and kindness, time and touch, presence and attention.

Over time, more than half of our gifts are hidden in drawers or trundled out to the dumpster. *"Hey, let's buy the preacher that picture of the praying hands."* I can't throw away "praying hands." That would be ... well, sacrilegious. I've got ceramic praying hands, paintings of praying hands, wood-carved praying hands, and praying hands that rotate and play "Sweet Hour of Prayer." By midlife, we're overwhelmed with clutter. By late-life, our families wonder what to do with the "stuff" when we're gone. Most of us don't need more stuff. We need more room.

Yet tradition and convention lead us back to the stores on the not-so-merry Christmas chase to find another perfect gift to give in the finest holiday tradition. Don't think me a "Scrooge" for suggesting that we ramp down the gift glut. The best gifts of all are not shrink-wrapped or barcoded, and God is not honored by our debts.

Joseph also went up from Galilee, out of the city of Nazareth,
into Judea, to the city of David, which is called Bethlehem,
because he was of the house and lineage of David,
to be registered with Mary, his betrothed wife, who was with child.
Luke 2:4-5 NKJV

Have you noticed that when you really want to keep something quiet, the information always seems to find its way to some mega-mouth with all the tact of a five-year-old child?

Mary's pregnancy was an issue that Joseph wanted to handle with gracious discretion (Matthew 1:19). It's tough to be discreet in a small town. Though he was comforted by angelic instruction, Joseph's quiet life must have taken a stunning turn when Mary turned up pregnant. You can bet that Joseph and Mary were the talk of Nazareth for a while. To complicate matters, the Romans launched a census. This meant that Joseph would arrive at the ultimate family reunion in Bethlehem with Mary on the threshold of childbirth – so much for keeping things quiet! The journey from Nazareth to Bethlehem covered some seventy-five miles. One can only imagine the harsh difficulties that Joseph faced. He must have been quite a man.

God chose him to be the protector of His only Son. His cameo appearance in the gospel stirs my curiosity. Matthew, Mark, Luke or John could have told us so much more, but they were focused on revealing Jesus to the world not as the son of Joseph, but as the only begotten Son of God.

Now there were in the same country shepherds living out in the fields,
keeping watch over their flock by night. And behold,
an angel of the Lord stood before them, and the glory of the
Lord shone around them.
Luke 2:8-9 NKJV

T'was the night before Christmas, and the world was a different place than the world we know. A tired Roman Empire, gutted by excess and debauchery, held a tenuous grasp from Spain to Asia Minor. Tyranny, slavery, injustice and poverty had come to dwell among the Jews, who reached their promised land but had lost their spiritual compass.

A diligent search of the Scriptures revealed that Messiah would come, and so, in the dark, barbaric night they waited – and prayed – and hoped, as they sharpened each point on the letters of law and smothered its soul with tradition. It was a tragedy – an unparalleled tragedy, that the ones who so diligently looked for Messiah were so blind and bound. They didn't recognize Him when God delivered Messiah in a Bethlehem stable.

Only 5.4 miles from the Temple where devout men cried for His appearance, Jesus was born. All of the teaching, all of the prophets, all that a seminary could offer in spiritual knowledge was at their fingertips. Yet the silent night of the soul continued in Israel while angels appeared to shepherds and wise men followed the star.

T'was the night before Christmas, and Jerusalem slept, so close to the manger – so far from the Master.

And she brought forth her firstborn Son, and wrapped
Him in swaddling cloths, and laid Him in a manger.
Luke 2:7 NKJV

Seth was the handyman at The Bethlehem Inn. He took care of the livestock, picked up and fixed up, and helped with the day-to-day running of the place. For his trouble he got pocket change, hot food, and a place to stay behind the kitchen.

Just after Seth hired on, he spent two weeks upgrading the stables. What had been little more than a cave was now a dry, covered lean-to with stall doors and feed troughs. Seth's father taught him how to craft simple farm implements, and Seth finished out the stable with a portable manger. Twice repaired and scarred from hard use, the manger had served as feed station, workbench, step-up, and tool box.

But on that special night, Seth hurried to clean out the little manger for a most unlikely use. On that special night, the manger would serve as a cradle. That "cradle" would be remembered for a thousand years and more. Jesus began making the ordinary extraordinary in the stable. He had that effect on everything, and everyone He ever touched.

God still chooses ordinary vessels for extraordinary service. On this Christmas morning, remember Seth's old manger. Christ is come to make something very special out of you. Merry Christmas.

Be still before the LORD and wait patiently for him.
Psalm 37:7 NIV

Take a vacation from television. You may never want to check your brain back into daycare again. Discover reading. Recover relationships. Uncover a talent. Enjoy a sunset. Banish inertia. Break an addiction. Renew your prayer-life. Expand your vacation to include the Internet. Trade "coms" for kids. Make your dining room a chat room. Try surfing (you'll need a board and an ocean). Avoid the "mouse" trap.

Instead of screens, try faces. Trade RAM and ROM for Dan and Ron. Now, let's take a radical step: Turn off your cell phone. Enjoy a few hours of solitude. Let someone else enjoy a few hours of solitude! Think before you speak. Diminish trivia. Study your Bible without interruption. No CD players allowed. Take the battery out of your beeper. Palm Pilots need to be firmly lashed to the dock. People aren't wired for the speed of sound and light.

We need time to think, contemplate, meditate, strategize, prioritize, and analyze. We need to be more active and less reactive. We need a true Sabbath rest. Living our lives in sound bytes and data bursts, we are robbed of wholeness and peace. Disconnect to reconnect with God.

...he who refreshes others will himself be refreshed.
Proverbs 11:25 NKJV

"Pastor, I'm leaving." On rare occasions those words have made me happy. Most of the time they are tinged with sadness. Almost everybody tells me that "God is leading" them elsewhere.

I was under the strong impression that He was all about building a church, not de-populating it. The questions always come: "Have I failed? Has the church failed? Is there a hidden offense?" I've come to grips with the fact that some people are only with you for a season. Some are God's scaffolding, sent to help a church through a growth phase, but many people leave unnecessarily. Relationship is usually at the core of an unwanted, unhealthy departure. Those departures should be rare. To strengthen the church we must strengthen relationships.

Connecting within the body of Christ should be a shared challenge. We must wage war against isolation and divisiveness. Our church services often leave people alone in a crowded room. People who feel "invisible" have a way of making themselves invisible on a permanent basis.

Is your church unfriendly? Is your church a weekly gathering of "alone" people? Fix it! If you are not part of the solution, you're contributing to the problem.

And there is no creature hidden from His sight,
but all things are naked and open to the eyes of
Him to whom we must give account.
Hebrews 4:13 NKJV

Having trouble balancing your checkbook? Are you off by a couple of bucks? Don't be too hard on yourself. The past twelve months revealed the inner workings of huge firms specializing in accounting. These firms, for all their expertise, have misplaced millions, even billions.

It really doesn't matter very much until someone calls for an accounting. Ignorance is bliss until past due notices and payable on demand filings begin to pile up at the door. This year may be remembered as the year that business America received its past due notice. Now the Congress is investigating, confidence is flat, CEOs are pointing fingers, scapegoats are in demand, and judicial amnesia has struck at the witness stand. The day of accounting ends with fines, jail sentences, ruined reputations, and bitterness all around.

It all serves to remind us that there is a day of final accounting coming for us all. The writer to the Hebrews said that, "We *must* give" an accounting. Are you ready to take the witness stand? Can you defend your life?

Settle all accounts now. Ask and receive forgiveness. Set your life course by the Book of Books. Live as one under subpoena: ready, even anxious, to close the case.

So shall my word be that goeth forth out of my mouth:
it shall not return unto me void, but it shall accomplish that
which I please, and it shall prosper in the thing whereto I sent it.
Isaiah 55:11 KJV

Biysk, Siberia: Book of Hope Distribution: Last night I heard the thunder . . . the thunder of Russian voices praying the sinner's prayer. Young and old, they prayed together. More than 700 came out for our crusade in a cold and drafty hall.

Our primary purpose is to distribute books, but sometimes God allows us to see the harvest. We were back at the hotel by 8:30 for a late dinner. Though tired, the team is excited. The power of the Word of God to change lives never ceases to amaze me. Our crusades are often chaotic. We arrive at a rented hall with minimal time to set up. Some crusades are filled with elementary school children. Some are filled with adults. The age of the crowd shapes our presentation. Plan "A" is often switched to plan "B" midstream.

We work through interpreters. Our time is limited. The invitation is given, and people respond. Is it effective? Ask Boris. Nine years ago he was running around after a crusade in Kraznoyarsk, trying to get every American's signature on his copy of the *Book of Hope*. Today he is a church leader and sometime interpreter for our teams. Boris found Christ through a distribution. I can't wait until tonight's crusade. I want to hear the thunder.

When pride comes, then comes disgrace,
but with humility comes wisdom.
Proverbs 11:2 NIV

I just nursed my computer through its first virus. The patient has recovered nicely, but I'm still a bit rattled at the prospect of losing my lifeline. I've set up a schedule with one of the nation's best virus doctors hoping to avoid re-infection.

My computer operating system has a feature I wish we could somehow apply to human beings; it's called "safe mode." When I run my computer in the "safe mode," I can tinker away under a greatly reduced risk of damage. "Safe mode" gives me the opportunity to try various strategies and cures with almost no down side.

I wish I had a "safe mode" for counseling. It would sure be nice to turn off the non-essential "programs" people are running, and float a few trial balloons to see if it fixes an ailing marriage, a financial disaster, or some relationship nightmare. Sometimes my suggestions are like gas on a fire. Sometimes they chill the room. What works in one situation fails in the next. In fact, God has provided a "safe mode" through repentance and humility that drops the volume and ferocity of a conflict to a curable level. Where humility is absent, a virus called rage infects everyone it touches.

Humble yourself. You're a lot easier to deal with in "safe mode."

For which of you, intending to build a tower,
does not sit down first and count the cost.
Luke 14:28 NKJV

There is nothing quite like a fresh start . . . unless you continue to do what you have always done.

New beginnings require a willingness to do better; to soar higher; to apply the lessons time teaches along the way. Most New Year's resolutions are stillborn for want of a plan to implement them. I bought a piece of hardware to install a wireless computer network in my home. It sat in a box for months. I didn't know how to install it myself, and I just didn't get around to scheduling time for a technically advanced friend to come over and get the job done. End result: nothing changed. I planned to lose weight, but I failed to join a club, or set aside time to work out, or put together a low-fat diet. End result: well – you can probably figure it out on your own.

It's easy to catch a vision. It's difficult to adopt new disciplines. Wishes are free. Changes cost you something.

Here we are at the threshold of another year. A new Daytimer gets us thinking about a new schedule; a new body; a new direction; a new challenge. Why not set one goal this year and establish ten steps to get there?

Next year you might be looking at a resolution that lived to see its first birthday.

Do you need Hope?

It's really **easy to receive** the
eternal hope of **new life in Christ!**

1. *Recognize that sin in your life separates you from a holy God,* who cannot be in the presence of sin.

2. *Accept the gift of Jesus Christ, God's only Son.* He gave His life as a sacrifice for our sins, receiving the punishment for them. The Bible says His blood washes us clean from our sins. Three days after His death, Christ arose from the grave to bring us into eternal life with God.

3. *Pray for forgiveness of sins.* If you confess that you believe Christ died for you and ask Him to forgive your sins, He will do it! Once Jesus has cleansed you from sin, God accepts you as His child and you will have eternal life with Him.

4. *Grow in God.* Once you have asked Christ for forgiveness of your sins, you are saved from sin and ready for new life in Christ. You will want to follow His example in water baptism, read your Bible and pray daily. Find an active church that believes the Bible, and there you will find help to grow in God.

5. *Write to us and tell us about your commitment.* We will send you the English-language "Book of Hope" to tell you more about Jesus, and we would be so happy to hear that you have accepted Christ as Savior.

book of Hope

3111 SW 10th Street · Pompano, Florida 33069 · www.bookofhope.net

book of Hope

1987 *In 1987, we were invited to give the Scriptures to every schoolchild in El Salvador, and God led us to create this harmony of the Gospels that tells the life story of Jesus.*

El Salvador *It had such an impact on El Salvador's nearly one million children, other Spanish-speaking nations began to ask for it — and soon there was a demand for the book in other languages as well.*

Translated *The "Book of Hope" has now been translated into dozens of languages and produced in several age-specific editions … all clearly show children how to accept Christ as Savior.*

Public Schools *Around the world we give the "Book of Hope" to students, usually right in their public school classrooms.*

Crusades *Often we sponsor citywide Hope Fest crusades in conjunction with book distribution, so entire families can come to Christ! We have even planted new churches this way.*

100 Million *In September 2000, we placed the "Book of Hope" into the hands of the 100 millionth child to receive it — and in 2001, we distributed over 33 million!*

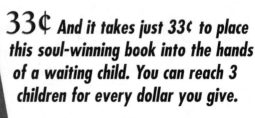

33¢ *And it takes just 33¢ to place this soul-winning book into the hands of a waiting child. You can reach 3 children for every dollar you give.*

We welcome your help today in this destiny-shaping ministry!

TOP 10 REASONS
to Consider a Gift Annuity

1. Guaranteed life-time payments
2. Payments are fixed
3. Payments are tax-free return of principal
4. Immediate income tax return deduction
5. Avoids Capital Gains tax
6. Very favorable rates

7. No investment worries
8. Avoid probate and federal state taxes
9. Protected from creditors
10. The joy of giving to Book of Hope – reaching children with God's Word

If you would like to learn more about a gift annuity that would provide these benefits for you and reach children around the world with the *Book of Hope*, call Mike Medley at 1.800.GIV.BIBL (448.2425) or just check the Annuity box on the enclosed coupon.

You can find out more about charitable gift annuities at the ministry website **www.bookofhope.net.**

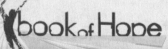

Which is worth more to you?

The eternal souls of the children of the world are worth far more than any amount of money ...

... and through the *Book of Hope*, you can tell the kids about Jesus in a wonderfully cost-effective way: every dollar places the *Book of Hope* into the hands of three students somewhere in the world!

Your dollar might reach:

• A teenager like Volodya in Russia. He received the *Book of Hope* when he was 14, and today at 25 he is a pastor!

• A little girl like Sunni in India. When she brought the *Book of Hope* home from school, her family became the first family in her entire village to believe on Jesus!

• And a young woman like Pinkie from South Africa who had left her hometown for the big city of Johannesburg and survived there by sleeping with various "boyfriends." The *Book of Hope* brought her to new life in Christ!

Their souls are worth far more than anything a dollar would buy you. Why not reach out to them today?

Send your best gift with the enclosed coupon to:
**Book of Hope, 3111 SW 10th Street
Pompano, Florida 33069**

book of Hope

1.800.GIV.BIBL (448.2425) • www.bookofhope.net

book of Hope
Ministry Response Form

www.bookofhope.net

Return this form to send your gift, request more information, request your free video, or send your comment to the Book of Hope ministry!

_____
Name

_____
Address

_____
City   State   Zip

(   )   – _____   _____ @ _____
Phone   Email

❑ **I want to help bring God's Word to the children of the world!**

Please use my contribution to place the *Book of Hope* into the hands of waiting students. I have enclosed:

❑ $25 to reach 75 students   ❑ $50 to reach 150 students

❑ $100 to reach 300 students   ❑ $_____ to help as much as possible.

❑ Please send me more information on:
   ❑ *Affect Destiny Team missions*   ❑ *Estate planning/charitable annuities*
   ❑ *Other:* _____

❑ Please send the free video:
   ❑ *The Book of Hope Story*

❑ My comment/prayer request: _____

_____
_____
_____
_____
_____

Please return to:
Book of Hope • 3111 SW 10th St.• Pompano, Florida 33069 • 1.800.GIV.BIBL *(448.2425)*